Listening to *Stephen* read

Listening to *Stephen* read

Multiple perspectives on literacy

KATHY HALL

OPEN UNIVERSITY PRESS
Buckingham · Philadelphia

Open University Press
Celtic Court
22 Ballmoor
Buckingham
MK18 1XW

email: enquiries@openup.co.uk
world wide web: www.openup.co.uk

and
325 Chestnut Street
Philadelphia, PA 19106, USA

First Published 2003

A catalogue record of this book is available from the British Library

ISBN 0 335 20758 8(pb)   0 335 20759 6(hb)

Library of Congress Cataloging-in-Publication Data
Hall, Kathy, 1952–
    Listening to Stephen read: multiple perspectives on literacy / Kathy Hall.
        p.   cm.
    Includes bibliographical references and index.
    ISBN 0-335-20759-6 – ISBN 0-335-20758-8 (pbk.)
    1. Reading – Case studies.   2. Reading – Ability testing – Case studies.
3. Miscue analysis – Case studies.   I. Title.
LB1050.42 .H35 2002
372.41—dc21   2002072265

Typeset in 10/12 pt Bembo by Graphicraft Limited, Hong Kong
Printed in Great Britain by Biddles Limited, Guildford and Kings Lynn

To the memory of my father, Frank Kavanagh, who died a few days after the manuscript was completed. From him I learnt the importance of time.

CONTENTS

ACKNOWLEDGEMENTS

Over the time it takes to research and write a book, one receives help from many people. I would like to express my gratitude to the many people who have helped me in bringing this book to completion. First, I am truly grateful to Stephen and his teacher for their kind cooperation, both of whom have to remain anonymous to protect their privacy. I want to express my deepest appreciation to the eight academics who participated in the project – Ann Browne, Barbara Comber, Henrietta Dombey, Teresa Grainger, Mary Hilton, Laura Huxford, Jackie Marsh, and David Wray. My thanks, too, to other academics who contributed to the symposium on this theme at the United Kingdom Reading Association Conference in Oxford in July 2000. Thanks especially to Fidelma Healy-Eames of the University of Limerick for her participation in that event. I also wish to thank the library staff of Leeds Metropolitan University for their speedy response to requests for research articles. To my colleagues at LMU I am indebted for support and encouragement over several years, especially those in the Centre for Educational Research and Research Training, Richard Bailey, Jon Tan, Paul Clarke, Nick Sutcliffe, Austin Harding and Christine Allan, and also to my sisters, Ann Kavanagh and Breda Kirwan – all offered helpful suggestions about various aspects of the project. I am indebted to Shona Mullen and Anita West at Open University Press for their support in publishing this book. Acknowledgements and thanks for permission to reprint the text of the children's book *Bear* are due to the publishers, Hodder and Stoughton, and to the author, Mick Inkpen. Above all, my grateful thanks to my partner Tom Smith for his unfailing understanding and support.

INTRODUCTION

What this book aims to do

Whether you are a literacy educator, a student teacher, a school adviser/inspector, a teacher educator, a literacy researcher, or just interested in the reading process, this book invites you to develop your own perspective on reading. It seeks to help you acquire a deeper understanding of the reading process and especially the theoretical underpinnings of different approaches to fostering reading in the classroom. Written primarily for teachers, teacher educators, and student teachers, it aims to help you not only with the selection of teaching strategies for the development of reading but also with an understanding of the theoretical rationale for particular approaches. The book will bring together issues of practice, pedagogy and theory in such a way as to encourage you to apply your understanding to your own personal context and to consider your own and others' practices, policies and theories with more discernment and insight.

It aims to support you in understanding the variety of possible teacher responses to classroom evidence about readers. It is intended to help people move away from a simplistic 'either–or' position with regard to reading practice and theory, to one that acknowledges that theories, teaching, and policies are not so conveniently labelled or pigeon-holed. It seeks to do this by moving from practice to theory rather than the other way round. It has two key features: first, the sense of being 'at the chalk face' – beginning with the reality of the concrete situation of a particular classroom, child and teacher; and second, the attempt to reveal assumptions, to define terms and to resist attempts to polarize and pigeon-hole.

Evidence that literacy educators and researchers hold different perspectives on reading can be found in debates about what counts as literacy and how to develop it. In 1995 the *Journal of Research in Reading*, for example, devoted an entire volume to a consideration of definitions of literacy, while how best to teach literacy has been a focus of debate for decades (e.g. Chall 1992; Goodman 1992; Oakhill and Beard 1999). An important underlying assumption of this book is that there is no 'one' right approach, philosophy or method of developing reading that is likely to be accepted by everyone and my intention is not to chase after some elusive right answer. Rather my intention is to promote understanding of multiple perspectives on reading and its development.

Origin of the book

Professionally, I, along with many others, have found the critical incident or the case or the story a very powerful means of teaching and learning especially in situations, like teaching, where the ultimate aim is professional action. Hence the initial focus on one child as a reader. The specific attention to multiple perspectives on reading stems from several experiences. In 1995, when working at Canterbury Christ Church University College, I was charged with the task of preparing a document on reading for an Ofsted inspection. This document had to represent the large and diverse lecturer team's pedagogical philosophy on reading and also needed to be in line with narrower, politically-driven agendas at the time about reading. The difficulty, not to say impossibility, of this task brought home to me the complexity of the theoretical underpinnings of reading practice and policy and how we so frequently underestimate the scale of this complexity in teaching, in policy making and in research. I resolved at that time to write something that would support teachers, teacher educators, and student teachers in recognizing the theoretical nuances of reading practice and policy. More recently, I participated in a conference in the United States where a variation of the approach I am using here was the basis of a seminar convened by Yetta Goodman (1998). In my view this was extremely effective in terms of making the abstract concrete, which is essentially what I am trying to do here. The experience, even more recently, of convening a symposium for the United Kingdom Reading Association's Annual Conference in Oxford in July 2000 in which I used a similar approach prompted me, finally, to write this book. Indeed the response I obtained from the people I approached to participate in the UKRA symposium (some of whom also participated in this project), as well as the audience participants, suggested that this was a valuable way to proceed.

Database and approach

The book begins with the practical, authentic context of one child – Stephen – in one classroom in a regular primary school in England in the first year of the twenty-first century. On getting permission from all the relevant partners (i.e. Stephen himself, his mother, his teacher and the headteacher of the school) I video-recorded Stephen reading and retelling *Bear* by Mick Inkpen to his teacher. I then transcribed the entire recording in full and conducted an analysis of the miscues or the errors that Stephen made. This database along with some biographical information about Stephen then became the vehicle through which I planned to probe different perspectives on teaching strategies and theoretical understandings of the reading process. I approached eight well-known and distinguished literacy educators and asked them to participate in the project. Participation involved viewing the recording, reading the transcript and being interviewed. I asked all eight scholars the same four, key questions:

1 What do we know about Stephen as a reader?
2 What else would you like to know about him?
3 What should his teacher do to enhance his reading?
4 What theoretical perspectives underpin your suggestions?

I audio-recorded and later transcribed the interviews with all the scholars and returned the transcripts to them so they could amend, confirm or extend their responses in any way they wished. All the scholars selected for the project have written extensively on literacy, all have key positions in teacher education and/or have a national profile in terms of influencing official policy and practice in schools. All have a background as class teachers. The scholars were selected on the likelihood that across the group, a variety of emphases on reading, reflected in a diversity of suggested ways of fostering reading in the classroom, would emerge. I also expected to find a good deal of consensus across these scholars' thinking. I was not disappointed on either count.

On the basis of the interviews I was able to pair those scholars who were alike in some key respects in their responses to the questions. This paired arrangement provided me with a launching pad from which I could describe and analyse, in more detail, four major theoretical perspectives on reading. This means the book is divided into four major parts, each part consisting of a brief introduction, edited transcripts from two reading scholars, and a discussion of fundamental issues raised through these transcripts.

Why oral reading?

Reading aloud remains part and parcel of everyday classroom reading practice. It is used by the teacher as a way of monitoring a child's progress and development as a reader. It is also used as a way of developing successful reading strategies, of raising awareness of and introducing new strategies. Classroom teachers and reading specialists use oral reading to make pedagogical decisions about pupils. Similarly, researchers often use oral reading to gain insights into reading development or the reading process itself. However, teachers, reading specialists and researchers differ on the importance they attribute to factors like accuracy, fluency, word recognition, phonemic awareness, phonics, the socio-cultural context of reading, and so on (Goodman 1998). How a reader is heard depends on how such factors are conceptualized by the listener.

There are deliberate omissions in relation to the wider area of reading. I was aware that the evidence presented about Stephen to our scholars could have been different and different questions could have been asked of the interviewees. It was my expectation that some of the scholars would challenge the evidence that was collected and this is part of the book's particular interest – in inviting different perspectives on the reading process, it invites different interpretations on what counts as valuable evidence of reading achievement.

Pen portrait of Stephen and his learning context

We start here with a pen portrait of Stephen and then describe the teaching approach his teacher used with him and the class in general.

Stephen is 8 years old and in Year 3 in a big school, located in a working-class area of a large city in England. He is the elder of two children. He is described by his teacher as much loved by caring parents and as a child who is quiet and reserved in manner but who is not withdrawn. He loves the school breaks and gets on well with the other children in the class. He has two or three special friends with whom he spends much of the break time. His mother is a friendly and supportive person who frequently visits the school and who participates in school events. Stephen is eager to please his teacher; he agreed readily to allow me to record him reading to his teacher – we also recorded five other children most of whom were from the same class and reading ability level and who, incidentally, revelled in the opportunity to be on video. Just before the recording Stephen talked to me and to his teacher about what he was doing in class that morning, he smiled a little and seemed rather shy. He had a cold that day. His teacher told me afterwards that he said he was worried about reading as he was afraid he wouldn't *know the words*. He was keen to leave when the recording was over as the bell had gone for break and he wished to get out and play.

Stephen's Year 3 class of 28 children has a considerable ability spread, having two children who have a statement of special educational need and several who reached Level 3 in the standard assessment tasks at the end of their previous year in school (Year 2). Most of the class had obtained Level 2 in reading and writing. Stephen himself had obtained a Level 1 in both reading and in writing in the national, externally set assessment tasks. Level one in reading is described as follows:

> Pupils recognise familiar words in simple text. They use their knowledge of letters and sound–symbol relationships in order to read words and to establish meaning when reading aloud. In these activities they sometimes require support. They express their response to poems, stories and non-fiction by identifying aspects they like.

The typical pupil is expected, at the end of Year 2, to achieve at Level 2 in those assessments. Stephen's teacher believes that in May of Year 3 he could just about be described as working at the next level which is described as follows:

> Pupils' reading of simple texts shows understanding and is generally accurate. They express opinions about major events or ideas in stories, poems and non-fiction. They use more than one strategy, such as phonic, graphic, syntactic and contextual, in reading unfamiliar words and establishing meaning.

Over his period in Year 3 Stephen has struggled with literacy tasks in general and with reading in particular.

Although he finds reading a challenge Stephen is not so weak a learner or a reader as to meet the criteria for having a statement of special educational need, in which case his teacher could draw on specialist support and resources to help him. He is not untypical, therefore, of a sizeable minority of children in most classrooms in primary schools. Primary teachers will readily identify with the demands placed on Stephen's teacher in providing the necessary support for him in the context of a relatively large and mixed-ability class. So the key reason for selecting him as a basis for this book is that his and his teacher's situation typifies very many situations in mainstream classes up and down the country.

His teacher uses a variety of approaches to teach reading in her classroom. She uses a mix of approaches: she develops her pupils' word attack skills through an emphasis on phonics and context cues and she uses word games and work books with all the class, but especially with those who are finding reading difficult. She uses graded, commercially produced reading schemes as well as real books. Children have opportunities to read to their teacher individually on a regular basis, i.e. several times per week, and this is especially the case for the weaker readers. These children listen to tape recordings of books and are encouraged to read the book as they listen to the tape. Time is also spent on choosing books and on silent reading. Reading and writing are integrated and one is seen as enhancing the other. In the light of the National Literacy Strategy, which teachers are increasingly encouraged to adhere to, the teacher this year is placing much more emphasis on whole class teaching, on text-based work and on word-based activity in line with the requirements of the National Strategy.

Before presenting the text that Stephen read and the miscue analysis and retelling, some background information on miscue analysis is important.

Miscue analysis

Developed by Kenneth and Yetta Goodman in the US over thirty years ago, miscue analysis is a technique that provides insights into a child's oral reading approach. It provides a descriptive, qualitative account of a child's reading strategies. It is based on the idea that the errors or miscues that children make while reading aloud provide valuable information about the way they use various reading strategies to work out what the print says. The miscues are what the child says when something other than the words in the text are offered (Goodman 1973). The thinking is that if we can relate the miscues to what should have been read we can begin to understand the extent to which that child is an effective reader. That means we can work out the extent to which s/he is able to use the following cues:

- orthographic (print cues or the look of the letters and word on the page);
- phonic (print cues or knowledge of the sound of the letters/words);
- semantic (meaning cues or using knowledge and experience of stories and of written texts to predict events); and
- syntactic (grammar or the ability to draw on knowledge and experience of patterns in oral and written language to predict text).

Goodman also suggests that better readers make use of both the linguistic contextual information (syntactic and semantic cues) and orthographic and phonic cues (sometimes combined and referred to as graphophonic cues), whereas poor readers tend to make use of graphophonic information only. But, as will be discussed later, this is a controversial point.

It is important to note that miscue analysis is based on a particular perspective on reading – often described as psycho-linguistic. This perspective interprets reading as an interaction between language and thought to construct meaning from text. It sees the reader as a chaser-after-meaning, as someone who is actively engaged in meaning making. It sees the reader as processing the text using successful strategies and/or those which may be unsuitable to the understanding of what is on the page.

In developing miscue analysis the Goodmans were establishing new ways of thinking about reading, ways that were seeking to move beyond what we often describe as barking at print. Miscue analysis was one way that helped to develop new theoretical approaches to reading and the teaching of reading, and shifted the focus from word calling to reading comprehension. It created a new way of viewing the errors a reader makes; it moved away from the correct–incorrect paradigm. This approach was revolutionary as it viewed the miscues the reader made as instances of reading, rather than instances of mistakes or errors, and so they became valid evidence of the reading process that merited scrutiny (Bloome and Dail 1997). Just as the expected or accurate responses the reader made were viewed as instances of meaning making, so the unexpected or inaccurate responses were viewed as the product of the same meaning-making orientation.

More recently, Goodman *et al.* (1987) and others (Black and Paulson 2000) have extended the use of miscue analysis in a way that more directly involves the reader in reflecting on the miscues made by asking the reader to comment on them. This is called retrospective miscue analysis and it provides yet further insights into how a child is reading. Miscue analysis is not without its critics (Bloome and Dail 1997), but more of that later.

Over the years since the Goodmans developed the technique of miscue analysis, others have modified it and adapted it (Arnold 1982; Moon 1990). The form used with Stephen is a further adaptation. Based on the same reading perspective as miscue analysis, the running record is similar to miscue analysis – it is also an observational, diagnostic technique. Devised by Marie Clay (1985), the running record refers to three main reading strategies – 'meaning', 'structure' and 'visual'. 'Meaning' corresponds to semantic cues above. Clay asks, Does the child use meaning? 'Structure' corresponds to syntactic cues above – it is about grammar. The teacher is asked to consider the question: Is what the child says grammatical? 'Visual' corresponds with orthographic cues above – the question is, Does the child use visual cues from the letters and words? Clay also refers to phonic cues and self-correction.

Several books offer guidance on how to conduct a miscue analysis and/or a running record (Wixon 1979; Arnold 1982; Clay 1985; Barrs *et al.* 1988; Moon 1990; Campbell 1993). The book *Reading Miscue Inventory* by Goodman *et al.* (1987) describes the original version and is worth consulting while Robin Campbell's *Miscue Analysis in the Classroom* (1993) describes not just how to conduct it in the classroom but also describes and discusses more recent versions of it like the running record and retrospective miscue analysis.

There are four main steps in carrying out a miscue analysis (assuming you are not going to video- or audio-record the proceedings):

1 Select a text of about 200 words on which to base the analysis. Make a copy for yourself to record the miscues as the child reads.
2 Before the child starts to read, discuss the purpose and method with the child so she understands you are both working together to improve her reading.

3 After the child reads the story ask her to retell it in her own words, asking some open-ended questions to probe understanding and comprehension of the text.

4 There are several ways of coding the miscues. The coding for Stephen's miscues is given on the text below.

Stephen's reading, retelling and miscues

Included here is a full transcript of Stephen's reading, retelling and miscues. The text on which the miscue is based is presented in Appendix 1 without any annotation of miscues. It is presented here with the miscues indicated and the retelling included.

NAME: Stephen

CLASS/AGE: Year 3/8 years

DATE: 11 May 2000

CODING

Substitution: line through the word and substitution written in.

Self-correction: line through the word and all attempts/correction written in.

Omission: circle round the word omitted. 'T' over the word when told by the teacher.

Insertion: word written in.

Hesitation or Pause: indicated by the line numbers based in turn on the audio counter.

Repetition: the repeated word is underlined.

What the teacher said or did is indicated in brackets.

Bear by Mick Inkpen

Stephen selects this book from a choice of six spread out on the table. He turns all the pages in the book before he decides that this is the one he would like to read.

Jackie, his teacher, asks how they should proceed – whether she should read first, then for him to join in or for him to start on his own. He decides Jackie should start reading first.

Jackie points out the author's name and the list of all the books he has written which are listed inside the first page.

They agree that Jackie will start reading by herself, then Stephen will read with her and then he will read on his own.

Jackie starts reading:

A small whoosing sound.
Then a plop!
A bounce.
And a kind of squeak.
That was how the bear landed in my baby sister's playpen.

Have you ever had a bear fall out of the sky, right in front of you?
At first I thought he was a teddy bear. He just lay there, crumpled on the quilt.
Then he got up and took Sophie's drink. And her biscuit. That's when I knew he was real.

The bear climbed out of the playpen and looked at me.
He rolled on his back, lifted his paws and growled.
He seemed to want to play.

I put him in Sophie's baby bouncer.
He was very good at bouncing, much better than Sophie.

Do you want to join in?

They read together:

I sneaked the bear into the house under the quilt. At bedtime I hid him among my toys. 'Don't you say anything Sophie!' I said. 'I want to keep this bear.' Sophie doesn't say much anyway. She isn't even two yet.

Stephen now reads on his own:

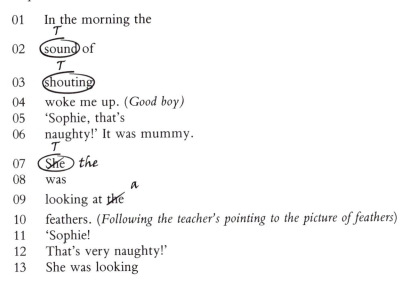

```
01   In the morning the
           T
02   (sound) of
           T
03   (shouting)
04   woke me up. (Good boy)
05   'Sophie, that's
06   naughty!' It was mummy.
           T
07   (She) the
08   was                    a
09   looking at the
10   feathers. (Following the teacher's pointing to the picture of feathers)
11   'Sophie!
12   That's very naughty!'
13   She was looking
```

14   at the
15   . . . .
16   . . . .
17   . . . .
18   . . . .
19
       T
20   (scribble). (*What sound does it start with?*) *1. sc*
21   Then
   T *the*
22   (she) looked at the
23
24
25   potty. (Teacher points to the picture)
26   'Sophie!'
27   she said.
28   'Good girl!'
29   But I don't
30
31
32
33   (think) *1. the* (Teacher says 'But I don't . . .) *2. think*
34   it was Sophie. (*Good boy*)
       T
35   I'm (sure) it
36   wasn't Sophie.
37
38   It
39
40
41   definitely *1. d.e.f (try) 2. dee f ee (def-in-e) 3. definitely (definitely)*
42   wasn't Sophie.
43
44   I took the bear to
45   school in my
46
47
      T
48   (ruck) (*Try the first bit*) *1. rr*
49
      T
50   (sack)

51 (Everyone) _T_
52 wanted
53 to be my
54 friend.
55 (Does) he _1. Did_ _T_
56 ~~bite~~?' _1. ba 2. bite_ (Good boy)
57 they said.
58 'He doesn't bite me,' ~~I~~ said. _1. he 2. I_
59 'What's his name?' they said.
60 'He doesn't have one'.
61
62 We
63 (kept) _1. keep_ (Good try) _T_
64 him
65 (quiet) all _T_
66 day
67 ~~feed~~ing him our _feed-ing_
68 lun~~ches~~. (Our lunches) _lun-ches_
69 He liked
70 the peanut butter
71
72 sand
73 wiches best. (Sandwiches)

Retelling 075–103

J: *Could you tell me what you've read already? What happened in this story?*
    Can you tell me what happens in the story? How does it start?

S: It starts with the teddy bear . . . goes . . . up . . . he goes down . . . he
    bounces . . . then he squeaks . . . and the little boy (*inaudible but sounds*
    like 'that was keeping him') . . . and it was morning . . . (*not clear*) there
    was a big row (*not clear*) before dark . . .

J: *There was a row, what had happened?*

S: Sophie was there too . . . writing on the wallpaper

J: *Poor Sophie! What else did . . . happened?*

S: And . . . before that . . . she'd gonna be sittin' on the toilet but she
    didn't go

J: *Who had been doing these things?*

S: The teddy bear.

J: *The teddy bear and then what happened after that?*

S: Then they went to school . . . and then

J: *Who went to school?*

S: The little boy

J: *The little boy, um*

S: and then . . . the other kids . . . they tried to be his friend because he had a teddy bear

J: *Yea. And so what did they do then?*

S: And then . . . the bear had peanut butter sandwiches and he liked them the best.

J: *Right. Do you like peanut butter sandwiches?*

S: Shakes his head

J: *You don't like them at all. Have you tried them?*

S: Yea

J: *I like peanut butter sandwiches. You remembered that story so well. You remembered everything. You're doing really really well Stephen. Will we read a bit more?*

Stephen now reads on his own:

104 A̶f̶t̶er *1. Af 2. After* (Good boy, after)

105 school my friends

106 came to

107 the house.

108 'Where is

109 he?'

110 they said.

111 We played with the bear

112

113

114 (be
115 hind) *1. be* ᵀ

116 the

117 (garage) *1. ga 2. ga-ra 3. grack* ᵀ

(*Real good try, garage*)

118

119

120

121 We made a

122

123

124

125

track

126 tunnel . . .

1. bir-da 2. bir-ad 3. a bird

127 a bridge . . .

(Teacher says *What's going on over here?* as she points to the bridge in the picture) *4. a bridge*

128

129 and a jump!

130

131 When the car came back

132 the bear had gone.

133 We looked and looked

134 but there was no bear anywhere.

135

136 At bedtime Sophie

137 wouldn't go to sleep.

138 She didn't

139 want her elephant.

140 She didn't want her rabbit.

141 She

142

143 threw *1. the 2. the-u 3. thr-au*

(*Threw, good try*)

144 them out of the cot.

145 I

T

146 (gave) *1. ga 2. ga* (*her my*)

147 her my

148 (second)

149 best pig.

150 She threw it out.

151 'Sophie! That's

T

152 (naughty)!' said mum.

153 But Sophie just

154

T

155 (howled). *1. how-led*

(*Sophie just what? Stephen says 'I don't know what that says. Teacher supplies the word. He repeats it*).

156

157 She *wants* wanted the bear.

158

159 CRASH! BANG!

160 It was the

161

162 *1. mid-del 2. middle* middle of the night. (*Good boy*)

163 SMASH!

164 CLANG! *1. cl-ang 2. clang*

165 The (noise) *T* *1. no*

166 was coming from the kitchen.

167 We crept *came* downstairs

168 and peeped *1. peep-ed 2. peeped*

169 (through) *T* *1. the-ou*

170 the door.

171 *I* It wasn't *at*

172 Burglar. *ba-ug-al-r*

J: *Will we read it together?*

S: *Yea*

Jackie and Stephen read together:

It wasn't a burglar. 'Bear!' said Sophie. 'Naughty!' So today a serious man in a serious hat came to look at our bear. He wrote something in a big black book. 'Will you have to take him away?' I said. 'We nearly always do,' said the man. He pointed his pen at my bear. 'But,' he said, 'this bear is an Exception.' 'This bear,' he went on, 'has fallen quite unexpectedly into a storybook. And it is not up to me to say what should happen next.' 'So can we keep him?' I said. 'Ask them,' he said. And he pointed straight out of the picture at YOU. And you thought for a moment. You looked at the man. You looked at the bear. You looked at Sophie. You looked at me. And then you said . . . 'YES YOU CAN!' So we did.

Plan of the remainder of the book

The rest of the book divides into four parts, each part offering a critical account of a particular perspective on reading. Part One offers a psycho-linguistic perspective on reading. Part Two takes a cognitive-psychological stance. Part Three considers reading from a socio-cultural perspective. Part Four views reading through a socio-political lens. Each part begins with two scholars' interpretation of Stephen as a reader, their suggestions for how he might be advanced as a reader, and the theory underpinning their practical suggestions. I decided to include the full transcript of each interview for two reasons. First, to give the fullest account offered by these distinguished literacy educators. Second, to allow the reader access to the context in which they made particular comments, particularly those comments that were selected for elaboration and discussion in the subsequent parts of the book. Depending on the slight variations of the interview context, these transcripts have combinations of subheadings and questions. A detailed discussion is then offered of each major perspective.

Part Two is rather longer than any of the other parts for the practical reason that this perspective has had a long history and has generated considerably more research on reading and, perhaps more importantly, has informed the current policy context in England more than any other reading perspective. Each part also considers official literacy curriculum in England, namely the National Literacy Strategy, in the light of that particular perspective.

The Conclusion draws together the main themes of the book and highlights some major implications for practice and for policy.

PART ONE
A PSYCHO-LINGUISTIC PERSPECTIVE

INTRODUCTION TO PART ONE:
A PSYCHO-LINGUISTIC
PERSPECTIVE ON READING

This first part explores some of the major ideas underpinning a psycho-linguistic perspective on reading. It begins with transcripts of the interviews conducted with Ann Browne and Teresa Grainger. Before picking up on and discussing some of the recommendations of our two scholars, I will offer a brief historical tour of the events and circumstances that led to the rise to prominence of a perspective that defined reading as a problem-solving activity. I will discuss what became known in the US as the 'whole language movement' and what in the UK was termed 'real books'. The writings of the original proponents of these ideas will be analysed and the positive contribution that this approach to reading makes will be considered. The difficulties and criticisms associated with this perspective on literacy will also be signalled and this discussion leads into Part Two. Throughout, connections will be made to the thinking of the two reading scholars, Ann Browne and Teresa Grainger, and to the classroom practices associated with this school of thought.

ANN BROWNE'S OBSERVATIONS, SUGGESTIONS AND THEORETICAL PERSPECTIVES

Profile of Ann Browne

Dr Ann Browne is a senior lecturer in education at the University of East Anglia where she works with trainee and practising teachers on primary language and literacy courses. Her main research interests are in English and Early Years Education. Her publications include four books about early years literacy: *Helping Children to Write* (1993), *Developing Language and Literacy 3–8* (1996), *A Practical Guide to Teaching Reading in the Early Years* (1998) and *Teaching Writing at Key Stage I and Before* (1999).

What follows is an edited version of a face-to-face interview I conducted with Ann in November 2001.

KATHY HALL (KH): *First I want to thank you very much for agreeing to participate in this project, for studying the video of Stephen and for giving me this interview. Perhaps we can start by reminding ourselves of the four questions – the first concerning what you think you know about Stephen, based on his reading and retelling and based on the very brief profile you got of him, the second concerning what more you would like to know about him, the third issue focusing on your suggestions for taking him forward, and finally, I would like to ask you about the theoretical perspectives you bring to bear on your interpretation of Stephen and how to help him. Shall we start with what you feel the evidence tells you about Stephen as a reader?*

Ann Browne (AB): Yes. He seemed very uncertain selecting the book, he grabbed the first book, *Funny Bones*, first of all, and didn't look at the others. Then his attention was drawn to those others and he grabbed one, the one that he subsequently read, *Bear*. He didn't look for authors, didn't look at the blurb, didn't look at the titles and, when asked to explain his first choice, he said he thought the book looked funny. So he may have been familiar with that book as it is a very familiar book for young children but you know the style of the illustrations would have given that and you wouldn't have to do much analysis to work out that this is a humorous book. So I think he was missing out a whole lot of strategies for choosing books. He didn't predict the content of the book at all, he didn't say 'Oh, it's about a bear', or 'I think this is about skeletons.' So he wasn't connecting to things that he was interested in, so very limited in that way, suggesting that he was very inexperienced at selecting books on his own. But this may be something you'd want to know more about – how much experience he's had at selecting books and making book choices and what is his knowledge of picture books and authors. And by Year 3 in fact you would expect it should be quite extensive and, looking at the environment he was sitting in, which was a very positive literacy environment, you'd think he would have this but I had questions about that.

Then in the introduction to the reading, the part where the teacher was reading, here Stephen was really focused. And it was really lovely to see that, he was intently looking at the words and apparently intently listening to the teacher's reading and that suggested to me that he was very interested in books and reading and he wanted to know what was in this book. And that was very positive.

Then we had the next bit when he joined in. He was invited to join in and he had sufficient confidence to join in which was again very positive to see, and he had interest, so that reinforced that intentness with which he'd been following the reading.

Here I started to analyse what he could do in terms of the processes and skills of reading. He had a good sight vocabulary of simple words, simple function words like 'it', 'was', and 'I', and mostly he got 'the'; he muddled it up a bit with 'she' but he mostly got it. Those little words like 'might' and 'be' – he was fine on all of those. He made some use of phonic strategies, for example, he got 'definitely' by sounding that out and partly he used it with syllabification as well, he was chunking it as well as using individual sounds. He was able on occasions to self-correct, not very frequently, but he did it, so again suggesting that he was wanting to make meaning but also suggesting maybe that he was wanting to get the words right which I think was quite a preoccupation of his. He substituted words which retained the meaning very closely like keeping the parts of speech, so he was using his knowledge of syntax. Again an example was 'did' and 'does' in line 55 and 'keep' and 'kept' later on in the reading so very positive in that he could draw on a number of reading strategies.

What he didn't use were the picture cues, the illustrations, the teacher pointed those out to him on a couple of occasions I think, so he wasn't using all the available cues that were there for him. He also read very slowly and that's what suggested to me that maybe he had a preoccupation with trying to get everything absolutely right. So the question then is, was he understanding what he was reading?

Then the next section of the reading is the retelling and I think at this point it was clear that he hadn't really understood what he'd read. He'd missed the subtleties of the text. He hadn't understood that this was a story about a real bear, that Sophie was getting the blame for something the bear had done. His teacher supported his retelling but even so there were quite a lot of misunderstandings. So that supposition that I had about his pre-occupation with decoding is confirmed for me by this.

So then taking all of that evidence from the selection to the retelling what I conclude is that he lacked confidence as a reader. He was hesitant and concerned with the words in the text; maybe that was interfering with his understanding. He liked humour and he wanted to be able to read, whether that was because he wanted to be able to read or whether he wanted to please his teacher, again I'd be uncertain about that. So that's a summary about what I think he could do.

KH: *Yes, thank you very much and now that brings us to what other evidence you would like to have about him. What more you would like to know about him?*

AB: I suppose I had lots of questions as you always do about an unknown child and these are not in any particular order but rather were generated by watching the tape. I'd like to know how he would tackle simpler texts because actually this one was quite a demanding text, it was a subtle story, it wasn't very obvious, there were undertones within it. And so I would like to know how he would tackle a simpler text which would, if you like, demand less understanding and have less words to be concerned about.

I'd like to know what kind of opportunities he has in school to respond to texts, to express ideas about books, to discuss books. I'd like to know what provision there is and how he participates within that in the class-room. I'd like to know what opportunities there are for him to read texts that he enjoys, that have a connection with his interest, with his life, and I think, in what you wrote, the teacher uses reading schemes as well as picture books for the children. But where he is on his choices between these would be interesting to know, and whether he has opportunities to select books himself or if the books are selected for him.

I'd like to know more about him as a child, about his interests, whether he ever reads books that are related to his interests, and maybe other reading material, maybe outside school, whether he reads comics, magazines about computers, cars or whatever he might be interested in. I'd also like to know how he reads familiar books, books that had been shared with him or prepared before he reads them, whether he then understands them better. And about how much practice at reading he gets in and out of school, although there seems plenty of opportunities within the classroom, and his mother I think was particularly interested in his education, but what in reality all that means in terms of time and experience of reading he gets.

And I'd like to know why he wants to read. Does he understand what reading is for, or does he want to read to please his teacher, or to please his parents? What is his understanding about reading, about the purposes of reading, the pleasures of reading? Does he see reading models at home, the out of school experiences? Does he see it as a purposeful activity? Is it presented to him as purposeful and happening beyond the confines of the classroom? So there was just a brainstorm of things, that I'd like to know a bit more about.

KH: *Thanks, Ann. Is it okay to move on now to some of the suggestions you have for his teacher?*

AB: Yes, well just before that, I thought that there were positive things about his teacher that I would like to mention, that are important to mention. This is especially important if you give a huge list of things that might be done, it suggests there were huge gaps in what's provided and I would want to acknowledge that there were positive things. His teacher was very warm and encouraging with him, and she did respond to what he was doing, and she noticed what he wasn't doing as well, so hence pointing out the illustrations, reading words for him, and from your notes there is a rich reading curriculum in the classroom so lots of good things going on.

But what do I think could be provided then? It would be important to think through the question: what does Stephen need, what precisely does he need? Rather than just a general reading programme, he needs a programme that's matched to his particular needs, and that relates to the sorts of things that he's not doing so well, which is not understanding, and not having a large sight vocabulary for his age. For example, he could be encouraged to revisit books that he knows. He needs his confidence building up in reading, so that he's less stuck on deciphering every word, so if there were familiar books, maybe that would be helpful. He could make his own books that were of interest to him, that again would give him confidence when he was reading them, because he'd have written them himself.

He could read with friends because he seems to be quite sociable, in that he has a close-knit group of friends. Have reading partners and work with friends, work with friends at the computer on reading and on writing. Have opportunities to respond to books maybe in group reading, but maybe in projects on author studies, collections of books in the classroom.

Teach him book selection strategies, help him to select his own books and encourage him to keep a list of books he has selected. Look at the choices he makes and see whether there is a pattern, then see how you could use that to pick more books that would interest him or take him elsewhere in his reading. So find out what interests him really, match books to his interests and ability, because that book was difficult.

Provide specific phonic teaching matched to his needs so, for example, on line 143 there was the 'oo' sound and the long vowel sounds in 146 that he didn't seem confident with, so there would be two things you could be quite specific about in relation to phonics teaching. Encourage him to guess when he's reading, encourage him to guess at words that fit the context, so they're not random guesses, encourage him really to take a chance, to speed him up, and to use the context of what he's reading. Enlarge his sight vocabulary, start to push him on beyond the functional simple words through games like lotto, snap, and computer games. Writing would help there too.

Provide introductions to books for him. Ensure that the title is looked at, that the content of the book is predicted, and that the author is noted. Ask him, for example, if he knows any other stories by this author. Ensure that the blurb is looked at before the reading begins, so that he's in the frame of mind for reading, so he's a bit familiar with what might happen, before he embarks on any reading.

Other things you might consider are using tapes with a friend so he gets the experience of complete stories, retelling stories using tapes and story props, taking tapes of books home, seeing if you can find an author that interests him, basing cross-curricular activities around a book, which would then provide opportunities for him to revisit books and become confident with books. Build up a little core of books that he's familiar with and feels strongly about. Read with him, do more of what the teacher was doing at the beginning of the tape, so paired reading with an adult would be good. This could be with a classroom assistant, a parent or a volunteer.

I would find out what he reads at home. As a hunch, because he said he likes humour, joke books and comics might be a good starting point for some reading material for him. Writing a joke book could be a way in to the making of a book for him.

Challenge his understanding of books so when he's asked to talk about a book he's read, if he's misunderstood, challenge that, in a positive way obviously, perhaps saying 'But I don't think that happened', 'Why do you think that happened?' etc. so that he's really focusing on the meaning. Demonstrate the use of illustrations, perhaps in shared reading activities, so those were just again a brainstorm of ideas.

KH: *Thanks very much, Ann. Can we change tack just a little bit now and move away from the helpful, practical suggestions to the thinking and the theory underlying all those observations and the suggestions you offered his teacher. I'm thinking particularly of your own work and the major influences on your own thinking about reading development.*

AB: I don't know whether to start off with the people who influenced me or with where I start when I'm thinking about children and learning, or both.

KH: *Yes, I like the idea of starting with the children and their learning and how you would want to progress learning?*

AB: Okay, right. I think it's important to try and understand how learners learn and to have that as an overview, and then take how learners learn and try and put yourself in the place of the child learning. So, thinking in a general sense then, you have to have a reason for learning; you learn most effectively if there is a purpose. Children need to know what it is they're learning to do, so that they're clear on what it is. They need to believe that this learning that they're undertaking makes a difference to them, and to their lives, that it adds something to what they've got already. Relevance is important. So that is really a starting point. Did Stephen really understand what reading is for and does he really know what he's embarking on, and does he know what reading could be to him? This brings in the question really of what his exposure to reading outside school is like and whether it is clear to him what the function of reading is, so that would link in with those observations.

Then there is respecting children as rational curious beings who are always eager to learn, but knowing that they are also eager to please. Young children are so eager to please, and this can get in the way almost of them learning, and you're not quite sure what it is, whether they are eager to learn or eager to please. All children have an intense ability to learn and a belief that they can do it.

I would always emphasize that reading is one of the language areas, and how we learn lessons about reading development from how children learn to speak and communicate, and acknowledging again that ability they have to communicate in so many ways and to take lessons from oral language learning. So consequently the importance of believing that they will learn to read and they will learn to write if they can see these activities as communicative activities. That would then take me into what is clearly, and what has been a big influence on me, which is the work of Smith and Goodman and the whole-language approach. Yes, they did influence me terrifically, and continue to do so. That again would link in with how I started to look at Stephen's reading and look at the way he used context and syntax and look at the other strategies. So that whole miscue idea and the retelling. What is the understanding – that's the whole purpose of reading; it isn't reading unless you've understood what you've read, and Goodman and Smith so emphasized this.

And then I think other people like Gordon Wells and his work on oral language – that would link, too: what he was saying about how well children learn language in real contexts and where parents encourage learning in a natural and purposeful way. It's so important to provide models for children. So you have to think of real contexts for this child to read in, i.e. the social dimensions, working with friends, and the choice of resources that would be more real to him. And this relates to what was loosely associated with Liz Waterland – but she didn't start it off – that is the apprenticeship approach. Here we have the adult and child learning together, and the child learning, in a supported way, from an adult and the child becoming more and more competent and taking over, and taking more responsibility when they become confident and competent at what they're doing.

Don Holdaway was an influence too. He saw learning to read as a social activity, one where you made links between learning at home, learning at school, the idea of shared reading. And again the process being very supported – giving children lots of ways into reading, giving them a set of books that they are familiar with reading, letting them read, supported by other children, by adults, returning to books to read them again. And learning the skills within the context of reading the whole or complete text, and a text that is an interesting text, an important text and an enjoyable text, one that's been selected pretty carefully for its child-appeal but also for its quality.

Henrietta Dombey has influenced me too in her work in trying always to put phonics, particularly, within a context of all the other things that need to go on. She's particularly good I think at saying Don't dismiss phonics, phonics has a place but it always needs to occur within a context. Yes, I think she has got a very balanced view of phonics and a very realistic one and you'd never want to dismiss any of the strategies that might help children to read anyway. So it's important, I think, to recognize that there is a number of strategies that we need to teach children. And she has been very sane and good about that.

And then at a more theoretical level the work of Stanovitch would have influenced me. However, he can be very dismissive of whole-language exponents, even though he very often writes that he's not being critical of them. But I find him being very critical of them, somewhat dismissive even. But his thinking on top-down and bottom-up models is useful. His notion of an interactive model of the reading process, that is that all the strategies have to work together, and you don't need to start at a top-down or bottom-up but you acknowledge that all of them are important, has been useful. Although I said he's very critical of whole language, when he talks about his models then I think he brings everything together, sounds a bit of a paradox there, actually, that.

KH: *Do you mind if I ask you something which I didn't really plan but it just arises from what you're saying about integrating top-down and bottom-up models of reading. I was just wondering what you thought about the National Literacy Strategy in the light of those possible tensions between bottom-up and top-down approaches.*

AB: I really have mixed feelings about this, Kathy, actually, you see, as I think you can work with the Literacy Strategy if you want to, because of the division into text, sentence and word level. You can use the text in pretty much the way, say, Don Holdaway was saying. And if you have an understanding of the reading processes, then you can select your objectives in a way that still makes a very meaningful approach to the teaching of reading. But I think that, sadly, at Key Stage 1 and before, the emphasis within the Literacy Strategy is on phonics and on the word-level work. There are more word-level objectives and that is pushed as if it's the solution to the development of reading and writing. But if you ignore those directives we're getting and just look at the framework and you ask 'How can I make this into a sensible teaching programme?' then you can make it work, I think. Maybe that's a bit of an answer really – how can I make it into something? Maybe you shouldn't have to make it into something.

If you think about the range of texts that children have to engage with, that could be wonderful, and the real push that there is now on poetry within the Strategy, and that's really exciting, could be exciting. But it's become reduced really because of the word level. I think what's so sad about the NLS is that there was a real opportunity to improve practitioners' understanding of the processes of reading and this hasn't happened. It has just become a mechanical thing, this is what you do and a question of this is how you do it. And so I think many people haven't had the time or maybe even the knowledge to be able to use it in a way that enables them to teach in a more holistic way. I suppose there are all sorts of contradictions in there, aren't there? What's happening is I don't see my students – and I think my students learn from the teachers they are working with – I don't see them trying to understand what their children are doing; they're more preoccupied with what they have to teach the children, so it's become a teaching thing, rather than a learning thing. I worry about that.

Increasingly I think it is the lack of understanding of the advocated teaching strategies that interferes with the success of the Strategy. Shared reading, shared writing and guided writing could be very powerful teaching and learning strategies. They have been in the past, but I don't think there is sufficient understanding of them – why they are powerful and how they can support and extend children's learning – and so they are not being used to best effect by many teachers. If they were used in the way suggested by Holdaway and exemplified in the CLPE book on shared writing, and if guided writing was seen as an opportunity to engage with children and support their discoveries about the processes of writing, particularly those relating to composition, i.e. like Graves' idea of a group writing conference, they would be far more powerful. As it is, all these methods of organizing literacy teaching are often limited to teaching children about phonics and spelling and have often become an end in themselves. They are filled with missed opportunities. Children are spending too much time on the bits and pieces of reading and writing and are getting bored with the routines. They are being taught the skills and are not aware of the joys and uses of literacy and consequently many of them do not see the point of becoming readers and writers. When children feel this, there is the danger that they will fail to learn or develop their abilities beyond what is acceptable in school or use and enjoy their skills outside school.

KH: *Well thanks very much for that. Is there anything else I should ask or anything you want to say?*

AB: Well, there is actually. What I was thinking about as I was driving here today, Kathy, and thinking about this meeting, is that one of the influences on me is the literature about writing. And how writing develops, and seeing the developmental aspects of writing and then linking that with reading, and that makes it very real to me. Reading work like that of Ferreiro and Teberosky, and seeing that developmental continuum of language learning which is very visible in writing and then knowing that there is a developmental continuum in reading. Development in reading is supported, well, it's imitative and supported as it is in writing and then the reader becomes more and more competent and more and more familiar with the way the writing system works and that would have affected how I see the development of reading.

KH: *Do you mean that they become more and more competent in all the modes of language when you say that?*

AB: Particularly connecting their development in reading with their development in writing. The feedback they get and the support that they get and the teaching that they get that is targeted to what they don't know yet but yet the support is there for what they do know and working in that way with children is so important, I think.

KH: *And writing is very much your area of interest too, isn't it?*

AB: Yes it is.

KH: *Ann, again, thank you very much.*

TERESA GRAINGER'S OBSERVATIONS, SUGGESTIONS AND THEORETICAL PERSPECTIVES

Profile of Teresa Grainger

Teresa Grainger is a principal lecturer in education at Canterbury Christ Church University College, where she runs the MA in Literacy and Language and coordinates the PGCE primary English programme. Her research interests are focused on the language arts: storytelling, poetry, drama and literature as well as pedagogy. Her books include *Traditional Storytelling in the Primary Classroom* (1997), *Resourcing Drama 5–8* (2001a) and *Resourcing Drama 8–14* (2001b) both with Mark Cremin and *Inclusive Educational Practice: Literacy* (2000) which she wrote with Janet Tod. Teresa was president of the United Kingdom Reading Association (2001–02) and is editor of the refereed UKRA journal *Reading: Literacy and Language*.

This is an edited version of a telephone conversation I conducted with Teresa Grainger in January 2002.

KATHY HALL (KH): *Thanks, Teresa, for agreeing to do this interview by telephone. I'm aware that you couldn't access the visual information, that you are basing your observations and suggestions only on the transcript and the background notes. What do you think we know about Stephen from this limited evidence of him as a reader?*

TERESA GRAINGER (TG): I can't see his hesitations. I'm focusing more on what he's saying, what he's doing with words. I don't think this invalidates what I'm saying but you've got to decide as you're doing the project. I do know the book – my children have it here at home. But in any case there are three things that I think we do know about him, things that I think are important. He's the oldest child, first son, and he's a sibling. In terms of his personality he is someone who is not ebullient.

Secondly, we do know some of his reading history. We know for example that he didn't achieve Level 2 at the end of Key Stage 1 reading assessment so he is not operating at the level expected of most children of this age. He seems to lack confidence in himself as a reader. He expressed a fear of not knowing the words before the recording. I was interested in this expression of anxiety – he was afraid that he wouldn't know the words. He is word-conscious then, perhaps, and he is hesitant.

Thirdly, through the miscue exercise you can see some of his skills. He's reliant on phonics, I think, and on segmentation and blending within that. He is also very reliant on the teacher – there were very many words supplied for him. And this is where I might have got more informa-tion from the visual evidence as his face may well tell a lot about him – whether he was trying to have a go for example. He struggled with some of the words and the teacher frequently supplied them. Sometimes she said 'sound it out' but mostly she supplied it. I think we know he's be-come over-reliant on particular skills and uses these at the expense of others. Yet he had a good understanding of the story and did seem to engage with it. He knew it was 'in the dark' and he knew what was going on. And this rather surprised me as I thought it was at odds with his reading. So in the retelling he does seem to have grasped the meaning but he doesn't have the confidence to have a go when he's stuck on a word, he just waits to be supported – he waits for the teacher to supply the word. These were the points that struck me in relation to what we know from the evidence.

KH: *Thank you, Teresa. Can you tell me what evidence you'd like to have; what would you like to know about him as a reader?*

TG: I'd like to know more about his reading habits. I'd like to know if he reads at home. I'd like to know what he does in class during quiet reading time. Does he read or does he fiddle around? Does he flick over the pages? Does he look at the pictures? What are his preferences – does he have any and we don't know that. What kind of reading material does he like if he's given a choice? What authors would he know or choose? Would he go for an Inkpen or a Burningham? If there's a reliance on schemes in the school, and I gather there is, then what level of the scheme is he on? How conscious is he of where he is in relation to others in the class – would he choose a book to be seen to be the same as his mates in the class who may not now be on the scheme?

And in terms of his reading record I'd like to know what his self-assessment of his own reading is. I'd like to know if he really has a desire to read. Does he enjoy reading?

Although he retells as requested, he does so because his teacher asks. He seems eager to please his teacher. He's assiduous, he reads the words as she asks. Also the teacher does a retell rather than a reflection and a retell – there is little discussion and debate. He remembered the story, to use her key word which gives us an insight into what she thinks you should do after the reading, that is remember it in order. She draws attention to picture cues but she draws attention to sounds at least three times. The remembering and the focus on sounds seemed to be most important to her. There was a tendency on her part, then, to attend to the 'small shapes' rather than attend to the bigger picture.

KH: *Could you say a bit more about that, Teresa, what you mean by 'small shapes'?*

TG: A couple of times the teacher draws his attention to the pictures but mostly she draws his attention to the words, the sounds of the words and so on. She tends to concentrate on the 'small shapes'. But to be fair to her she's doing a miscue analysis, and in a strict miscue analysis one might offer no support at all. And this may have been a conundrum for her. She seems to have combined an ordinary one-to-one reading encounter, which I know it isn't, with a miscue – all the time aware you are videoing her. She has a tendency to say 'What word is that?' – and I'm not saying that's not appropriate, but she might occasionally have highlighted words within words. Now of course she may have done that. I know I can gesture with my finger to the visual cues without literally saying 'Look at that.' Then the child feels he has made the decision himself – but as I didn't see them reading together, I'm less confident about this point. Equally she doesn't stop to discuss the book, she doesn't interrupt to engage with the meaning of the text – now this is what I would call a 'big shape'. I know it was a test situation but her inclination was only to use two elements – prompt for visuals or prompt for sounds. And she didn't encourage him to recognize parts of words. She didn't encourage him to read on to help him get the word. She's probably thinking 'This is a miscue analysis and I musn't interrupt.' The bit about the peanut butter was great, now this kind of interaction could have happened during the reading although one doesn't want too many breaks as this would interrupt the story too much.

The other thing in relation to this is the affirmation – his teacher is good at affirming and encouraging him. But I think she overdoes the 'good boy'; she says this several times, especially when he sounds a word out. I think you might want to extend such interruptions into a moment's discussion

– 'Do you think he would bite? I wouldn't like it if a teddy bear bit me etc. Do you think he did bite? Let's read on and find out.' That kind of thing makes a difference to the next bit of the text I think, and I think it's better than 'good boy' as you create the desire to know rather than only affirming that he has read words correctly. And I have to say 'good boy' sounds rather patronizing to me anyway. But then I know it's easy to be critical when it's not you. So really the point I'm making is that I would suggest the teacher might pay more attention to the meanings, interpretations, rather than focus too narrowly on the accuracy of the words. In other words I'd recommend more emphasis on the 'big shapes' and less emphasis on the 'small shapes'.

KH: *Okay, thanks for that.*

TG: Getting back to what else I'd like to know about Stephen. I'd like to know what his attitude to reading is. He might well sit in 'read aloud' time and be an avid listener, or he might fiddle with his shoe laces. I'd like to know a lot more about his commitment to reading. So I would like to know more than 'his word' as it were, which I think is what we mainly got in the miscue transcript. I would want to see his behaviour, what he actually does, and I'd like to know about his interest in reading at home.

I'd also like to know what the parental support is like. Does he read at home? Does he read independently? Does he read to his sibling? Does he read aloud? It sounds as if his mum is helpful and supportive but this doesn't always mean parents know how to support in the best way. Is she asking him to read to her or is she reading with him, are they reading together? She's a supportive mum clearly and I'd like to know what kind of guidance parents are offered by the school in this regard.

Last thing I'd like to know – and this probably should be the first thing I mentioned – that is what he is like as a person. I'd like to know about his personality, his interests, his tendencies, what gets him going. I believe strongly that we can hook children in who aren't yet capable and committed or confident if we work through their interests, by finding the subject matter that ensnares them in some way. Not all children are going to be confident to pick up, say, a Harry Potter book and read it, but what I would at least want is that they would come to the idea of a book in your hand as not being a negative thing. If he has rollerblades, a skateboard and so on then perhaps he'd read material about his hobbies; would he look at a catalogue or a book about his interests? In this way one could tempt him into reading via his interests and begin to get a handle on the kinds of narrative texts he might enjoy.

KH: *So what do you think his teacher should do to advance him as a reader?*

TG: I think the first thing to do is put this evidence alongside other knowledge about him as a reader along the lines I was suggesting just now. A miscue is not enough of course, it only really looks at the cueing systems although it should encompass comprehension and response as well. The other sorts of evidence should come from a reading conference, from observations of him in the classroom, talks with his parents – all of this to get a bigger picture of him. Then one could devise a plan for him and indeed for others who may have a similar profile. The teacher should develop a series of specific aspects to take him forward. She might draw on the support of a classroom assistant here, his parents, herself working in a one-to-one with him where she can, but this will not be so easy. So she might group him with some others who also need the same kind of support and here I would make use of guided reading.

However, a point I would emphasize is that the specific support planned for him should be set within a wider culture of language and literacy. I think there's a danger in thinking that the specifics can be done separately – this work should be integrated into a wider programme of literacy development that prioritizes meaning in a literature-rich classroom environment.

In relation to the specifics it would be sensible to use the key pedagogies of shared and guided reading in particular, and within these the teacher would need to extend his cueing systems. He doesn't seem to be aware of the cueing systems he's using. And I think this could be done in shared and guided reading contexts where peers can discuss the cueing system they use. I'm not suggesting he needs that terminology but I do think these kinds of sessions can develop metalinguistic awareness. Provide opportunities for children to articulate what they do when they're stuck – 'I read on to the end of the line when I'm stuck on a word' etc. He's not looking for words within words, he's not guessing what's coming next in the text. Sometimes he made errors as if he wasn't sure what the sense of the sentence was. And this would need to be tackled in those kinds of sessions where children talk about what they do as they read and are specifically taught strategies.

I think his teacher might develop his sight words more thoroughly – he's not using graphic knowledge well. I would suggest lots of games for this.

My sense is that he's probably come through a strong phonics diet and that's fine, but he doesn't know what to do when he meets a word that is phonetically irregular, he waits to be told what it is. And as I've said before, he is preoccupied with the words – he hasn't struck out on his own; he's not making his own guesses using a range of context and visual and semantic cues; and here he needs to be supported a lot more. He needs a wider range of strategies for tackling the words *and* he needs to know he is doing it. What I mean here is that in the guided reading sessions she needs to help him become aware that he's been taught how to read forward, to check the picture cues and so on, that he can do those things when he comes to an unknown word; then he can practise these strategies at home. It's as if 'knowing' the words is the only part of the reading process for him.

What I think his teacher should be aiming for is for him to become increasingly independent as a reader. To get more confidence he may well need highly patterned language like one finds in the Dr Seuss books – that he can read independently, and have some fun with. He might be encouraged to engage in poetic performance. He could, for example, work with one or two friends on putting a poem on tape, using expressive voices, and interpreting the poem in some way. This could involve using highly patterned verse, which would give him the freedom to read some text well. Equally he could tell stories onto tapes. He's not likely to want to be in the story chair himself and be a teller, but if he's working in a group and he knows he's going to have a part to play, a role to perform with his mates, he might begin to engage more with the meaning, with fluency and expression.

I believe strongly the teacher needs to read aloud to him (and to the class), and develop his awareness of authors. Reading partnerships would also be good for him – where, for example, the Year 5s partner with the Year 3s. This would be excellent support for him because he certainly doesn't want to be placed in a position where he is exposed. This arrangement benefits everyone but it especially benefits the weaker readers. All of this should be happening, I think, within a wider context of a classroom that celebrates authors, that emphasizes reading and writing for meaningful purposes. The 'additional literacy support' could be used for his specific difficulties but none of this will work unless it's set within a context of meaningful engagement with literature profiled in the classroom.

KH: *What kind of theoretical framework do you draw on in making all these recommendations?*

TG: I take a Vygotskian view of learning – a social interactionist perspective. The learner must appreciate the purpose of what he's doing if he is going to develop as an independent reader. If he doesn't understand the purposes and have his own purposes for reading, he's only going to continue to develop in those contexts in which he's being supported. I'm also very influenced by reader response theory, and the author–reader–text triangle as well as the work done at the Institute of Education (London) (e.g. James Britton, Harold Rosen, and Margaret Meek) and Donald Graves, the Goodmans, and Frank Smith. I'm interested in the author–reader–text triangle. I would locate myself within the whole-language movement but I would also say that within the whole-language movement there's a range of people and views. For example, I think it's important to get a balance between implicit and explicit teaching/learning – I'd like children to discuss their cueing systems. I don't think Goodman himself suggests children discuss reading strategies, and the NLS supports such a stance. Teachers don't have to own this knowledge – we can share it and I think there is much scope for the use of retrospective miscue analysis – this helps children make their own independent moves forward. For me reading is a problem-solving business and I believe children need to see this, to self-correct etc. But to bother to problem solve, to bother to self-correct, you've got to know there's meaning to be had, and you've got to value this. So we come back to the purpose of the enterprise and how children learn this through engagement and interaction. After all, if reading is anything it's thinking about meaning.

We need to make sure that we are integrating not only the modes of language, listening, speaking, reading and writing, but also developing children's skills, understanding, knowledge and attitudes. Okay, naming the phonemes might be a significant piece of knowledge to have, but without a wider framework we're in danger of developing the skills at the expense of the fundamental enterprise of making meaning. We can easily increase knowledge about language but we need to ensure that children are able to make good use of this knowledge in creative applications and for their own purposes, and in my opinion this is not what's happening nation-ally at the moment – at least in the case of writing. The holistic develop-ment of the individual is important and we shouldn't neglect it.

KH: *Many thanks, Teresa. I very much appreciate the time you've taken to study the evidence and to talk to me.*

READING AS A
PROBLEM-SOLVING ACTIVITY

Introduction

How would we describe some of the theoretical underpinnings of the observations and suggestions of our scholars so far? Each of them highlighted some of the theorists and theories that have informed their judgements and understandings of the reading process. Each of them drew on a range of literature and thinking about language and about learning. It is certainly not my intention here to suggest that these scholars can be conveniently pigeon-holed or categorized into a particular camp – if anything, this book shows just how futile, crude and simplistic such an approach would be. You might well wonder, then, at the title of Part One, which does suggest a particular perspective on literacy. My explanation is this. You can usefully consider the observations and suggestions of our scholars against some of the major perspectives that have informed the field of reading. You can begin to detect the relative impact on their thinking of these various perspectives and how they differ in the emphasis they place on different theoretical principles. You can begin to work out what theories seem to be heavily influencing their ideas and suggestions, and by so doing you can begin to formulate your own theoretical perspective which, I suggest, is very likely to draw on more than one or even two major perspectives. This is perfectly reasonable, given that all these perspectives are attempting to describe the same process. This part of the book looks at reading through a psycho-linguistic lens and it refers back to our scholars' suggestions from time to time in order to trace the influence on them of this particular stance. Psycho-linguistics is the interdisciplinary field of psychology and linguistics in which language behaviour is studied.

Whence the psycho-linguistic perspective?

The linguist Noam Chomsky (1965) revolutionized the study of language when he demonstrated that comprehending language was not a matter of linking up the various meanings of adjacent words. This kind of linear processing was the basis of the behaviourist psychologists' accounts of language comprehension that had prevailed for some fifty years before. Children did not simply imitate the language they heard, Chomsky suggested. Language was far too complex to be acquired in this way. He postulated a nativist view of language acquisition in suggesting that humans are innately predisposed to acquire the language of their environment. Children naturally acquire the language of the home by sheer exposure, he observed, and they become good users of oral language long before they start school. Moreover, they become proficient in oral language without direct instruction. In Chomsky's view, humans had to be equipped with some cognitive device for working out the complex rules of language – how else could you explain this remarkable achievement?

Many in the field of reading, especially psychologists, then began to wonder if Chomsky's observations about oral language could also be applied to written language. This was how a psycho-linguistic position on reading came about. While Chomsky had argued that children were innately equipped to learn language, psycho-linguists went on to demonstrate that children were active learners who worked out the rules of language for themselves. When a child says 'I eated my dinner', or 'I can see two sheeps' s/he is inferring that you put an event in the past by adding 'ed' to the verb and that you make a noun plural by adding 's'. So mistakes in their oral language give insights into the way children were inferring the rules. Could there be parallels in written language? Do children learn how to read and to write in much the same way as they acquired oral language? Could learning to read and to write be natural?

Reading as natural and as a constructive or problem-solving activity

These questions exercised several literacy researchers but perhaps few more so than Kenneth and Yetta Goodman and Frank Smith. Kenneth Goodman argued that the mistakes, or what he termed 'miscues', children make while reading are better viewed as information about the comprehending process the reader is going through than mistakes to be eliminated. They should be viewed, he argued, as indicators of how the reader was making sense of the text. He concluded that, because children were better able to read words in story contexts than in word lists, they were using context knowledge to support comprehension and word identification. It's important to note that reading, according to Goodman, depends not only on the text but also on what the reader brings to the text in the form of previous knowledge, not just of language, but knowledge of the world itself. He says:

> Reading is a constructive process: both the text and the meaning are constructed by the reader. That means that at any point in time there are two or more texts during reading: the published text and the reader's text. In the transactions, both the reader and the text are changed. The reader's knowledge and schemata are changed, and the text is changed as the reader constructs it to fit expectations and world knowledge. In this emerging consensus, what the reader brings to the text is as important as anything in the text. Comprehension always depends on the reader's knowledge, beliefs, schemata, and language ability.
>
> (Goodman 1992: 358)

Overall, emphasis is placed on the meaning that learners themselves want to communicate.

His close observation and analysis of actual reading behaviour led him to describe reading as 'a psycho-linguistic guessing game' (Goodman 1967). Here he laid out the elements of language that he thought readers used to construct meaning from texts. He suggested that readers draw on three cue systems simultaneously to make sense of text: graphophonic, syntactic, and semantic cues. He said:

> The readers of English I have studied utilize three cue systems simultaneously. The starting point is graphic in reading and we may call one cue system 'graphophonic'. The reader responds to graphic sequences and may utilize the correspondence between the graphic and phonological systems of his English dialect . . . The second cue system the readers uses is 'syntactic'. The reader using pattern markers such as function words and inflectional suffixes as cues recognizes and predicts and structures . . . The third cue system is 'semantic'. In order to derive meaning from language, the language user must be able to provide semantic input. This is not simply a question of meaning for words but the much larger question of the reader having sufficient experience and conceptual background to feed into the reading process so that he can make sense out of what he's reading . . .
>
> (Goodman 1973: 25–6)

By using all these cue systems readers could minimize uncertainty about unknown words and meanings. Since readers are viewed to be naturally motivated to make sense of texts, Goodman saw no reason to distinguish between a word-identification phase and a comprehension phase in reading nor to isolate any single cue system for separate training or development. He said 'We can study how each one (cue system) works in reading and writing, but they can't be isolated for instruction without creating non-language abstractions' (Goodman 1986: 38–9).

Similarly, Frank Smith's *Understanding Reading* (1971) argued that reading was not something that you are taught, but rather something you learned to do as a consequence of belonging to a literate society and he postulated that there were no special prerequisites to learning to read. He said 'The function of teachers is not so much to "teach" reading as to help children read' (1971: 3). For him, you learn to read by reading and you learn to write by writing. In line with Goodman's notion of reading as a psycho-linguistic guessing game, Smith suggested that reading was a matter of making informed predictions about a text based on what readers already knew about how language works (syntactic and semantic know-ledge) and what they knew about the world (semantic knowledge). His idea was that the reader develops hunches or hypotheses about upcoming words in a text and then confirms what the word is by sampling only a few features of the visual display. He advanced the controversial idea that reading was only incidentally visual – he minimized the role that graphic information plays in reading, saying:

> The more difficulty a reader has with reading, the more he relies on the visual information; this statement applies to both the fluent reader and the beginner. In each case, the cause of the difficulty is inability to make full use of syntactic and semantic redundancy, of nonvisual sources of information.
>
> (Smith 1971: 221)

And two years later he reiterated the secondary importance of visual informa-tion in saying 'It is clear that the better reader barely looks at the individual words on the page' (Smith 1973: 190). By nonvisual sources he meant readers' prior knowledge of the context and of the way language works. He argued for the importance of these sources of information so readers could make good predictions and so they would not have to rely too heavily on visual information, thus losing sight of the meaning.

Even more controversially, Smith (1973: 105) claimed that 'readers do not use (and do not need to use) the alphabetic principle of decoding to sound in order to learn to identify words'. To reiterate Smith's position: in coming to the text with expectations and a disposition to predict, readers sample just enough of it to confirm or reject their predictions. As will be demonstrated below, this take on reading and, in particular, the status Smith (and others) attributed to graphophonic knowledge have since been challenged and found to be inaccurate.

Basically psycho-linguists, like the Goodmans and Smith, view writing as paralleling oral language, differing only in mode. In 1980 Yetta Goodman claimed 'Language development is natural whether written or oral. It develops in a social setting because of the human need to communicate and interact with the significant others in the culture' (Goodman 1980: 3). Written language is seen as having the same functions as all other forms of language (listening, speaking) which include the need to inform, to communicate, to interact with others, to learn about the world and so on. In other words, language, whatever its mode, serves a purpose for the learner; young children learn to talk because it is useful and functional for them. So the argument goes that if written language is also seen as functional, then children will learn to produce (write) and understand it (read) in much the same way. And just as oral language is learned without direct teaching, so too written language could be learned without direct intervention. In this country several theorists advocated greater links across the various modes of language and they raised awareness of the power of language as a medium of learning (e.g. Barnes *et al.* 1972; Britton 1972; Barnes 1981; Corden 2000).

The Goodmans (1979) actually assumed that there was only one reading process, that is that all readers, whether beginner/inexperienced or fluent/experienced use the same process, although they differ in the control they have over the process. They assumed a non-stage reading process, in other words. In their view the major advantage experienced readers have over inexperienced ones is their better knowledge of language and of the world. As such, skilled readers, it was thought, relied less on orthographic information.

The teacher's role in this model involves two things: first, creating a climate in which children would be interested in using reading and writing – as Newman (1985) put it, offering 'invitations' to learn – and second, enabling children join the 'literacy club' as Smith (1992). In this view reading development is best fostered through exposure to text that is rich in natural language and through helping the reader attend to meanings and contexts. It is assumed that controlling the vocabulary of texts or attending to parts of words would not pay dividends; that in fact such an approach would limit opportunities for learning.

In this context Wade (1990) debated the inadequacies of the reading schemes of the time in this country, providing an instance from one in which reading in reverse order from line eighteen to line one, rather than from line one to eighteen, appeared to make as much (or as little!) sense. He argued that the short sentences, the simple vocabulary and repetition of sounds, words and ideas limited the reader's meaning-making and prediction potential. Similarly Margaret Meek (1988) criticized the disconnective text, the insubstantial characters and the lack of interest or suspense in the train of events in reading schemes, contrasting this with the richness of language and satisfying plots associated with children's literature.

Because reading is seen to develop 'from whole to part, from vague to precise, from gross to fine, from highly concrete and contextualized to more abstract' (Goodman 1986: 39) this perspective on the reading process is often thought of as a 'top-down' model of literacy development. Whole stories are seen as better than sentences and sentences are seen as better than words (Holdaway 1979). Dividing language into smaller and smaller parts or subskills jeopardizes clarity, meaning and simplicity, it is assumed. While the teaching of 'basic language skills' is not ruled out, it is recommended that they are developed within a wider language context which can make vital contributions to the efficiency and organization of the classroom for learning. Both Ann Browne and Teresa Grainger stressed this point about integration and sense of purpose in their deliberations about Stephen. In fact both scholars gave this the status of a principle of learning. They spoke about the importance of purpose, relevance and of intrinsic motivation. Ann asked: 'Does he understand what reading is for?' and Teresa's unease about the teacher's affirmations for word accuracy shows her contention that reading and learning are largely based on intrinsic motivation and personal relevance rather than on extrinsic rewards and the proddings of others.

Principles of whole language and real books in the classroom

Psycho-linguists, such as those noted above, and the literacy scholars and teachers who are persuaded by their thinking, believe that all language is used for authentic purposes and that language, whether oral or written, is best if it is learned for authentic purposes. Whole language refers to the teaching of reading and writing using complete texts in communicative situations, in contrast to skill practice or isolated language drill. The assumption is that the model of acquisition through real use (not through practice exercises) is the best model for developing literacy. This is the way Goodman's popular book *What's Whole in Whole Language* (1986: 24) summed it up for teachers and parents:

> Why do people create and learn written language? They need it! How do they learn it? The same way that they learn oral language, by using it in authentic literacy events that meet their needs. Often children have trouble learning written language in school. It's not because it's harder than learning oral language, or learned differently. It's because we've made it hard by trying to make it easy. Frank Smith wrote an article called '12 Easy Ways to Make Learning to Read Hard'. Every way was designed to make the task easy by breaking it up in small bits. But by isolating print from its functional use, by teaching skills out of context and focusing on written language as an end in itself, we make the task harder, impossible for some children.

The key principle is that literacy development should be consistent with language development in general and this means adhering to the following principles in the classroom:

- whole, real functional language;
- authentic speech acts and literacy events;
- ownership for the learner;
- use of literature and other authentic language in reading;
- choice of topics in a wide range of genres for writing;
- integrating language modes i.e. listening, speaking, reading and writing;
- integrating language and content in the curriculum;
- building on the language, culture, and experience of learners.

(Goodman 1992)

Frank Smith (1978) summed up the implications for the classroom by identifying two basic necessities for learning to read: the availability of interesting materials that make sense to the learner and an understanding adult as a guide. Margaret Meek (1982: 9) endorsed this stance, saying 'A book, a person and shared enjoyment: these are the conditions of success.'

So the nature of the texts is important (Meek 1988) and so too is the nature of the interaction occurring around texts. The use of texts based on natural language, i.e. real books rather than commercially produced reading schemes or basal readers, is important. One proponent, Liz Waterland (1988), suggested that you can test the suitability of the language by asking whether the book can be read aloud by a fluent reader in a natural manner. In her view the language used should be natural, predictable and meaningful to the child.

In the whole-language classroom, emphasis is placed on empowering the learner. Goodman (1986: 26) expressed it as follows: 'Language development is empowering: the learner "owns" the process, makes the decisions about when to use it, what for and with what results . . . literacy is empowering too, if the learner is in control with what's done with it'.

Harste (1989: 245) claimed that 'whole language is essentially a theory of voice that operates on the premise that all students must be heard'. And Goodman (1992: 359–60) argued that 'learning is at best diminished and at worst drastically changed when it is controlled by the teacher'. Teachers, he says, should seek to 'mediate' rather than intervene. He exemplified the role of the teacher by suggesting that he or she should discuss book choices with pupils, they should offer a range of ideas to help pupils select writing topics. The teacher is encouraged to promote pupil discussion, to invite the pupils' own ideas and get them to consider possibilities rather than give them an algorithm or a ready-made solution.

In sum, what the psycho-linguists sought to get us away from was the notion – that had prevailed for so long in the development in reading in schools – that reading is a linear process of letter-by-letter deciphering, sounding out, word recognition and finally text comprehension. It is not a linear process, they insisted, but a meaning-building (constructivist), problem-solving one.

Interactive activities with authentic texts

A typical day in a whole-language classroom might include work in personal journals, small group discussion of curriculum events, 'quiet time' for reading, 'show and tell', conferences with the teacher or volunteer on recently read or written books, read alouds, and class and group responses to literature. Teresa Grainger and Ann Browne recommended several approaches for Stephen's teacher that fit with the above principles. Typical interactive activities indicative of classrooms committed to whole language and real books would include the following:

- Shared reading experiences through reading of 'big books', i.e. books with print and illustrations large enough to be seen by everyone in a group – originated by Holdaway (1979). This encourages readers to join in reading with the teacher and, as they become familiar with the books, to discuss the illustrations, the contents, the language, etc. This collaborative activity is especially good for modelling reading for beginner readers.
- Hearing children read and sustained silent reading in which the teacher can guide, encourage and facilitate reading development (Campbell 1990).
- Teacher reading stories aloud to the class – this is especially good for developing understanding of how books work and how language works, for learning new words and syntactic structures, and for learning the pleasure of reading (Meek 1988; Fox 2001).
- Literature circles – for example, discussion of one piece of literature that everyone has read; discussion of related texts; discussion of texts from the same genre e.g. mystery stories; the circle may focus on literature by a particular poet or author; discussion of work of a local author who then visits the group; discussion of literature written by class members (Calkins 1986; Harste and Short 1991).
- Literature response activities – book sales involving pupils in creating a commercial to sell a favourite book to the class; pupils to create murals, pictures, paintings, collage, sculpture, mobiles, posters; pupils to perform dramatized versions of the literature or create a puppet show; writing or dramatization of the story to involve the creation of new endings; telling the story from the point of view of one of the characters; journal or letters to be written from the perspective of one of the book's characters; pupils to create a newspaper based on the time period and the happenings in the story; pupils to interview one another about their responses to the story; pupils to research the life of the author (Harste and Short 1991).

- The use of reading and writing workshops (Graves 1983) and the 'author's chair'[1] (Graves and Hansen 1983), conducting writing/reading conferences (Calkins 1991).

The above suggestions are all heavily oriented towards constructing meaning from and responding to literature. Underlying literature-based teaching is the theory of *reader response*. Reading is viewed as a dynamic interaction between the reader and the text. Enjoyment of the reading experience is important and this is prioritized over gathering facts or details from what is read. Traditional teaching of comprehension was largely based on questioning pupils about its literal contents. Teresa Grainger wanted Stephen's teacher to focus more on the relationship between the text and his life and less on low-level questions and in this she was drawing on 'reader response theory'. She would encourage teachers to ask pupils questions to explore feelings about the text and to make links between the text and their own lives.

Rosenblatt (1991) proposed the idea that one reads from one or two stances. One stance she called 'aesthetic', which occurs when the reader is focused on what he is living through during the reading event – the reader is attending to the words <u>and</u> to the qualitative overtones of the ideas, images, situations and characters that are being evoked in him as he reads the text. The second stance Rosenblatt described is 'efferent'. This is a stance concerned with the information the reader takes away from the text. These two stances are not mutually exclusive but, according to Rosenblatt, when reading literature the predominant stance should be aesthetic. That is, literature should be read primarily for the enjoyment of the experience. Approaching literature from an efferent stance she says gives the impression that stories should be read for facts and analysis. For this reason she urges teachers to dwell in the experience of reading and to prolong the aesthetic experience through the kinds of activities listed above – drawing, writing, drama, dance and discussion.

Reading in a whole-language classroom would not typically include learning at sound–symbol correspondence for its own sake or using artificial tasks such as worksheets, although mini-lessons may be offered on different aspects of the reading or writing task in order to enable learners to achieve their purpose within the task. Phonics, for example, would not be taught explicitly or systematically. Phonics teaching is usually integrated into meaning-based reading and writing activities and done incidentally as teachers decide it is needed. Whole-language teachers typically provide phonics instruction as part of invented spelling activities. But whole-language theory regards letter–sound relations (which is referred to as graphophonemics) as just one of three cueing systems – the others being semantic/meaning cues and syntactic/language cues.

Teaching of such mini-lessons would be a response to children's needs in relation to an authentic literacy task. Isolating skill sequences is out and slicing up literacy into grade- or class-appropriate skills, objectives, or out-comes is unacceptable in this model. So too is simplifying texts by control-ling their sentence structures and vocabulary, or organizing them around phonic patterns. This view of teaching is in direct contrast to direct instruc-tion or objectives-based instruction which relies on the breaking down of written language into subskills and parts and pre-planning teaching to teach these subskills (Stahl 1997). The problem classic whole-language theorists have with the kind of pre-planned, systematic and subskills-oriented approach is that they think this runs counter to children defining the pur-poses for their literacy activities. It is thought to disempower the learner.

Before moving to a discussion of the impact of the whole-language move-ment on classroom practice it is worth noting that our two scholars, while subscribing to the principles of whole language, do not reject the importance of explicit teaching of language skills provided this is done in a way that maintains an emphasis on meaning and understanding of the text. For example, Teresa Grainger talked about explicit teaching in a rich context of literacy study. Ann Browne said Stephen needed specific phonic teaching in some aspects and she and Teresa said he needed more sight word training.

Influence and impact of the psycho-linguistic perspective

In England the whole-language or real books approach harks back to the 'language experience' approach that was initiated by the Schools Council Initial Literacy Project known as *Breakthrough to Literacy* (Mackay *et al.* 1978). This initiative emphasized the learner's active engagement in the comprehension and construction of authentic texts and sought to reduce reliance on textbooks. In a sense, therefore, the stage had to some extent been set for the adoption of whole-language practices in schools.

Research on practice, however, revealed that teachers typically did not abandon more traditional methods of teaching reading, including the use of schemes and the teaching of word attack skills and phonic knowledge. But the politicization, during the 1980s and 1990s, of education in general, and of reading in particular, polarized the debate about teaching methods. So you had journalists who were only too eager to suggest that teachers expected pupils to pick up reading in school, without any guidance or structure (Phillips 1990), and others, who should know better, who claimed, on the basis of spurious evidence, that an apparent fall in reading standards was down to the adoption of whole-language methods (Turner 1990). In 1996 an official, but controversial, report on the teaching of reading in inner London schools claimed that the systematic teaching of phonics was a 'significant omission' in practice (Ofsted 1996: para. 16). My recent reread-ing of that report and other studies of practice (e.g. DES 1990) convinces me that the principles and practices of whole language were elements of a broader repertoire of teacher practices that sought to balance direct teaching of word recognition skills with an emphasis on meaning-based approaches through the use of good quality literature. There is no doubt that the principles and procedures associated with whole language impacted on teachers in this country and teachers found the ideas liberating and engaging. Ann Browne and Teresa Grainger are especially persuaded by the arguments of this stance on literacy. David Wray, whose interview transcript is presented in the next part of the book, acknowledged its impact on him as a teacher and although he now, like Ann and Teresa, has reservations about aspects of the movement, its ideas undoubtedly resonated with him. Laura Huxford too, as will be demonstrated, draws on psycho-linguistic theory in her interpretation of Stephen's learning needs.

The other side of the Atlantic would seem to have embraced whole language more readily and more exclusively. Commenting on the rapid rise of the whole-language movement in America, David Pearson (1993: 504) said:

> Never have I witnessed anything like the rapid spread of this recent movement [whole language] away from mechanistically driven and toward child-centered approaches to teaching reading. Pick your metaphor – epidemic, wildfire, manna from heaven. The movement has spread so rapidly throughout North America that it is a fact of life in literacy curriculum and research.

Some have argued that whole language/real books is both a philosophy and an instructional approach, with the aim of motivating and interesting learners in the process of learning (Bergeron 1990). However, Newman (1985), in contrast, argued that it is not a method of instruction in the conventional sense but that it is a philosophy. Watson (1989) suggested that whole language is difficult to define because most whole-language advocates reject definitions and those who seek definitions, she claims, usually disapprove of the approach in the first place.

To some extent the difficulty associated with definition arises because whole language is perceived as a democratic concept that allows for individual interpretation and variation – it is seen as a concept that is not applied universally; 'it represents local, rather than universal, truth' (Gunderson 1997: 237). In addition, the strong emphasis of psycho-linguists on response to literature, rather than on reading achievement as measured by standardized achievement tests, adds to the difficulty of evaluating it. Response to literature and motivating children to become avid readers are more complex to assess than reading attainment in the more traditional sense of decoding and literal comprehension.

Despite the above definitional difficulties, some researchers have sought to compare whole-language approaches with more traditional methods involving the use of direct instruction and reading schemes and also to assess it against its own aims. In general it would appear that the results of these studies are mixed, with some showing gains and advantages for whole language and others showing disadvantages (Stahl *et al.* 1994). There is some evidence to suggest that whole-language approaches may have an important function early in the process of learning to read, but that as the child's needs shift, they become less effective (Stahl and Miller 1989). It seems too that the literacy skills tapped by standardized tests take longer to learn in whole-language classes than in more traditional classes (Gunderson 1997).

The psycho-linguistic model certainly placed unprecedented emphasis on motivating learners to become readers and writers. We are familiar with the criticism that, while producing pupils who can read, schools are less good at turning out those who do read. There is sound evidence that a literature-oriented approach promotes children's independent reading as well as their understanding of the story genre (Morrow 1992) and that it fosters the use of comprehension strategies and positive attitudes towards reading (Guthrie *et al.* 2000).

Of particular interest, in my view, is the debate about the impact on minority groups, for example children from economically disadvantaged backgrounds. Stahl and Miller (1989) found no study involving the latter that particularly favoured whole language. The explanation for the apparent lack of effects favouring whole language with disadvantaged pupils may be that such children may need more than that which whole language provides. Stahl (1999) suggests that children who come from homes where there is a great deal of support for literacy may fare better in whole-language classrooms since these pupils will already have acquired experiences that match the need to make choices in the literacy-rich environments they encounter in school. In contrast, pupils who come from homes where there are few books, where they are not read to, and where alphabet games are not features, may not have the necessary skills to take advantage of the learning opportunities on offer. The assumption here, of course, is that whole-language classrooms exhibit continuity with life in middle-class homes and discontinuity with life in working-class homes.

This thinking also fits with Lisa Delpit's criticisms of indirect or process teaching approaches more generally. She argues (1995) that some pupils are likely to interpret this pedagogy as doing nothing or it may, at best, remain a mystery to them since their expectations of how teachers ought to behave conflict with the facilitative, indirect role that they actually get. It could also be that the high regard that some minority groups have for teachers as powerful authority figures indicates that they rely on and expect direct teaching from their teachers. The logic here is that while whole-language classrooms may well work for middle-class, mainstream pupils, they may not work for culturally and linguistically different pupils because they may have different expectations regarding teacher role. However, I must add that, intuitively sensible though this line of argument is, I could find no study that provided evidence of this so it must be taken as a hypothesis awaiting refutation or confirmation by research.

The counter-argument here is also compelling. That is that pupils who depend on schools to become literate are probably most in need of authentic literacy experiences. Lots of drill and skill-based activities may well fail to help these pupils to become thoughtful readers, and people for whom reading matters in their lives. Of course this doesn't mean that the opposite is the answer for these pupils (Hiebert 1994). We return to this point later when we explain and discuss 'top-down' and 'bottom-up' models.

The National Literacy Strategy and a psycho-linguistic perspective

Current literacy policy in England is influenced by the psycho-linguistic perspective discussed above, specifically in its acknowledgement of the various cueing systems that learners need in order to become effective readers. First, a brief introduction to the National Literacy Strategy (NLS).

The NLS was introduced into primary schools in England in 1998, and although it is not legally binding like the National Curriculum, teachers and schools are strongly urged by national policy makers to adhere to it. The vast majority of schools now implement it. Its introduction was controversial as it marked a departure from what had obtained prior to it insofar as teachers up until 1998 could determine what teaching practices and mode of organization to use in the classroom to develop literacy. Its introduction followed more than a decade of debate about supposedly poor standards of literacy in primary schools.

Termly teaching objectives for each year of the primary age range are described in detail in the Strategy. A structure for time and class management of a daily Literacy Hour is specified: it is expected that for at least 60 per cent of the time pupils should be working with the teacher. Three broad elements of literacy are the focus of the Strategy:

- word-level work (phonics, spelling and vocabulary);
- sentence-level work (grammar and punctuation); and
- text-level work (comprehension and composition).

It is clearly stated that successful reading depends on a range of strategies. The 'reading searchlights model' (DfES 2001: 1) describes how each of the four searchlights (phonic knowledge, knowledge of context, grammatical knowledge, and word recognition and graphic knowledge) 'sheds a partial light, but together they make a mutually supporting system' (DfES 2001: 1). It is in this regard, I think, that the psycho-linguistic perspective shows its greatest influence on the NLS.

The Strategy adds that of these approaches, phonic and graphic knowledge should be prioritized. This is not in line with whole-language principles but we return to this in more detail in Part Two when we discuss other evidence made available through the cognitive–psychological school. There are several references to the importance of the application of this knowledge so it is meaningful to the learner and this fits well with the whole-language model, but the fundamental principle of breaking down language into elements to be studied separately from context of application is not consistent with whole language.

The NLS represents quite a different model of literacy pedagogy than that espoused by whole-language theorists. Kenneth Goodman, for instance, had argued that whole language gives teachers the power to make decisions; he said 'It shifts power from teachers' manuals to teachers' (1989: 214). The NLS, in contrast, is highly dependent on manuals, partly explained by the fact that content and teaching are so heavily emphasized. This too is in sharp contrast with whole language – as Yetta Goodman (1989: 114) said, The focus of whole-language curriculum is not on the content of what is being studied but on the learner.' She adds that 'this does not minimize the importance of content; rather it represents the belief that content can only be understood and seriously studied when learners are . . . participating in deciding what will be learned'.

Several researchers (e.g. Dombey 1998a, 1998b;Wray 1998; Hall 2001) expressed reservations about various aspects of the NLS, not least the reduction in teacher autonomy and professional judgement that it represented. The scholars interviewed in this part of the book show a similar concern, especially Ann Browne who alerts us to the potential dangers of diverting teachers' attention from children's learning.

Overall the psycho-linguistic perspective had a number of significant influences on the field of reading. Pearson and Stephens (1994), who themselves could not be described as part of the whole-language or real books movement, identify four major influences of the impact of the psycholinguistic perspective on the field of reading. Although they were referring to the United States, these influences apply equally in this country in my view. In focusing on meaning making, the psycho-linguistic stance on reading encouraged us to value literacy experiences much more than we had in the past. And the past here is not so distant – it is worth reminding ourselves that several official reports of literacy practice in this country during the 1980s had urged teachers to devote more attention to imaginative aspects of reading and texts. For example in 1982, referring to the fact that 5-year-olds were introduced too quickly to published reading schemes, the inspectors stated 'The children spent a good deal of time decoding print with the result that they read mechanically and with little understanding . . .'(DES 1982: 5). This same survey of first schools commented on the unproductive time spent by 50 per cent of the schools on

English exercises which stifled individuality. This despite the fact that as far back as 1975 the Bullock Report had said that 'explicit teaching out of context' is of little value (DES 1975: 172). Official reports in the late eighties (DES 1988, 1989) confirmed the importance of children's literature and their response to literature in the development of the intellect and the imagination. In practice this meant that teachers were more likely to be critical of decontextualized, work-book exercises on specific letter-sound correspondences, syllabification exercises and routine comprehension activities.

Secondly, the whole-language movement made us value texts based on natural language patterns, especially those designed for use with beginner readers, thus enabling emerging readers to draw on their knowledge of language to predict meanings and words. This meant that texts that were based on high-frequency, short words, such as Example 1 below, were no longer so valued and, similarly, those based on phonic elements, such as Example 2 below, became less common.

Example 1	*Example 2*
Run, John, run.	Nat can bat.
Run to Dad.	Nat can bat with the fat bat.
Dad will run.	The cat has the fat bat.
Run, Dad.	The rat has the fat bat.
Run, John.	Nat has the fat bat.
See them run.	Bat the bat, Nat.
	(Pearson and Stephens 1994)

Indeed, current reading schemes in use in this country incorporate texts that to a greater or lesser extent mirror children's literature.

Third, the psycho-linguistic perspective made us more aware and sensitive to children's efforts as readers. As Pearson and Stephens (1994: 29) put it, 'Errors became generative rather than negative' and showed us more of the workings of the child's mind, allowing the teacher and the learner to understand more about the reading strategies being used and not being used. In attending so much to comprehension, it correspondingly de-emphasized pronunciation and recitation. The influence of the psycho-linguistic school of thought in relation to the emphasis on children's reading cueing systems is evident in *English in the National Curriculum* (DFE 1995) and as stated above in the National Literacy Strategy.

One reading researcher in the United States concluded that over the 1980s and early 1990s in the US, there seemed to have been a shift in interest from seeing reading as comprehension to seeing reading as a personal response to quality literature – what he terms 'reading-to-enjoy' rather than 'reading-to-learn'. Referring to what teachers emphasized prior to the psycho-linguistic era, Stahl (1999: 18) claims that this shift is a significant one:

The shift from Reading-to-Learn to Reading-to-Enjoy is a profound one. Whereas the emphasis in the directed reading activity was getting facts from text, first narratives and later expository text, shifting to text-based and reader-based inferences, the emphasis in whole language classes is on response to literature, without assessing any understanding at the literal or inferential level. The result can be that children's discussions wander from the text itself to a discussion of issues around the text.

There is no doubt that reading-to-enjoy is a vital aspect of the psycho-linguistic school. Over the 1980s concerns remained in England about the inadequacy of practices in relation to reading-to-learn, especially in the use of information texts (e.g. DES 1989) and this was an issue that exercised researchers and policy makers that are not so easily located in this school of thought. We take up some of these issues in the next part of the book.

Psycho-linguistic theory helped us appreciate the significance of know-ledge of likely linguistic sequences in text – the probabilities of not only letters in words, but also words in sentences, sentences in paragraphs, and larger genres of text. By giving us miscue analysis and by highlighting reading as a constructive process, psycho-linguists gave us, respectively, a means of examining the reading process and a theory of reading that were distinct from previous ideas about reading.

Note

1 One chair in the classroom is designated as the author's chair and pupils sit in this special chair to share their writing. The focus is on celebrating completed writing projects, not on revising the composition to make it better.

PART TWO
A COGNITIVE-PSYCHOLOGICAL PERSPECTIVE

INTRODUCTION TO PART TWO:
A COGNITIVE-PSYCHOLOGICAL
PERSPECTIVE ON READING

Part Two considers reading from a cognitive-psychological perspective. First the interpretations and recommendations of two further distinguished literacy educators will be presented. These particular scholars have made a major contribution to current literacy policy in England. They draw on psycho-linguistic ideas in their recommendations and suggestions but a major thrust of their thinking is informed by a cognitive-psychological theory of literacy.

Following the transcripts of our two scholars, the following themes will be considered in some detail: the stages learners go through as they become more sophisticated readers, the practical implications for the classroom of this evidence, phonological and phonemic awareness, and comprehension development and reading to learn. Finally, this part will consider the impact that the cognitive-psychological approach has had on policy and practice.

LAURA HUXFORD'S OBSERVATIONS, SUGGESTIONS AND THEORETICAL PERSPECTIVES

Profile of Laura Huxford

Laura taught mainly in primary schools and children with special educational needs. She also taught and led pre-service and in-service teacher education courses at what is now the University of Gloucestershire. She used miscue analysis extensively in courses to enable teachers to understand how children orchestrate strategies when reading. Her PhD was about young children's developing reading and writing. She became Director of Training for the National Literacy Strategy in 1998. Since then she has produced *Progression in Phonics*, *Developing Early Writing*, *Grammar for Writing* and the *Additional Literacy Support Programme* within the NLS.

What follows is a summary of Laura's observations of Stephen. Her recommendations to his teacher are outlined and the theoretical rationale underpinning those suggestions is highlighted. Laura participated in the symposium at the United Kingdom Reading Association's annual conference in Oxford 2000 in which a group of scholars presented their interpretations of Stephen as a reader and how he could be supported. These participants only had the video and transcript evidence of Stephen's reading and retelling at that point – they did not have any other information about him or his learning context. What follows is based, for the most part, on that presentation, on Laura's own notes of her presentation and to a lesser extent on an interview I conducted with her some time later. I was especially interested in Laura's response to the four key questions:

1 What do we know about Stephen as a reader?
2 What else would you like to know about him?
3 What should his teacher do to enhance his reading?
4 What theoretical perspectives underpin your suggestions?

Laura's first impressions of Stephen

Laura described her first impressions of Stephen as follows:

> He is willing and even keen to flip through the books on display but
> he's a shy, slow, hesitant reader expecting the teacher to tell him words
> he doesn't know. He makes little attempt to use any cueing systems
> other than occasionally sounding out words. He gives the impression
> he may have been drilled in phonics at the expense of other strategies.
> He is probably reading too slowly to make sense of the text – i.e. the
> context strategy searchlight cannot come into play. His ability to retell
> some of the narrative may have been dependent on the pictures or
> from hearing the book read before. It is unlikely he is making much
> sense out of the text.

What Stephen appears to be able to do

Following a closer examination of the video evidence, Laura listed all the
knowledge and skills that Stephen appeared to have. In doing this she
speculated about the thinking that Stephen was engaged in as he read.

- *Word recognition*: He read correctly most of the words; many were high-
  frequency words but he also read naughty, woke, school, friend, peanut,
  and anywhere. These could be in his sight vocabulary; some may have
  been deduced from the text if he were making meaning. He was particularly able on words with apostrophe omission e.g. doesn't, wouldn't,
  didn't, wasn't, that's, don't. He picked up the word threw on its second
  appearance.
- *Phonics*: He showed he could make correct letter to sound correspondences and could blend consonant–vowel–consonant (CVC). He was prepared to have a go at other words and knew that building words from
  letters was an option e.g. af/ter.
- *Grammar*: Stephen used grammatical knowledge. Where he did make an
  error, the error was almost always grammatically plausible, e.g. She was
  looking at the feathers (07–10). He substituted The for She (07) – a new
  sentence could start with The – and later he said a for the (09). Other grammatically plausible errors and self-corrections included: did for does (55),
  he for I (58), keep for kept (63), track for tunnel (126), came for crept (167).

- *Context*: Stephen is reading for meaning. Instances where Stephen's substitutions indicated that he had obviously understood what he was reading and was trying to continue to make sense are came for crept (167) and track for tunnel (126). At 07 where he substituted The for She, he stopped reading. We don't know what he was doing in that pause. He had read The but wouldn't read on even though the teacher's finger was on the next word was. Could it be that he realized that The was would not make sense? He read was without hesitation on subsequent occasions. A similar situation occurred later with the words she and looked (22). He said the again and refused to read on to the word looked even though he knew the word, as evidenced by his reading it correctly later in the text.
- *Orchestrating the strategies*: Most of the substitutions had a similarity in at least the initial letter indicating that Stephen was combining his knowledge of letters with another strategy either grammatical or contextual (or both).

What Stephen appears not to be able to do

Laura identified four key areas of reading in which Stephen showed himself to have particular weaknesses.

1 He was reluctant to have a go at the longer words which were not in his sight vocabulary either by guessing from the context or sounding out. He tended to expect the teacher to tell him.
2 He didn't correct himself very often, but he didn't make many errors to correct as he was told most of the words he didn't know.
3 He may have been using word-building strategies i.e. analogy, chunking in some of the words he read correctly, but we have no way of knowing. But he didn't have an effective strategy for tackling long words. If he attempted them at all, he tended to start at the beginning and say all the letters. He didn't appear to know the vowel digraphs except possibly ee (feeding) e.g. he sounded out threw as thr – e – w. In summary, he is at a fairly basic level in the use of phonics i.e. he can blend CVC words and knows that word building is an option.
4 He wasn't reading with much expression or sense of meaning. Although he was reading most words correctly, there were still too many which he needed to pay attention to, to get fluency.

Comparing first impressions with in-depth analysis

Laura compared her initial impressions with those she obtained through her more detailed and close observation of Stephen reading and retelling to his teacher.

Contrary to first impressions, Stephen must have been getting the sense out of this book, not just in an overarching way from the pictures but word by word, otherwise he could not have made errors which were semantically/grammatically plausible with such consistency. Furthermore, he was concerned to make sense – as indicated by the refusal to read the next word when he knew what it was (page 9). Nevertheless, he was manifestly not imparting meaning to the listener and his interest in the book (perhaps in reading) was not evident. What appeared to be a reasonable grasp of phonics was probably much more limited. He showed that he could read CVC words and he tried to sound out other words but often he didn't have the phonic knowledge to recognize digraphs or a strategy to deal with two-syllable words.

Evidence Laura would need to make a more informed judgement

These are the questions that Laura posed in relation to the evidence she would like to have about Stephen in order to make a more informed judgement about him as a reader. She would like answers to all these questions.

1 Was this his typical reading behaviour?
2 What support was he having at home?
3 What was his attitude to reading? For example, does he ever read voluntarily?
4 Did he enjoy reading 'information' books?
5 Does the teacher use shared and guided reading with the class?
6 What was the classroom reading environment like?
7 How often did he read – to an adult? – independently?
8 How recently had he learned to blend CVC words?
9 Could he write CVC words and words with adjacent consonants?
10 Had he been systematically taught vowel digraphs?
11 What strategies was he being taught for tackling two-syllable words?

What his teacher might do

Laura went on to describe the teaching approach Stephen's teacher might use to advance his reading skills and attitudes. She says:

1 If he's alone in the class in his apathy to books, appeal to his interests, provide appropriate material, write notes to him, fix up a fax/email correspondent.
2 If the class is generally unmotivated in reading, get going with something exciting – use drama, get them involved with communicating

outside the class – generally create genuine and exciting purposes for reading and writing.

3 Model reading strategies in shared reading.

4 Get him to remind the rest of the group of the range of reading strategies in guided reading and expect him to demonstrate his use of them. At first show him what strategies he is using; later, ask him what strategy he thinks he is using. Encourage him to cross-check with another strategy when he has figured out an unknown word e.g. if he has used a couple of letters and then deduced the rest from the context, make sure he matches the word on the page with the word he said and then get him to tell you sounds for all parts of the word. This is a way to becoming autonomous by teaching himself how words are formed.

5 Give him books with fewer words he has to tussle with. He was at frustration level with this book. He shouldn't need to wonder about more than one word per sentence. If he is given a book with more new words than this, they should be primed in some way before or as he reads.

6 Find a way to increase reading 'bulk' by either using a buddy system in school or establishing a regular reading slot at home (or both).

7 Place him on the appropriate Additional Literacy Support (ALS) module: in the phonics programme he probably needs vowel digraphs, tackling long words, and past tense verbs.

8 Fluency building: ask him to find the next full stop and to read to it.

9 Read to the class a lot, including non-fiction.

10 Find plenty of excuses to write – writing will spur his ability to decode better than anything and may well be the key to motivation.

11 Make the whole business fun!

Underpinning reading theory

Laura noted that much of the theory underpinning the above analysis is contained in the research reviews by Marilyn Adams (1990) and Clay (2001). The observations and suggestions also draw on the work of Chomsky, Ehri, Frith, Goodman, Holdaway, Rumelhart, and Stanovich.

I would suggest that the theoretical perspective of all these researchers could be conveniently described as straddling the psycho-linguistic and cognitive–psychological perspectives on the reading process. In view of Laura Huxford's professional role it is not surprising that these theoretical perspectives also strongly underpin the National Literacy Strategy. These perspectives are explained and discussed more fully below.

DAVID WRAY'S OBSERVATIONS, SUGGESTIONS AND THEORETICAL PERSPECTIVES

Profile of David Wray

David Wray taught in primary schools for 10 years and is currently Professor of Literacy Education at the University of Warwick. He has published over 30 books on aspects of literacy teaching and is best known for his work on developing teaching strategies to help pupils access the curriculum through literacy. This results in such innovations as the Extending Interactions with Texts (EXIT) model to guide the teaching of reading to learn, and writing frames to help with the writing of factual text types. His work has been made an integral part of the National Literacy Strategy at both primary and secondary levels. His major recent publications include: *English 7–11* (Wray 1995); *Developing Children's Non-Fiction Writing* (Wray and Lewis 1995); *Writing Frames* (Lewis and Wray 1996); *Extending Literacy* (Wray and Lewis 1997); *Writing Across the Curriculum* (Lewis and Wray 1998); *Literacy in the Secondary School* (Lewis and Wray 1999); and *Teaching Literacy Effectively* (Wray *et al.* 2001).

This is an edited version of a telephone conversation I conducted with David in February 2002.

KATHY HALL (KH): *Thank you, David, for agreeing to do this interview by telephone. I appreciate the time you've taken to participate in the project.*

What do you feel we know about Stephen as a reader?

DAVID WRAY (DW): The first thing is the lack of confidence which is apparent from the very beginning. I thought that was an interesting feature. He started off very lacking in confidence and hesitant, but as he got going, and in the second bit of reading, he was doing very well. He got a bit of a head of steam going. He recognized some words in that second section that were much more difficult I think than some he didn't recognize in the first section. Once you get going, it's confidence really and this is what happened with Stephen here, I think.

There's quite a bit of reliance on context especially picture cues. Although there was some evidence that he was using phonics I thought what he wasn't doing terribly well is blending. He was able to recognize initial sounds and sounds by themselves, but pulling them together seemed to be the difficult part of it for him. Even though he read that first section very hesitatingly, it was quite impressive how much he remembered from it. And that wasn't what I'd expected from looking at the video. I thought he would have remembered much less of what he'd read because the reading was so broken and so hesitant, but he did seem to understand the story quite well and could retell reasonably well, I thought.

So those are the kinds of things I think I would pick up about him as a reader.

KH: *Thanks for that. What else would you like to know about him?*

DW: I would like to know how he would read in rather less stressful circumstances. He was being videoed and also he was reading out loud. Reading aloud is stressful for many kids and this is part of the theory I will come onto later. It seems to me that reading aloud is not always the same as reading to yourself and you perform differently in the two contexts. And Stephen here is put under some stress and I want to know how he would read in less stressful circumstances, when there isn't such pressure.

How does he respond to reading? I'm thinking of things like: can he follow written instructions? When he's read descriptions in a story can he draw a reasonably accurate picture of what he's read? Can he use written information in his own subsequent writing? Those sorts of things are ways of getting at how kids read which don't require that oral performance. Those are the things I would like to know. I'd like to see him in different circumstances in order to know what he understands from his reading. I'd like to see him in situations that do not require oral performance.

If I were his teacher I would want to look more closely at his blending to see whether there were any contexts in which he could blend more effectively. I would want to look at what kind of circumstances I would be able to devise, and what games and activities I could devise to help him to do that, so the blending is something I'd want to work on.

KH: *What should his teacher do?*

DW: Three things.

First make the reading experience predominantly less stressful than it seems to be here. He clearly lacks confidence and I think his confidence needs building up by experience of success and it seems to me that success is the crucial thing. He has to experience reading as a good and pleasing experience. And that's not going to be the case if it's always going to be a performance. I think his teacher needs to give him lots more experience of reading silently and then having to do some follow-up activities to use what he's read. So that's the first thing – using comprehension in a different way.

The second is a technical thing and that is to work on his blending. Hopefully not decontextualized exercises but he does need some intensive work on pulling sounds together and making words.

Thirdly, and this is probably the one you would expect from me, I'd like to see him given a wider choice of reading. I'm always struck when kids are asked to choose in that context – there were five or six books on that table but not one of them was non-fiction. They were all storybooks. We haven't seen this child necessarily at his best because it may be that non-fiction texts would allow him to perform better. And teachers very often do that, they often assume that reading a story is the be-all and end-all, and it's not. There's lots that kids can read and choose to read by themselves. And so his teacher needs to give him wider choice and broaden the range. She might find texts that he is quite keen to read and willing to give more attention and energy to.

KH: *What theoretical perspectives underpin your suggestions?*

DW: The one I already mentioned – that is that I think reading aloud is different to reading silently. And I suppose miscue analysis has led us to think in this kind of way, that we assume that by analysing how a child reads aloud in response to a text would actually get us a very good picture of the reading strategies the child is using and so on. But I think we can be misled by this sometimes as it seems to me that by reading silently you can use quite different strategies to get at meaning and it can all take place much faster in a way. Miscue gives only a partial picture about reading. That's one theoretical thing I guess.

There's a more general thing about children's progress, and this is not just relevant to reading, it's relevant to learning anything. I think children have to succeed. It seems to me that the job of the teacher is to make sure that kids succeed at something. Of course there's an instructional role, but teachers need to make sure that children can do something well and help them to know they can do it well. I'm sure this isn't the normal experience that Stephen has of reading. Clearly his teacher is very concerned about him and they have a very close relationship – you could tell that from the tape. But if that was his experience of reading then it's no wonder he's struggling. It's really highlighting what he doesn't do well. It makes the whole business a very painful thing to engage in so to help children do well they have to be allowed to succeed. Teachers have a responsibility to ensure that happens whatever it takes – whether it means reading very very simple texts, whether it means doing what she did do in fact, that is reading along-side, choral reading. And that's not just about reading; it's about learning generally.

And the third thing is what I would call privileging story, privileging narrative. And that's almost universal in primary schools, that kids learn to read on storybooks. It seems to me this is just so wide off the mark for many of them. And there is a gender thing; many of them, particularly boys, would respond much better to reading if it was about the kinds of worlds that they mentally inhabit themselves. When I think of my own 4-year-old who obviously is not reading yet, but when he chooses texts or things to talk about they're always about soldiers and cars and typical boys' things. They're all factual things, they're not fiction that he's engaged in. He's engaged in listing and naming and pulling things apart and looking at them. Now I want him when he starts reading to be allowed to choose texts which relate to his own interests, those predilections about how you interpret the world. And we often don't do that especially for boys – we offer a biased view of what counts as reading.

KH: *Can I just ask you about the people who influenced you most in your thinking?*

DW: A number of people influenced me. My initial introduction to literacy was done by Goodman and Smith – there's no doubt about that. These were the people whose ideas really struck home with me when I was a teacher and I was lucky enough to hear Ken Goodman speak at an UKRA conference when I was still teaching and it just made so much sense in terms of what I was seeing my kids doing and nobody had ever talked quite like that to me before, introducing those ideas. Obviously having looked at it in more detail I think there are parts where the Goodman ideas are not quite right – we've learned more, but that whole new take on what reading was about, it just opened my eyes. I would be a different person if I hadn't been introduced to Ken Goodman's ideas. And Frank Smith as well; Frank Smith is very challenging, looking at common sense and then saying, hang on, is that so common?

The other thing that got me into this whole business in the first place was doing an Open University course many many years ago, called reading development, and going on to do a diploma in reading development at that time. A lot of people of my generation around the country did that course at the time. It produced a commonality of our experience and our philosophies I think, and that again introduced me to the whole idea of comprehension and what understanding was about. Context use – all those sorts of things in reading – and the fact that it wasn't just about saying things out loud and getting the words right, it was about understanding what you were doing, that was the crucial thing. Now of course I had thought about those things as a teacher but I hadn't really thought about them seriously so it was that course and I guess it was people like John Merritt who led that course – such people were very influential.

More recently I have been influenced by Marilyn Adams and she does have a new line on things and her ideas open your eyes to things we often forget.

KH: *And your own work over the years, the various projects you've done, for example the project on effective literacy teachers – presumably all that has shaped your thinking?*

DW: Yes, and here it's different kinds of people shaping one's thinking. Our work on non-fiction – that changed my thinking – obviously I had a feeling it was very important. It was working alongside teachers in classrooms who were inspiring their kids to do wonderful things. You might go along to a teacher and say I read this idea in an article, I wonder if you'd like to have a go and see if it works, and you come back two weeks later and they've done brilliant things with it – much more than I could ever do. I could list at least a dozen teachers' names who have been significant in that area of non-fiction. So it is teachers in classrooms that influence you there, more than any major theoretical insights. It's finding practical ways of responding to the theory that's the real challenge because the theory can't always be applied easily.

The effective teachers of literacy project – this was a privileged experience, being in classrooms with teachers who were very good at it, who were doing things far better than I could, how they kept all those different demands going, they were doing some staggering work.

KH: *Thank you very much.*

WORDS MATTER

Introduction

While the scholars whose suggestions we have presented so far clearly draw on psycho-linguistic perspectives in their interpretations of Stephen, to varying degrees they also incorporate suggestions that have a basis in cognitive psychology. For them there is no discontinuity or conflict in this eclecticism but what is interesting is the way they draw that balance, i.e. the relative emphasis, for example, placed on meaning and code breaking and the relative emphasis placed on systematic teaching of word recognition and on responding to print.

This section considers reading from a cognitive-psychological perspective; it reviews the contribution to our understanding of the reading process offered by this perspective; and it considers its impact in current policy. The point of this discussion is to invite you to develop a critical awareness of what this position on reading is, to understand the debates and unanswered questions and, on that basis, to begin to connect policies and practices on reading with their theoretical origins.

I will begin by summarizing some of the more controversial messages that the psycho-linguistic school of thought had delivered and go on to present an account of the findings arising from cognitive-psychological research on reading that questioned some of those messages. The extent to which some of our experts subscribed to the cognitive-psychological research is already evident in the interview data but we will revisit their specific suggestions occasionally in the light of a fuller account of the theory.

Although you have only had interpretations of Stephen and his reading needs from four scholars so far, you will have noticed that all of them (and indeed others whom we introduce later) referred to the need to improve his word recognition level and to develop his fluency in reading. Effective teaching in decoding and fluency is critical for Stephen and pupils having this kind of difficulty need high-quality and explicit decoding strategy teaching. You may have other readers who have adequate decoding facility but still read slowly, without much intonation, expression or emphasis. They may pronounce all the words right but still struggle to read. The cognitive-psychological perspective on reading has made a considerable contribution to our understanding of what is involved in these processes.

I have already stressed the major contribution that the psycho-linguistic approach made to our understanding of reading and its development. But if you also look at reading through a cognitive-psychological lens, you are likely to extend the range of strategies in your teaching repertoire.

Five major questions can be usefully debated now. These are:

- To what extent can we characterize the reader as progressing through stages, or is a non-stage model acceptable and what are the pedagogical implications of this?
- What is phonological awareness and what is its significance?
- How are phonological awareness and phonic knowledge developed?
- What has cognitive psychology taught us about developing comprehension?
- What has been the impact of the cognitive-psychological perspective on reading in England?

Throughout the various sections, the practical implications for the classroom will be integrated into the discussion and references will be made to our scholars' suggestions. There are also separate sections on key aspects of practice.

Cognitive-psychological concerns about the psycho-linguistic stance

As we saw, wholeness, authentic language, meaning and reader response are the hallmarks of the psycho-linguistic view. It is one that involves both text and context. Frank Smith, in particular, contended that context cues played the major role in comprehending text. Moreover, its philosophical principles of empowering learners, of positioning the learners as agents of their own learning and of the status attributed to the learners' responses to literature all contributed to a child-initiated and interest-initiated (as opposed to teacher-centred) pedagogy, and to some considerable resistance to teacher-driven or objectives-led curricula and to direct teaching or skills reinforcement. All of this was criticized within cognitive psychology as operating on assumptions that empirical evidence did not support. In other words, as far as some cognitive psychologists were concerned, it lacked scientific backing.

Reading acquisition as stage or non-stage?

One of the major areas of debate in reading has been about whether children progress through reading stages or whether the reading process is essentially the same for the experienced and the novice reader. This is a point that often distinguishes those taking a strong cognitive-psychological perspective from those adhering to a psycho-linguistic stance. Drawing on the work of Juel (1991), the difference between those two positions, in relation to stage or non-stage, can be conveniently summarized in a table as follows:

Table 1   Stage and non-stage models of reading development

Stage model (cognitive-psychological)	Non-stage model (psycho-linguistic)
There are qualitative differences between experienced and beginner readers. Readers go through different stages which are characterized by the addition of more efficient ways of identifying words.	Reading process is the same for all readers, regardless of reading experience, but there are differences in the control readers have over the processes, that is how they use the cues available to them.
There are differences in the processes readers go through, not just differences in the control that readers can exert over the processes.	These differences are quantitative, not qualitative. They depend on quantitative growth about knowledge of language (syntax) and the world (meaning).
Word identification is the key to comprehension. And knowledge of orthography is more important in that essential task than syntactic or semantic knowledge.	Reading is more dependent on knowledge of the world and of language context than it is of knowledge of the printed word i.e. orthographic knowledge is less important.
Maximal orthographic information is used. The efficient use of orthographic knowledge leads to better comprehension.	Minimal orthographic information is used.

Source: Morris *et al.* (1996)

   Non-stage models emphasize the importance of oral reading and minimize the role of decoding skill in learning to read. For those proponents reading material should be rich in meaning and language quality. The stage proponents, on the other hand, attribute priority to early learning of spelling–sound correspondences. Therefore they emphasize texts that have some degree of controlled vocabulary in order to make the alphabetic system as explicit as possible. Cognitive-psychologists view the understanding of the alphabetic nature of written language as key and that is considered the major hurdle for the beginner reader. It's important to emphasize though that both schools of thought view reading as a search for meaning and as a goal-directed activity. They agree on the destination, so to speak, but disagree on the journey to that destination.

There are several stage models in the cognitive-psychological literature (e.g. Gough and Hillinger 1980; Chall 1983; Frith 1985; Ehri 1987; Ehri and Wilce 1987) and, although they all differ in some minor respects, they are essentially the same in relation to one important aspect. That is, they all accord huge importance to decoding or deciphering words. On this there is undoubted consensus. Moreover, stage models demonstrate that over time the child does actually learn to read in qualitatively different ways. Because of the scale of the consensus regarding both the significance of deciphering words and the staged process of reading acquisition, I have decided that it is not necessary to discuss the minor differences in the various stage models here, fascinating though these are in some respects. This is because my main concern is to demonstrate the contribution that the cognitive-psychologists made to our understanding of the reading process and to enhance appreciation of the theoretical perspectives that our scholars bring to bear on their suggestions for reading development in the classroom.

A stage theory of reading acquisition and how to progress to the next stage

It is, however, appropriate to discuss just one of the stage models as illustrative of the field. Henrietta Dombey (Part Three) and Laura Huxford both referred to at least one stage theory in their discussion of the theory informing their suggestions for Stephen. I will take the work of Linnea Ehri and, to a lesser extent, that of Marilyn Jager Adams as an example, not least because Laura Huxford's account of what Stephen's teacher might do to support him is heavily influenced by their work. Laura refers to both Ehri and Adams as having influenced her thinking. David Wray also talked about the importance of the work of Adams.

What Ehri found so mysterious is the way readers are able to look at a word and immediately get its meaning without any effort at decoding the word. Just sight of the word triggers immediate recognition. How do beginner readers then acquire the ability to recognize words rapidly and automatically? How is it that readers are able to store and remember new words easily after very few encounters with those same words? Ehri spent over two decades researching these questions or variations of them.

Sight word reading, she argues, is used the most because it is fast and automatic. In using the term sight word reading, Ehri is clearly referring to the processes that learners acquire as they learn to read. She dispels some common misconceptions about sight reading. One is that only irregularly spelled words are read by sight. Instead she emphasizes that all words, including those that are easily decoded, become sight words once they have been read several times. Second, her work (and that of other 'stage' theorists) suggests that, contrary to popular belief, sight word reading is not a flashcard method of teaching reading, but rather a process of reading words by accessing them in memory. However, teachers will be familiar with the use of 'sight word' as a teaching method whereby sight words are understood to mean the high-frequency, irregularly spelled words pupils are taught to read as unanalysed wholes, often on flash cards (e.g. 'once', 'their', 'come'). And third, she dispels the notion that sight word reading involves memorizing the visual features of words like their shapes and that it has nothing to do with letter-sound correspondence. She strongly rejects this, saying 'Mature forms of sight word learning are alphabetic and phonological at root' (Ehri 1995: 117).

The key to sight word reading, Ehri discovered, is a process she termed connection forming. Connections are created, she says, that link the written forms of words to their sounds and meanings and these connections are stored in the reader's word memory (or lexicon). The stage aspect of her theory derives from her further discovery that different types of connections predominate at different points in development. The notion of connectionism is common among stage-reading theorists (e.g. Stanovich 1992). Ehri's thinking is that advances in reading ability occur as new processes or strategies for word identification are used by the reader.

It is interesting that in so many of her writings (e.g. 1991, 1994, 1995, 1999) Ehri begins by noting that there are many ways to read words other than by sight but she says these ways are only used in the case of words not known by sight. One way, other than sight reading, is decoding or phonological recoding. This refers to the process of transforming graphemes into phonemes and then blending the phonemes into pronunciations. Another way is reading by analogy and this refers to the process of using known sight words to read unknown words that share letters, e.g. recognizing 'slant' by analogy to 'plant'. In this she is drawing on the research, now very familiar to teachers in Britain, of Bryant and Goswami. Yet another way is reading by predicting which refers to the process of generating sensible guesses about words based on context cues or on initial letters or both. In this of course she is clearly drawing on the insights made available by Goodman and others of the psycho-linguistic school.

Pre-alphabet phase

Because of its significance in all the stages of reading acquisition, Ehri uses the word 'alphabet' in her labels for the four stages she theorizes that children go through as they learn to recognize words by sight. The first phase, the pre-alphabet phase, describes a time when the learner stores in memory connections between selected visual cues and words. Such cues might be single visual cues to remember the word, like a thumbprint appearing next to a word as revealed in one study (Gough and Juel 1991), or the location of the word on the page, or the shape of two round eyes in the word 'look'. Letter–sound connections are not involved at this stage. When children in this phase recognize print in their environment such as fast food restaurant signs, they do so by remembering the visual cues that go along with the print rather than the actual words themselves (Ehri 1994). Children connect to the meaning or the idea and not the actual word, so frequently they offer variable rather than precise wordings – semantically appropriate substitutions. The child is minimally dependent on graphic information at this stage and maximally dependent on context information.

At this stage what's important is that the beginner reader has lots of quality literacy experiences in order to appreciate print's communicative function. Essential would be the opportunity to listen to stories, the opportunity to see print being used for meaningful purposes, for example dictating a story or a message while the teacher writes it down, reading and writing greeting cards etc. (Sulzby and Teale 1991). Other suitable classroom activities to expose the child to print at this stage might include drawing the child's attention to print in the environment; labelling of classroom objects; and use of big books where they can see, and perhaps follow, the print as the teacher reads.

Partial alphabetic phase

Once learners acquire some knowledge of the alphabet system, however, sight word reading shifts into a partial alphabetic phase. Now connections are made between letters in written words and sounds in the pronunciation of those words. 'Partial' is used to describe this stage because the learner attends only to the most salient letters – usually the most salient letters are the first and final ones of the word. To remember sight words by this means, learners need to know the relevant letter–sound correspondences and they need to be able to segment initial and final sounds in words. To move pupils on from the first to the second phase, it seems they should be helped to notice shared sounds in words, to segment initial sounds in the pronunciation of words, and to recognize that letters symbolize initial sounds in words.

Phonemic awareness is necessary at this stage. Because of the significance of phonemic awareness in the development of early reading and because of the unique contribution that cognitive-psychology contributed to our understanding of this phenomenon, a later section is devoted to its development.

Phonic knowledge is also important for this stage and I will also discuss that more fully later.

A good way to progress children who are at this stage would be to balance the emphasis on sense making and the development of alphabetic knowledge while at the same time encouraging the child to use multiple cue sources. As a child is reading, Marie Clay (1989) suggested these four cue sources might be emphasized to good effect:

1 Sense and meaning: Does it make sense?
2 Visual cues: Does that look right?
3 Letters/sounds: What would you expect to see?
4 Structure, grammar: Can we say it that way?

The advantage of the partial alphabetic phase over the earlier stage is that it provides the beginning of a system to support memory. Knowing the alphabetic system greatly supports the task of noticing and remembering relevant connections between written words and their pronunciations.

Full alphabetic phase

Once learners get full knowledge of the alphabetic system, complete connections are formed between graphemes in spellings and phonemes in the sounds of words. The full alphabetic phase is reached when readers realize that most graphemes symbolize phonemes in the spelling system. Unknown words can now be identified by attending to all the graphic information. Unknown words can be read because the reader can now transform unfamiliar spellings of words into blended pronunciations.

The early part of this stage is characterized by lots of sounding out and concentration on the letters. At the beginning of this stage, Chall (1983) suggests, the child may glue to print by which she means that the child's attention may be overtly directed to spelling–sound relationships. She also described it as grunting and groaning because children often hesitantly go through a text calling words aloud. Stahl (1997) describes this as fixed on print. In my view this is exactly where Stephen is – he is placing great emphasis on accurate decoding of words. In general, the distinguishing feature of this stage is that spellings become bonded to pronunciations of words in memory.

One obvious advantage of representing sight words more completely is that word reading becomes much more precise (Ehri 1994). Learning to decode (or decipher) is vital for moving from rudimentary reading to reading large numbers of words.

Cunningham and Cunningham (1992) argue that invented spelling during writing has potential for developing children's orthographic knowledge. They suggest activities such as 'Making Words'. This is an activity in which children are individually given some letters that they use to make words. Children make between 12 and 15 words, beginning with two-letter words and continuing to three-, four-, five-, six-, seven-letter or longer until the final word is made. The final word includes all the letters they have that day and children are usually keen to figure out what word can be made from all the letters. 'Making Words' is an active, hands-on, manipulative activity in which children discover sound–letter relationships and begin to see patterns in words. They also learn that changing just one letter or a sequence of letters changes the whole word.

Another strategy that could be used for readers in this and the earlier phase was developed, tested and found effective by Gaskins *et al.* (1996/97). The Benchmark Word Identification (BWI) Program sought to enable pupils to use key words to decode unknown words. This is how they went about achieving this. They selected about 100 words for pupils to analyse during the school year, chosen according to key criteria. The words contained spelling patterns that are frequent in English and that cropped up frequently in children's books. They contained the full variety of initial consonants, digraphs, and blends that beginning readers would encounter in their books. For example, the word 'truck' was picked to represent the letter pattern '-ck' and the 'tr' blend. They then taught three or four key words per week using explicit teaching that included the following:

- stretching out the pronunciations of words to analyse constituent sounds in the words;
- analysing the visual forms of words;
- talking about matches between sounds and letters;
- noting similarities to sounds and letters in other words already learned;
- remembering how to spell the word.

All of these word analysis approaches were modelled to develop the pupils' metacognitive awareness and control over their word learning, and these word analysis approaches were applied as necessary as they read connected text with the familiar letter patterns. These texts were first read to pupils as they point and follow, then they were echoed and choral read. Finally the children read all or parts of the text on their own. The teachers discussed with pupils why they were learning words in this way. To quote how one teacher spoke to her class: 'We fully analyze words, because if we get into our heads every single letter for a word matched to every single sound, we will be able to get the word back out when we want to read it or write it again' (Gaskins *et al.* 1996/7: 250). The pupils were encouraged to become word detectives. Phonics rules were not taught, but pupils were encouraged and expected to generate and verbalize their discoveries about the make-up of words. Their induction processes about regularities of the spelling systems were guided and supported – they were not left to discover the spelling system on their own.

Consolidated alphabetic phase

Eventually the concentrated attention to the letters in words permits the learner to bypass such explicit use of spelling sound correspondences. As sight words accumulate in memory through repeated experience of reading a letter sequence that represents the same phoneme blend across different words, letter patterns recurring in different words become 'consolidated' into what Ehri calls 'multi-letter units symbolizing phonological blends' (1995: 117). Knowing, say, 'ing' as a consolidated unit makes the job of forming connections to learn the new words, 'coming', 'swimming', 'playing', 'interesting', 'exciting' etc. so much easier. Juel's research (1991) demonstrates that fluent readers only revert to previous stages when faced with a rare or foreign word and then they mimic the beginner reader at an earlier stage.

Larger letter units are valuable for sight word reading because they reduce the memory load involved (Ehri 1994). What seems to have happened at this consolidated alphabetic phase is that the application of spelling sound information becomes rapid and automatic and context-free. This is so because readers at this stage can use analogies, they can learn to read unknown words by applying their knowledge and memory of the composition of known words. It's no longer necessary to reflect on word recognition at this stage – the process of recognizing words has become automatic. And since the learners in this phase are now free from deliberate attention to word identification, they can devote their attention to meaning and the content that is read.

What the stage theorists, with their emphasis on connectionism, drive home to us is that, first, the recognition and comprehension of a word compete for the short-term memory capacity that is available; second, the more effort required to decode a word the less capacity there is to support comprehension; and third, it follows therefore that the more automatic the decoding process is, the better is the understanding of the word.

Another advantage of this phase is that the whole process is speeded up and, of course, when many words can be recognized automatically the learner is more likely to engage in wide reading. Stephen has not reached this stage since for him reading appears not yet to be an automatic process. It is effort-full, not effort-less. He has to dwell on every word, deliberating over it and searching for clues to work out what it might be.

The transition to automatic word recognition occurs over several years. More than a decade ago Marilyn Jager Adams (1990) reviewed the field of early reading and, on the basis of very many studies, concluded that as children are exposed to more and more words and as they devote more and more attention to their patterns, they build up a network (or, to use Ehri's word above, connections) of relations among letters. This mental network holds vital information about the order in which letters typically appear.

For example, we know some letters frequently appear together, and so when one letter is recognized, this primes other letters in the mental network. As an example, this is how Adams (1990: 109) describes how the word 'the' is perceived:

> As the eye fixates on the word 'the', the letter recognition unit for the letter 't' receives direct, visual stimulation. In English, when the letter 't' occurs in the initial position of a three letter word, the next letter is extremely likely to be an 'h'. The strength of the associative link from the 't' to the 'h' should therefore be very strong and positive, resulting in considerable excitation of the 'h' unit. Thus as a consequence of the reader's having seen the initial 't', the 'h' unit reaches its own seeable level of excitation more quickly than had it been waiting on direct visual excitation alone.

Exposure to written words is so important according to the evidence reviewed by Adams. She speculates that the process of sounding out words draws attention to the orderings of individual letters, speeding up the formation of networks. Her research (and that of others) casts serious doubts on the role of context (e.g. picture cues) in reading. Indeed this body of research demonstrates that excessive use of context may hinder children's development of orthographic knowledge. We will return to the classroom implications of some of these ideas later.

The notion of reading as constrained reasoning

We are already familiar with the notion of reading as reasoning and problem-solving oriented, following Goodman's description of reading as a psycho-linguistic guessing game and the whole language theorists in general emphasizing context cues (i.e. semantic and syntactic cues); see Part One. Indeed, long before that, even as far back as 1917, Thorndike had argued that reading is best thought of as reasoning. In the light of the above account of sight reading and the work of those cognitive-psychological theorists who see reading acquisition occurring in stages and highly dependent on alphabetic knowledge, it is worth reconsidering the fit between these two apparently different perspectives. To what extent do you think reading is actually a problem-solving activity, a psycho-linguistic guessing game?

In this regard I think the notion of reading as constrained reasoning is extremely helpful. It is a notion developed by Stanovich a decade ago (1992) in reviewing the state of the cognitive-psychological evidence at the time, but one that has had little publicity especially in the reading literature in the UK. However, several writers have drawn on the ideas underlying this notion (e.g. Harrison 1992) and indeed several of our scholars drew on

Stanovich's work in justifying their observations of Stephen and their suggestions for his teacher, e.g. Ann Browne and Laura Huxford.

To understand the notion of reading as constrained reasoning you must first appreciate and distinguish between two sub-processes of reading. One is the process by which a word activates its meaning in memory – or, to use the technical term, lexical access. Simply put, this is word recognition. The second is what happens after this process. This demarcation in turn neatly divides the reading process into parts that are 'like reasoning' and 'not like reasoning'. Lexical access in fluent readers, argues Stanovich, is not at all like reasoning or problem solving. He says this is 'a fast, obligatory, low capacity process largely uninfluenced by knowledge structures outside the lexicon or by higher-level cognitive expectations' (1992: 3). Post-lexical processes, or what happens after a word has been activated in memory, could be described as 'reasoning', he says, but even here the reasoning is limited or 'constrained' by the person's ability to activate the information associated with the word's orthographic, phonological and semantic representations in the first instance. If the word is not recognized quickly, then comprehension won't follow. This is so because comprehension requires the raw materials (working memory of the orthography) with which to operate efficiently.

Because comprehension of the text is limited by the outcome of lexical access, Stanovich says that reading is best seen as constrained reasoning. Such a conceptualization takes word recognition as 'the central subprocess of the complex act of reading' (Stanovich 1992: 4). Hence my title for this section of the book. Throughout his writings Stanovich (1991, 1992, 1995) constantly emphasizes that, although word recognition is central to reading, the ultimate purpose of reading is, of course, comprehension. He says 'Efficient word recognition seems to be a necessary but not sufficient condition for good comprehension . . .' (1992: 4). It is highly unlikely, he suggests, that excellent reading comprehension will coexist with deficient word recognition skills. Word recognition is a prerequisite to comprehension.

Cognitive-psychological message: the word is important

You will remember that the psycho-linguistic perspective on reading, described in Part One, ascribed great significance to context cues, and some theorists (e.g. Frank Smith) argued that visual information in text is sampled by the reader and is not necessarily of primary importance. Their perspective on reading is often described as 'top-down' because of the emphasis on context, on meaning, on the whole text, on response to text, on what the reader brings to the text in terms of expectations and prior knowledge etc. The constructivist metaphor was strong: the notion of the reader as constructing meaning was all-important.

The research discussed here so far together with other experimental psychological research using eye-movement technologies has demonstrated that readers do in fact attend closely to visual information. (These latter studies take a picture of how the eye moves and what it fixes on during reading.) Readers do not sample the text in quite the way that 'top-down' theorists had previously assumed. There are many studies published now that convincingly demonstrate that visual features of the text are not minimally sampled in order to confirm hypotheses, but instead are exhaustively processed, even when the word is highly predictable (Stanovich 1992). This suggests a 'bottom-up' approach. Moreover, these same studies demonstrate that learning the cipher is neither easy nor natural, thus suggesting that children need support in learning it and that they benefit from explicit and some systematic teaching.

Poor readers, in contrast to fluent readers, make the greatest use of context cues – they are forced to rely on context cues since they haven't the necessary word recognition skills. This finding also contradicts Smith's thinking as he had argued that fluent readers paid more attention to context. There is little evidence that the difference between good and poor readers lies in good readers' better use of context cues. Juel (1991) notes that there is in fact an upper limit to improvement in the use of context information. She says that 'at best skilled readers can accurately predict one quarter of the words in context and these are frequently function words which are of such high frequency anyway that context is rarely needed to recognise them' (Juel 1991: 774). Function words are usually forms of 'to be', articles and prepositions. On the other hand, content words (i.e. nouns, adjectives and verbs, those words that really carry the meaning) are predictable in running text only about 10 per cent of the time. These words then are the least accurately predicted and they require the most decoding skill.

The outcome of all this work is that models of reading acquisition have, over the past fifteen years or so, shifted away from 'top-down' assumptions and towards models that emphasize autonomous processing through connection making. In turn this has meant a tempering of the constructivist metaphor where the reader builds or constructs meaning and it has raised awareness of how the text itself constrains expectations and beliefs (Perfetti and McCutchen 1987; Stanovich 1991, 1992). Stanovich (1992) summarizes this shift by saying that it is increasingly recognized that strong constructivist assumptions do not square with what is now known about the effect of context on word recognition, that is, word recognition is less affected by context as reading skill develops.

While I think Stanovich's notion of reading as constrained reasoning, noted above, is helpful, intriguing and insightful, I am left with some unease in relation to his tendency to undermine, if not reject, the notion of reading as a meaning-building activity. And here I think it is useful to consider briefly the idea of 'big shapes' and 'little shapes' originated by

Myra Barrs at the Centre for Language in Primary Education (CLPE) in London and endorsed so strongly by Teresa Grainger and Henrietta Dombey in their interpretation of Stephen's reading.

Big shapes and little shapes

Teresa Grainger referred in some detail to the idea of 'big' and 'little shapes', recommending specifically that Stephen be given much more support in relation to the former. Drawing on the work of Anne Bussis *et al.* (1985) and Margaret Moustafa (1993, 1997), who see reading primarily as meaning-driven, Myra Barrs (Dombey *et al.* 1998) develops the idea of 'big shapes' and 'little shapes'. 'Big shapes' refers to the large-scale cueing systems that the learner draws on when making sense of print. This includes syntax and semantics as well as such large-scale structures as genres. 'Little shapes' refers to the small-scale cueing system of letters and sounds as well as other cues like spelling and punctuation, in other words, what is happening at the level of print. She and her colleagues describe reading as a 'multi-level process in which the reader attends both to the big shapes and the small shapes, confirming at each of these levels hypotheses that have been set up at the other' (Dombey *et al.* 1998: 2). The big shapes, she says, always have to come first since they are linked so closely with the meanings of texts. She and her colleagues see the 'little shapes' fitting inside the bigger ones, and, crucially, as best learned 'within the context of a familiar and supportive text, where other cueing systems help children learn to use the least familiar ones – the graphophonic cueing system, or the print' (1998: 2). Children have to orchestrate these different kinds of information as they learn to read.

So at this point you might well ask the question: who is right, the psycho-linguists who insist that reading is a 'top-down' process or the cognitive-psychologists, most of whom tend to see reading more as a 'bottom-up' process?

Top-down or bottom-up?

The use of context is important in reading, as the psycho-linguistic school demonstrated. Without context knowledge, readers would not be able to work out the relevant meaning of words nor would they be able to draw inferences about the text. But where they are less accurate is in relation to the use of context in the identification of words. Skilled readers do not use context cues much to identify words but they do use context to interpret words and sentences. Context is used for higher level processes of meaning interpretation rather than for word identification (Perfetti 1995). As already noted above, less skilled readers, by contrast, use context to identify words because they are not skilled enough to use word identification skills. The evidence from the cognitive-psychological literature shows that when *bottom-up* processes that result in word recognition are deficient, the learner compensates by relying more heavily on contextual information.

Marilyn Jager Adams's evidence (1990) is often cited to support 'bottom-up' teaching, and specifically phonics. Yet, in her seminal text *Beginning to Read* (1990: 421–2), she warns of the dangers of 'bottom-up' teaching. Referring to good quality programmes for the development of reading she observes:

> . . . good programs [do not] succumb to the simplistic hypotheses that letter–sound relations are the most basic of reading skills. Rather, with respect to the knowledge that is critical to reading, that which can be developed through phonic instruction represents neither the top nor the bottom, but only a realm in between. Before children will learn to read, they must learn to recognize individual letters. They must become aware of the structure of language, from sentences and words to phonemes. And, most important, they must develop a basic under-standing of the forms and functions of text and its personal value to their own lives.
>
> Finally, none of these programs embodies the misguided hypothesis that reading skills are best developed from the bottom up. In the reading situation, as in any effective communication situation, the message or text provides but one of the critical sources of information. The rest must come from the reader's own prior knowledge. Further, in the reading situation as in any other learning situation, the learnability of a pattern depends critically on the prior knowledge and higher order relationships that it evokes. In both fluent reading and its acquisition, the reader's knowledge must be aroused interactively and in parallel. Neither understanding nor learning can proceed hierarchically from the bottom up. Phonological awareness, letter recognition facility, famili-arity with letter patterns, spelling–sound relationships, and individual words must be developed in concert with real reading and real writing and with deliberate reflection on the forms, functions, and meanings of texts.

It should be clear by now that the answer to the question in the title of this section is that both are right, but that the whole-language theorists did not sufficiently recognize the importance of word recognition. The pedagogical issue for teachers is how to balance learning the cipher or the code and reading for purposes that are authentic for the learner i.e. for enjoyment, for finding out, etc. The psycho-linguistic school certainly raised our appreciation for the latter and the cognitive-psychological school undoubtedly raised our appreciation for the former.

Connie Juel (1991, 1999) offers helpful suggestions on how to deal with the tension between learning the code and reading for authentic purposes. The former requires building up the learner's spelling–sound knowledge with reading material that makes the alphabet system transparent and this suggests controlling the vocabulary that the child is exposed to. The latter, on the other hand, requires exposure to texts that are rich in vocabulary and meaningful in content. Juel (1999: 209) says 'it is wrong to abandon controlled vocabulary texts on the assumption that reading is a psycho-linguistic guessing game'. The question, therefore, is: how can we create controlled texts without making them so limited in vocabulary that they appear dull like example 2 on page 50? Juel offers two suggestions.

First, she suggests, the teacher might introduce together multiple letters that often correspond to the same sound (for example, the long *e* pattern in 'me', 'sea', 'see', 'neat', 'green', and 'Pete'). She suggests simultaneous teaching of different sounds of the same letters (e.g. 'how', 'bow') which will also promote a more varied initial vocabulary for stories. She cites evidence to show that concurrent teaching of two sounds for a single letter fosters better learning than the successive teaching of the two sounds. Second, she suggests that not all the words in a story need to be decodable exclusively on the basis of what has been taught in phonics. She recommends the addition of high-frequency words to the phonic texts and the use of patterned text and nursery rhymes. Well-known or very familiar texts can be read, she suggests, while drawing attention to the words that exemplify the spelling–sound pattern of the day.

Juel's own research suggests that a little phonic instruction goes a long way, especially when the books the children are exposed to contain a number of decodable words that can facilitate implicit learning. The message from Juel's vast amount of evidence is that, while phonics training is very important, the training should be focused and short-lived.

Elfrieda Hiebert (1994), on the basis of several school-based projects involving pupils who depended to varying degrees on the school to become literate, goes further than Juel in arguing the case for balance across 'top-down' and 'bottom-up' perspectives. Her research demonstrates the need for using both approaches. She summarizes her findings as follows:

Authentic literacy tasks can assist students in responding to and interpreting text in ways that build on their existing knowledge and extend to worlds beyond the classroom. These tasks can be created so that students take ownership of literacy and schooling, not just of individual texts. Students whose previous literacy experiences have emulated school literacy tasks thrive in these contexts. Authentic literacy tasks also allow students without extensive literacy experiences to participate more fully in literacy events. But, without contexts where teachers consistently model and guide, the students who depend on schools to become literate don't necessarily or automatically attain high levels of literacy as a result of authentic tasks. However, when authentic literacy tasks include guidance, most first-grade students who begin with little school-like literacy can become proficient readers and writers.

(Hiebert 1994: 404–5)

Over the nineties several researchers (e.g. Trachtenburg 1990; Spiegel 1992; Moustafa 1993, 1997) have demonstrated that teachers can and do combine both perspectives. How do you interpret the position adopted by our literacy experts on this topic? It seems to me that not one of them rejects the significance of attending to word recognition. Differences lie perhaps in the relative emphasis they place on word recognition with Laura Huxford tending to accord greatest priority to this aspect of reading. Later in this Part we will consider the extent to which the National Literacy Strategy reflects the thinking of the cognitive-psychological school. But now we will briefly revisit some of our scholars' suggestions for promoting Stephen's word recognition skill.

Teaching word recognition: Stephen and children like him

The cognitive-psychological perspective on reading is one in which word recognition is central, as reflected in the title of this Part of the book. It is noteworthy that most of our experts referred to Stephen's need in this regard. Although the emphasis they accorded overall to this varied, none could be said to neglect its importance. Ann Browne referred to the need to 'enlarge his sight vocabulary' and she suggested games like lotto, snap and computer games for doing this. This was echoed by Teresa Grainger. Both scholars also suggested writing should be integrated with reading so in writing sessions Stephen's attention should be drawn to patterns in words. Laura Huxford talked about the importance of 'orchestrating strategies' or helping him harmonize all the various reading cueing systems in reading, and how Stephen hadn't yet mastered this ability. Although he may have some skill in using word-building strategies like analogies, Laura said he didn't have an effective strategy for tackling long words, noting that he didn't know the vowel digraphs (except perhaps 'ee'). She would encourage his teacher to be very explicit in developing his word recognition skills. For example, she said the teacher could get him to talk about how he figured out an unknown word. She mentioned sounding out the parts of the word. David Wray said how if he were Stephen's teacher he would devise 'games and activities' to help him with blending. Henrietta Dombey, whose perspective we discuss further in Part Three, talked about helping Stephen to notice the morphemic and phonemic patterns in words. A morpheme is a root word, the basic part of a word to which affixes (prefixes and suffixes) are added, while a phoneme is the smallest element of sound that makes a difference to the meaning of a word. She also recommended the use of displays of word families.

To apply the recommendations of our scholars and the research discussed in this part of the book more broadly, i.e. to other children like Stephen, you would have to get a good sense of the child's word recognition along a continuum of written word knowledge, for example beginning consonants, word families, vowel patterns, multisyllable words. Then over time you would need to provide some systematic word study and find ways of applying this word study in meaningful contexts. Below are some principles and procedures from the work of Morris *et al.* (1998) which are probably familiar to teachers but which, nevertheless, have proved to be effective with struggling readers, and specifically with readers who have difficulty decoding.

- Determine the child's reading instructional level, that is the level where he is challenged but not frustrated.
- Find reading material that is of personal interest and significance to him.
- Foreground comprehension by informally discussing stories or articles as they are being read.
- Establish the child's word recognition: check for knowledge of and ability to apply beginning consonants, word families, vowel patterns, multisyllable words.
- Try out ways of getting him to practise reading on his own.

Four activities might feature strongly in such a child's literacy diet – Guided Reading, Word Study, Writing and Easy Reading. Guided Reading might involve you or a trained classroom assistant or parent helper and the child in reading alternate pages of a suitable text, stopping occasionally to check comprehension. After a few pages of this partner reading, the helper could ask the child to predict some aspect of the plot and then ask him to read silently the remaining three or four pages of the story. Encourage him to ask for help with difficult words. He could perhaps take the next chapter or several pages home on audiotape. This time his job is not just to listen to the recorded chapter but to practise reading it in preparation for an oral reading the next day, during which time the plot would also be discussed. Depending on the size of the book, the next section or chapter could be partner read and a tape of the next one taken home.

Every day have the child spend some time, say ten minutes, in word study. Table 2 offers an example of sorting vowel patterns.

But as indicated above in the description of the stages of reading development, there are several ways to decode words and the teacher needs to develop and be mindful of all of them. Five word identification strategies are summarized in Table 3.

Table 2 Word sort example

mat	*rake*	*card*	*(?)*
fan	made	park	fall
bag	face	far	ball
flat		dart	

name

Source: Morris *et al.* (1996)

Table 3 Word identification strategies

Strategy	*Description*
Phonics	• Pupils use their knowledge of sound symbol correspondences and spelling patterns to decode words when reading and spelling.
Analogies	• Pupils use their knowledge of rhyming words to deduce the pronunciation or spelling of an unfamiliar word e.g. 'creep' from 'sheep'.
Context, semantic and syntactic cues	• They use information from illustrations, from their prior knowledge of the subject matter and of the way language works.
Morphemic analysis	• Pupils apply their knowledge of root words and affixes (prefixes at the beginning and suffixes at the end) to identify unfamiliar words. They 'shed' any prefixes and suffixes and identify the root word first. Then they add the affixes e.g. 'trans-port', 'bi-cycle', 'tele-scope', 'centi-pede'.
Syllabic analysis	• Pupils break multisyllabic words into syllables and then use phonics and analogies to decode the word, syllable by syllable e.g. 'cul-prit', 'tem-por-ar-y', 'vic-tor-y', 'neg-a-tive'.

Source: Tompkins (1997: 169)

Writing might involve the child in selecting his own writing topics and expression of ideas should be prioritized over mechanical accuracy especially in the early weeks of focused teaching, and always in first drafts. Easy Reading could be part of everyday work in which he and a helper would start a story in school and he could finish the story at home.

Some teachers of the middle years of primary school notice that their pupils make little progress or actually lose ground in their reading development.

Some have argued that this is due to the increased demands of the curriculum, especially the unfamiliar vocabulary of informational books. However, more recent research along the lines outlined above (e.g. Chall *et al.* 1990) suggests that inadequate teaching of word identification strategies may be responsible. The problem is that for pupils like Stephen, practice in the context of repeated readings of predictable texts may not be enough. Some children simply do not notice individual words and teachers need to be more explicit in these cases.

They need Shared Reading plus. They need shared reading experience where the teacher reads a big book with pupils using a class set of books. The teacher models, i.e. reads aloud, while they follow along in their individual copies. Essential for children like Stephen are also both of the following: focusing on target words and using the target words in reading and writing activities. The teacher chooses one or more words from the class word wall for study. Having highlighting this word, teacher and pupil identify and list words with the same phonogram i.e. spelling pattern. Pupils write the words and/or add them to personal word banks/booklets. Pupils are also encouraged to notice the target words in books they read and report to the teacher when they notice the word. They use the target words in word posters and in books they write.

Since phonics is such key word identification strategy and since it is a topic that is controversial in reading debates, the next section deals with this in some detail.

Phonological awareness and phonic knowledge

Phonological awareness is probably one of the most significant developments in our understanding of the reading process in the past fifteen years. As one psychologist put it, 'Although phonological processing is not the only place to look for answers to the mysteries inherent in reading acquisition, it has been one of the most productive areas of inquiry to date in terms of advancing our scientific understanding of the reading process' (Blachman 2000: 495). Credit is due to cognitive psychologists for furnishing us with this understanding. In view of its importance, I will address three questions in this section. First, what is phonological awareness and how is it assessed? Second, why is this awareness important? And third, how can it and phonic knowledge be developed in the classroom?

What is phonological awareness and how is it assessed?

Simply put, phonological awareness is a general awareness of sounds in speech as distinct from their meanings. When that awareness includes an understanding that words can be divided into sequences of phonemes, this sensitivity is termed phonemic awareness. A phoneme is the smallest element of sound that makes a difference to the meaning of a word (Dombey *et al.* 1998). 'Cat' has three phonemes, /c/a/t/, and 'ship' also has three, /sh/i/p/. Phonemic awareness is the insight that every spoken word can be thought of as a string of phonemes. Because phonemes are the units of sound that are symbolized by the letters of the alphabet, an awareness of phonemes is important to understanding the alphabetic system, and therefore to the learning of phonics and spelling.

Phonemic awareness develops through other, less subtle levels of phonological awareness like noticing similarities between words in their sounds, enjoying rhymes and counting syllables. Spoken words can be phonologically subdivided at several different levels of analysis. These include *the syllable* (the word 'predict' has two syllables: /pre/ and /dict/); the *onset and rime* within the syllable (/pr/ and /e/, and /d/ and /ict/, respectively); and the individual *phonemes* themselves (/p/, /r/, /e/, /d/, /i/, /k/, and /t/) (Snow *et al.* 1998). The work of Goswami and Bryant (1990) highlighted the significance of the unit just below the level of the syllable i.e. the rime. The onset is the part of the syllable before the first vowel and the rime is the part of the syllable from the first vowel onwards.

The assessment of phonemic awareness involves tasks that require the child to isolate and segment one or more of the phonemes of a spoken word, to blend or build up a string of separate phonemes into a word, or to manipulate the phonemes within a word in some way, for example removing, adding or rearranging phonemes in one word to make another one. This is how a recent study, commissioned by the US Congress (Ehri *et al.* 2001), described how this kind of sensitivity could be assessed:

- *Phoneme isolation*, which requires the recognition of individual sounds in words, for example, 'Tell me the first sound in paste'.(/p/)
- *Phoneme identity*, which requires the recognition of the common sound in different words, for example, 'Tell me the sound that is the same in bike, boy, and bell'. (/b/)
- *Phoneme categorization*, which requires recognizing the word with the odd sound in a sequence of three or four words, for example, 'Which word does not belong? "Bus", "bun", "rug".' ('rug')
- *Phoneme blending*, which requires listening to a sequence of separately spoken sounds and combining them to form a recognizable word, for example, 'What word is /s/ /k/ /u/ /l/?' (school)
- *Phoneme segmentation*, which requires breaking a word into its sounds by tapping out or counting the sounds or by pronouncing and positioning a marker for each sound, for example, 'How many phonemes in ship?' (3: /sh/ /i/ /p/)

- *Phoneme deletion*, which involves recognizing what word remains when a specified phoneme is removed, for example, 'What is smile without the /s/?' (mile)

Why is phonological awareness important?

Research has now well established that phonological awareness is important in learning to read (Adams 1990; Blachman 2000; NRP 2000). It is both a precursor to and a consequence of reading. The most recent and systematic review of the evidence concluded that phonemic awareness is one of the best predictors of how well children will learn to read (Ehri *et al.* 2001). One example of the many studies reviewed in this project was one by Share *et al.* in 1984. Share and colleagues assessed pre-schoolers on several measures when they entered school – they took measures on each of the following: phonemic segmentation, letter name knowledge, memory of sentences, vocabulary, father's occupational status, parental reports of reading to children, and TV watching. They wanted to know which of these measures best predicted how well the children would be reading one and two years later. For each year in school, phonemic awareness was the top predictor along with letter knowledge.

Although not every child needs an explicit programme in phonological awareness, the reading teacher needs to know why such teaching is important as well as how and when to provide it.

How does phonemic awareness contribute to helping children learn to read? First of all, as already noted, the English writing system is alphabetic and it is not a simple matter to figure out that system. The thing is that words have prescribed spellings that are made up of graphemes symbolizing phonemes in predictable ways. The ability to distinguish the phonemes in the sounds of words so that they can be matched to graphemes is the key. And of course there are no breaks in speech which would indicate where one phoneme ends and the next one begins, thus accounting for the difficulty in doing this. Discovering phonemic units in speech is greatly facilitated, however, by some explicit teaching in how the system works – that is the conclusion of the recent review of the evidence (see National Reading Parel website (NRP 2000) for details as well as Ehri *et al.* 2000).

Understanding the alphabetic system requires an awareness that spoken language can be analysed into sequences of separable words and words, in turn, into sequences of syllables and phonemes within syllables. In other words all children need to learn about the segmental nature of print and how the sound segments are represented in print. Decoding words requires blending skill to transform graphemes into recognizable words. Reading words by analogy (e.g. recognizing 'camp' from knowing how to read 'lamp') requires onset–rime segmentation and blending skill. Also reading words by sight requires phonemic segmentation skill. As we saw above in relation to the final stage of reading, to store sight words in memory, children have to connect up graphemes to phonemes in the word and then retain these connections in memory (Ehri *et al.* 2001).

Although very many children seem to make these discoveries effortlessly on their own by listening to nursery rhymes, by playing oral language games and by having opportunities to write, very many other children do not seem to acquire such knowledge and skill automatically. It is likely that some children come to school having attained the prerequisite skills of reading, having had sufficient exposure to language and literacy play to trigger these associations or mental networks (Blachman 2000). It is also likely that, despite exposure to language games and all sorts of literacy experiences, other children remain phonologically insensitive.

Some explicit teaching is probably necessary for such children although again it is likely that a small amount of phonemic training goes a long way. Steven Stahl gives a fascinating account of one child, Heather, who was having difficulty learning to read in school. As part of her assessment, Stahl gave Heather a task which required her to remove a phoneme from a spoken word. He asked her to say 'meat', which she did. He then asked her to repeat it without the /m/ sound ('eat'). She said 'chicken'. Stahl was rather surprised at this. Then he asked her to say *coat* which she did, and then to try saying it without the /k/ sound. She said 'jacket'. As he studied her responses to several such tasks, he worked out that she responded to words only in terms of their meanings, and not as entities to be manipulated in themselves. For her, a little less of 'meat' was 'chicken' and a little less than 'coat' was 'jacket'. For most communication, focusing on meaning is necessary but for learning to read it is desirable to view words in terms of the sounds they contain (phonemic awareness) and in terms of their sound–symbol relationships (phonic knowledge).

Issues in the development of phonological awareness in the classroom

Before discussing how phonemic awareness might be developed in the classroom it is worth pointing out some issues involved in its teaching. Some of these issues have only very recently come to light and derive from the research of the National Reading Panel in the US.

Children who were taught only one or two phonemic awareness skills, e.g. segmenting words into phonemes, or segmenting and blending phonemes, showed stronger phonemic awareness and more strongly transferred to reading than children who were taught three or more skills.

I think this is a fascinating finding as it suggests that, as we hinted earlier, a small amount of teaching of phonemic awareness goes a long way. The researchers tried to explain this finding and they offered some interesting explanations. One suggestion they offered is that when only one or two skills were taught, more pupils actually mastered the skills that were taught. Another possibility they speculated on makes a good deal of sense to me. They suggested that teaching multiple skills (more than three in this case) impaired the acquisition of phonemic insight as children may have become confused about the underlying principle as they moved from one skill to the next, first breaking words into sounds, then blending sounds into words, then taking sounds out of words to say new words. In the light of this possibility, the research team sensibly advises teachers, who are using multiple skills programmes, to teach one skill at a time and to ensure this skill is mastered before moving on to the next one. Crucially, in my view, they also add that teachers should teach pupils how each skill can be applied in reading as soon as it is taught.

They also suggest that what is more important than the number of phonemic skills to teach is the issue of which skills to teach. Phonemic instruction should be appropriate for a child's level of literacy development. The work done with pre-schoolers for example should be much simpler than the kinds of manipulations done with older pupils. Drawing on the research of several other authors the National Reading Panel listed phonemic tasks in order, from easy to difficult:

1 First sound comparison: identifying the names of pictures, beginning with the same sound.
2 Blending onset–rime units into real words.
3 Blending phonemes into real words.
4 Deleting a phoneme and saying the word that remains.
5 Segmenting words into phonemes.
6 Blending phonemes into non-words.

The work of Goswami and Bryant had already established that children find it easier to recognize onsets and rimes than to recognize phonemes. Moreover, those children who could do this at 4 years of age learned to recognize words more quickly over the next few years than their counterparts who did not have this skill at 4 years of age. In addition, they found that those who could not recognize such patterns could quite easily be helped to do so through nursery rhymes, play with language, using alliteration and rhyme, games like *I spy* and so on.

By teaching children to link this knowledge of sound patterns with letter patterns and by helping them notice the internal structure of words, they learned to draw analogies based on these patterns between words they knew and words they did not know. Their research suggested that while children actually begin reading using only a visual approach to recognizing words, their awareness of onset and rime allows them to apply analogies in order to recognize new words. In the early stages of course they benefit from having those analogies pointed out to them. So children recognize new words, not so much by breaking down words or even building up words from their knowledge of phoneme–grapheme relationships, but by making analogies. Herein lies a self-teaching process that stands the beginner reader in good stead for future reading.

In deciding which aspect to teach or which approach to use, you have to take account not only of the difficulty of the task but also how your pupils are expected to apply that skill. In teaching the first of these above, for example, the intention is to alert children to the fact that words have sounds as well as meanings. The reason for teaching the second is to help beginner readers generate more complete spellings of words. And the reason for teaching phonemic blending is to help them combine letter sounds to decode words. As the research team make clear, teaching phonemic awareness effectively includes teaching the applications as well as the skill.

It is not possible to say how much time or how long teaching in phonemic awareness should last in order to be effective. Obviously individual learners will differ in how much teaching they need to acquire phonemic awareness. This implies that it is important to tailor teaching to pupil need by working out who has and who has not acquired the skills being taught. Children who are still having difficulty should continue with further skill development in phonemic awareness while those who have already acquired the skills would benefit more from doing other reading and writing activities. The NRP tentatively advise that the most effective circumstances may be teaching one or two PA skills with letters, especially blending and segmenting, in small groups of struggling readers or preschoolers for 5 to 18 hours (Ehri *et al.* 2001).

At least one reading expert questions this implication of the Panel's pedagogical recommendation, saying that it is tantamount to endorsing systematic phonics teaching in the early years. He queries the implicit assumptions that more is better and that earlier is also better. He also challenges the Panel's evidence on the grounds that there may be other ways of promoting this awareness. James Cunningham (2001: 333) argues that

> the burden of proof is with the Panel to show that research-based practices such as shared reading of books that play with sounds, writing with invented spelling, and teaching onsets using a variety of activities (key actions, students' names, and key foods or beverages) do not help most children develop the necessary phonemic awareness they need. Until this happens, the Panel's rush to standardization of how and when to best develop the essentials of phonemic awareness should be ignored or opposed.

My own understanding of early and more recent work of Usha Goswami (Goswami 1986, 2000; Goswami and Bryant 1990) on analogies in reading processes leads me to suspect that Cunningham's list of practices should certainly be part of phonemic work with children. Goswami's recent work (2000) on the relationship between a child's phonological awareness and lexical development points to the importance of the quality of the child's linguistic environment from infancy. Factors such as the clarity and frequency of the speech of care-taking adults and the efficiency of the child's linguistic processing – and the latter, she says, could be affected by factors such as the frequency of ear infections in early childhood – might all play an important role.

The point of referring here to Cunningham's response to the review of the NRP is to highlight some of the contested areas even within what is, arguably, quite a narrow area of reading. The scientific evidence presented by the NRP is strong in relation to the significance of phonemic awareness in children's reading development. This, in my view, has been well demonstrated with plenty of irrefutable evidence. But Cunningham's questioning of the NRP's interpretation of the pedagogical extension of that evidence is fair and valid, I think, since here we are in more messy research territory. The pedagogical evidence is not conclusive.

Issues in phonics teaching

We have already distinguished phonemic awareness from phonic knowledge. Phonics teaching is a way of teaching reading that emphasizes the knowledge of letter–sound correspondences and the ability to apply this knowledge to reading and spelling. Phonics teaching is designed for beginner readers in the primary years and for children having difficulty in learning to read. On the basis of our earlier discussion, it should be clear that phonemic awareness needs to be in place before phonic training starts.

Systematic phonics

The review by the National Reading Panel revealed that systematic phonics teaching makes a bigger contribution to children's reading development than programmes involving incidental or no phonics instruction. Systematic phonics teaching helped beginner readers acquire the use of the alphabetic system to read and spell words in and out of text. In addition, it contributed substantially to pupils' growth in reading comprehension. And it exerts its greatest influence in the early years i.e. reception and Year 1.

However, phonics teaching failed to exert a significant impact on the reading skill of low-achieving readers above Year 2. Given our profile of Stephen, it is worth pondering the explanations offered for this finding. The Panel suggests that phonics teaching provided to low-achieving readers may not have been sufficiently intense but the studies available for their analysis were too few to be definitive and future research will have to provide further evidence about the impact of phonics instruction on older learners. The existing evidence would suggest that a phonics route to decoding may not be the best approach for Stephen. The Panel concluded, 'There are many uncertainties surrounding the introduction of phonics instruction to children in upper grades who have already moved into reading' (NRP 2000: 2–114).

The Panel also suggests that perhaps the impact of phonics instruction could be enhanced by combining it with teaching that supports children in learning to read words in other ways, e.g. reading words from memory, reading words by analogy to known words, and reading words using spelling patterns and multisyllabic decoding strategies. The Panel also suggests that it may be important to include systematic teaching in reading fluency when phonics is taught to older children. In the light of Stephen's profile we will return below to more practical suggestions for developing fluency.

Phonics taught early proved much more effective than phonics teaching introduced after Year 1. The conclusion the evidence seems to support is that systematic phonics teaching produces its biggest impact on growth in reading when it begins in reception class or Year 1 and before pupils have learned to read independently.

But what is meant by 'systematic' here? Systematic phonics programmes teach phonics explicitly by delineating a planned, sequential set of phonic elements. A key feature distinguishing systematic from non-systematic phonics teaching is the identification of a full array of letter–sound correspondences to be taught (NRP 2000: 2–99). The array includes the major correspondences between consonant letters and sounds and also short and long vowel letters and sounds, and vowel and consonant digraphs (e.g. oi, ea, ou, sh, ch, th). It may also include blends of letter-sounds that recur as subunits in many words, such as initial blends (e.g. st, sm, bl, pr) and final stems (e.g. -end, -ack, -ill, -op). A systematic approach does not merely teach the alphabetic system but also offers practice in applying this knowledge in reading and writing. Teaching may provide children with text incorporating words that can be decoded using the letter–sound correspondences already taught or children might write their own text and read others' text using the letter-sounds taught.

Synthetic and analytic phonics

It is important at this point to distinguish between synthetic and analytic phonics. The former emphasizes letter-by-letter phonological decoding. What is emphasized is the phoneme. The teaching strategy here is to sound and blend the sequential letter-sounds. This is an example of what the teacher using this approach might do (Juel and Minden-Cupp 2001). For the word 'hat', she writes each letter, touches each one and asks the pupils to say each sound. Then they blend the sounds, as she makes a blending motion under the word. In other words children are taught to say the sounds of letters and blend them to decode unfamiliar words. A systematic phonics programme would typically begin by teaching children relations between individual letters and pairs of letters called digraphs (e.g. th, ai, ch, oi) and all 44 sounds or phonemes of the language (NRP 2000: 2–104).

An example of a synthetic phonics programme used in England is *Jolly Phonics*. Developed by a teacher, Sue Lloyd, in 1993 for 4- and 5-year-olds in their first year of school, the programme uses meaningful stories, pictures and actions to reinforce recognition and recall of letter–sound relations, and precise articulation of phonemes. There are five key elements to the programme:

1 learning the letter sounds;
2 learning letter formation;
3 blending for reading;
4 identifying the sounds in words for writing; and
5 tricky words that are high-frequency and irregularly spelled.

The programme promotes playful, creative, flexible teaching that fits well with whole-language practice (NRP 2000: 2–125) and leads directly to authentic reading and writing. A feature of *Jolly Phonics* is that children are taught hand gestures to help them remember the letter–sound associations. The value of mnemonics for teaching letter–sound relations to younger children is supported by research evidence (Ehri *et al.* 1984). Application of this principle is also found in *Letterland* (Wendon 1992), a programme designed to teach young children letter–sound associations. Here all the letters are animate characters that assume the shape of the letters and have names priming the relevant sound e.g. 'Sammy Snake', 'Annie Apple'. What this approach achieves is added motivational value for children – by making the learning into a game and playful, it guards against boredom and speeds up the learning process.

Analytic phonics avoids having children pronounce sounds in isolation to figure out words. Rather they are taught to analyse letter–sound relations once a word is identified. Analytic phonics can also refer to the process of identifying unknown words with analogy to the onsets and rimes in known words. (Some authors describe this as 'analogy phonics' – e.g. NRP 2000.) In this approach, the pupils are taught key words that contain common spelling patterns. The pupil is then taught to break an unknown word into its component onset and rimes and to search a word wall for known words with the same onset or rime. If 'hat' was an unknown word, the child might note the /at/, finding the known word 'cat' on the word wall and observing 'If I know "cat" then I know "hat"' (Gaskins *et al.* 1986 and Juel Minden-Cupp 2001). Examples of such programmes include Reading Recovery and the Benchmark Word Identification Program (Gaskins *et al.* 1986).

The jury is out as to whether phonic knowledge is best developed synthetically or analytically. (Juel and Minden-Cupp 2001: 5) say:

> There is now evidence that of those children who really struggle with decoding, some profit more from a synthetic phonics approach while others find an analogy approach easier to use as an instructional strategy . . . The optimal match of instructional strategies and linguistic units used in that instruction, for children with differing levels of word recognition skill, is far from clear in laboratory settings – let alone in classroom settings. Both the instructional unit (i.e. phoneme or onset and rime) and instructional strategy (i.e. sequential letter-by-letter decoding versus making an analogy to a key word) may differentially affect children.

However, Juel and Minden-Cupp's own subsequent work, based on classrooms, sheds some light on this question. They found that a structured phonics programme that included both onsets/rimes and the sounding and blending of phonemes within the rimes was very effective. Important to note here is that the rime unit had to be analysed into its component letter–phoneme correspondences, especially for those children who entered first grade with limited knowledge of letter sounds. So it seems both approaches are beneficial. The NRP review of the evidence found no significant difference in the impact of both methods; what seems to be important is the systematic approach to the development of phonic knowledge.

The message for educators, who, unlike researchers, have to make decisions that affect individual lives in the here and now and who cannot wait for research to offer definitive answers, is first, to be mindful of the state of the current knowledge base and second, to make a professional judgement based on that knowledge and their own professional context and set of learners. What is key perhaps is not to be dogmatic about how to develop this awareness, important though it is, but rather to be open-minded to the several possibilities for doing it effectively.

It would appear that when phonics is taught to children at the outset of learning to read and continued for some two to three years the children achieve greater growth in reading than do those children who receive only one year of phonics instruction. However, the evidence on this is but suggestive and not definitive. Further research will have to determine more precisely how long phonics teaching should last.

Developing phonological awareness and phonic knowledge in the classroom

Research discussed above shows that phonemic awareness is essential for understanding the alphabetic principle and for acquiring phonic knowledge.

In recent years there has been a proliferation of guidebooks, materials and programmes for the purpose of developing young readers' appreciation of the alphabet system via phonemic and phonic training (e.g. Adams *et al.* 1998; Dombey *et al.* 1998; Torgesen and Mathes 2000; DfES 2001; and Goldsworthy 2001).

Phonological skills can be developed incidentally through oral language, songs, rhymes, riddles, word play in stories, and invented spelling as well as games, activities and exercises (e.g. 'I spy') which draw attention to speech sounds. Most teachers probably use a combination of all these approaches. The key thing about all these activities is that they take place in a language-rich environment where attention is often turned to language itself. We cannot but notice children's natural propensity to experiment and play with sounds and the teacher can capitalize on this propensity to play with words separate from their meanings. Among the more practical ways of sensitizing young children to the sounds in language are children's books that deal playfully with speech sounds through rhyme, alliteration, assonance and so on. And among the best around still are the Dr Seuss books, although there are very many available. See Yopp (1995) for an annotated bibliography. The critical feature of such books is that they shift the child's attention from the message of the text to the language itself that is used to tell the message. Hallie Yopp (1995) suggests five sequenced things to do with such texts:

1 Read and reread the story for the pure joy of reading and sharing.
2 Comment on the language use and gently guide attention to the word play.
3 Encourage predictions of sounds, words or phrases and then ask the children how they arrived at their predictions.
4 Examine language use. Depending on the age of the children she suggests the teacher might explicitly point out and analyse phonemic features. For children aged 4 to 7, for example, the teacher might say 'What sound do you hear at the beginning of all those words? (Yes, the /k/ sound). Isn't it interesting how the author uses so many words with the /k/ sound? What are some other words that begin with the /k/ sound?'
5 Create additional verses or make another version of the story. Children can change the story yet maintain the language pattern to develop their own versions of the story.

Programmes designed to promote phonological awareness more directly than my descriptions above typically include activities to develop skills in rhyming, alliteration, syllable awareness, identifying initial sounds of words, identifying onsets and rimes, creating words from given onsets, identifying final sounds, sound blending, segmenting words into syllables and phonemes, exchanging phonemes to create new words and mapping phonemes to letter symbols. As already noted above, sound blending is easier than

phonemic segmentation, and exchanging phonemes and mentally mani-
pulating sounds in words is probably the most difficult skill to achieve.
Beyond the most basic level, phonemic awareness training can be fully
integrated with the teaching of letter–sound correspondences and related
whenever possible to the child's attempts at invented spelling.

The NRP review demonstrated that phonological training seems to have
maximum benefit when it is combined with teaching in letter–sound correspondences. Connections between speech sounds and letters need to be
thoroughly understood and applied to decoding. Key activities here would
include working with onsets and rimes in a way that facilitates understanding of the orthographic patterns of language (e.g. 'plant', 'slant', 'stamp',
'lamp' and so on). The activities provided in the classroom need to be
based on learner need as indicated by the stage they have reached in terms
of their reading development.

Stahl (1992) offers nine guidelines for exemplary phonics teaching. These
are summarized here.

1 'Builds on a child's rich concepts about how print functions'. Key here is
   that letter–sound teaching makes no sense to a child who does not have
   an overall conception of what reading is all about and what it is for.
2 'Builds on a foundation of phonemic awareness'. Phonemic awareness is
   easily taught but absence of it leads to reading difficulties.
3 'Is clear and direct'. Stahl encourages teachers to avoid ambiguity. He
   gives an example of a direct approach for teaching the /b/ sound in
   'bear'. He suggests that you show the word 'bear', in the context of a
   story or in isolation, that you point out that it begins with the letter *b*,
   and that the letter *b* makes the /b/ sound. This approach, he says, goes to
   the basic concept, which is that a letter in a word represents a particular
   phoneme.
4 'Is integrated into a total reading programme'. Phonics instruction, he
   suggests, should never dominate reading teaching. At least half of the
   time in a reading lesson, he suggests, should be devoted to reading connected text and no more than 25 per cent of the time should be devoted
   to phonics teaching.
5 'Focuses on reading words, not learning rules'. It is important to remember that effective decoders see words not in terms of phonic rules but in
   terms of patterns of letters that are used to aid word identification. Effective phonics teaching first draws attention to the order of letters in words,
   urging them to notice common patterns in words.
6 'May include onsets and rimes'. An example offered here is how children
   are taught to compare an unknown word to already known words and to
   use context to confirm their predictions. For example, when encounter-
   ing the word 'wheat' in a sentence, the pupil might be encouraged to
   compare it to 'meat' and say 'If m-e-a-t is "meat" then this is "wheat"'.

The pupil then cross-checks the pronunciation by seeing if 'wheat' made sense in the sentence. This approach is comprehension-driven but it does teach decoding effectively.

7 'May include invented spelling practice'. Practice with invented spelling does improve children's awareness of phonemes, which is an important precursor to learning to decode.

8 'Develops independent word recognition strategies, focusing attention on the internal structure of words'. The purpose of phonics teaching is to get learners to notice orthographic patterns in words and to use those patterns to recognize words.

9 'Develops automatic word recognition skills so that students can devote their attention to comprehension, not words'. Stahl suggests that once a child begins to use orthographic patterns in recognizing words and recognizes words at a fluent pace, then it is time to move away from phonics teaching and spend more time on reading and writing text.

Juel and Minden-Cupp (2001) offer very precise, research-based guidance in relation to teaching children who enter the first grade (Year 1) with minimal reading skills. Their evidence led them to conclude that such children have the greatest success with the following classroom practices:

1 Teachers modelled word recognition strategies by a) chunking words into component units such as syllables, onset/rimes, or finding little words in big words, as well as modelling and encouraging the sound and blending of individual letters or phonemes in these chunks; and b) considering known letter-sounds in a word and what makes sense.

2 Children were encouraged to point to words as text was read.

3 Children used hands-on materials (e.g. pocket charts for active sorting of picture cards by sound and word cards by orthographic pattern).

4 Writing for sounds was part of phonemic instruction.

5 Instructional groups were small with word recognition lesson plans designed to meet the specific needs of children within that group.

In this country, Henrietta Dombey and Myra Barrs argue in favour of 'whole-to-part' phonics teaching (analytic). They suggest that, rather than proceeding from the part to the whole (e.g. sounding out an unknown word), children are more likely to begin with a repertoire of known words and proceed from wholes to parts. Barrs says 'children come to understand how to break words down rather than how to build them up; their favoured approaches are analytic rather than synthetic' (Dombey *et al.* 1998: 1). The work of Goswami and Juel noted above would support this contention.

As has been argued several times in this book, there is empirical evidence for the value and importance of early, explicit teaching in word recognition. Likewise, there is evidence that pupils benefit from reading high-quality children's literature. So teaching phonics in association with children's literature maximizes learning opportunities. The major value of whole-to-part phonics teaching as described in Dombey *et al.* (1998) is that their whole-to-part framework integrates learning to read with real reading. Indeed there is conclusive evidence now that the most effective literacy teachers use a balance of approaches to the development of literacy and to reading in particular (e.g. Pressley 1998).

What about developing fluency? Stephen again

Fluent reading involves reading words accurately, rapidly, and automatically in a way that frees the reader's cognitive resources to concentrate on meaning. However, more recent conceptions of fluency also include the ability to group words appropriately into meaningful syntactic units for interpretation. Fluency requires the speedy use of punctuation and the decision as to where to place emphases to make a text make sense. The point is that readers have to carry out these processes rapidly and without conscious attention. Research evidence now shows that gradual, continuous improvement in reading speed happens through practice (NRP 2000). Moreover, there are two aspects worth identifying – accuracy of word recognition and automaticity of word recognition. In the early stages of reading the beginner reader may be accurate in word recognition but the process is usually slow and effortful. With increased practice and exposure to the words in the texts the pupil reads, word recognition continues to be accurate but improvements in speed and ease of word recognition are also evident. The teacher has to balance both of these processes – accuracy and speed/expression or fluency. Accuracy is not enough to ensure fluency and without fluency, comprehension may be impeded (NRP 2000: 3–8).

You will recall that the evidence to date on phonics suggests that older, struggling readers like Stephen seem to benefit less from phonics than their younger counterparts who have not yet started to read independently. The current thinking is that such children might benefit from phonics instruction combined with training in fluency. As virtually all our scholars observed, Stephen's reading lacked fluency most likely because he had to concentrate on the words due to his lack of word identification skills. Ann Browne referred to the need 'to speed him up' and Laura Huxford talked about 'fluency building'. Fluency is seen as an important marker of a proficient reader, yet teacher guidance on this facet of reading is quite rare.

Slow readers, by definition, read fewer words per given amount of time than readers who read at more normal rates. Thus, just to keep up with their classmates in the amount of reading done, these slower readers have to invest considerably more time and energy in their reading. So tackling fluency would seem to be a vital aspect of enhancing the reading proficiency of the struggling reader. Thinking of how slowly Stephen read and the fact that all our scholars referred to the need to enhance his fluency, I found the suggestions of Timothy Rasinski (2000) and Rasinski *et al.* (1994) very helpful.

First, this is how he described the negative consequences at classroom level of a hypothetical child like Stephen:

> Imagine yourself as a fifth-grade [Year 5] student who is assigned to read a 12-page chapter in a social studies book in school. Imagine also that you are a disfluent or inefficient reader. You read at 58 words per minute . . . or about half the rate of your classmates. You begin reading as best you can. Like most students, you are well aware of what is happening around you. You are about halfway through the passage, and you notice that many of your classmates have finished reading – they are done and you still have six pages to read. What do you do? Do you pretend to have completed the assignment even though you haven't read or comprehended the entire passage? Or, do you continue reading knowing that by doing so you will be broadcasting your lack of reading proficiency and making your classmates wait on you? Neither solution is very palatable, yet the problem is all too common. Even if an assignment were made for home reading, the 60-minute reading assignment for most students would become two hours of reading for you. Checking out of the reading club may be just around the corner. You may become a 9-year-old . . . who claims never or hardly ever to read for fun. And if you don't read, chances are your progress in reading will continue to decelerate.
>
> (Rasinski 2000: 147)

He and other reviewers like the National Reading Panel established that slow reading is associated with poor comprehension and poor overall reading performance. Citing research dating back over 60 years Rasinski suggests that faster readers tend to have better comprehension of what is read and tend to be, overall, better readers.

Some proven strategies for enhancing fluency include guided repeated oral readings, reading while listening or echo listening and reading in phrases. All these approaches have pupils reading passages orally multiple times while receiving feedback from peers, parents or teachers. These methods have been tried and tested by research and found to be effective. The problem for the class teacher, however, especially without the support of classroom assistance, is that all these methods were originated for use in one-to-one or small group settings. Rasinski advises, therefore, that teachers use other proven, classroom-based approaches. He suggests modelling fluent reading. Pupils need frequent opportunities to see and hear fluent reading and, often, less fluent readers miss out on hearing other, fluent readers read as they may be assigned to reading groups composed of non-fluent readers. Choral reading is another means that is suitable for the regular classroom.

Listening to tape recordings of a favourite book while following the text has the advantage of allowing pupils to work on their fluency independently. Henrietta Dombey specifically mentions this approach.

Laura Huxford suggested Stephen might look on to the next full stop, then read to that. There is evidence that marking phrases or sentences in the pupil's text with a slash aids fluent reading. Reading short texts such as poems, famous speeches, or popular songs marked in this way may support a more smooth phrasing. If, as in Stephen's case, the lack of fluency is due to lack of work recognition skill, then fluency is best promoted with materials that they find relatively easy in terms of word recognition. The use of easier texts allows the non-fluent reader to concentrate on expression. Both Ann Browne and Laura Huxford recommended the use of simpler texts for Stephen to avoid having him read at frustration level. It is important to find texts that are well within the reader's independent-instructional range in order to promote fluency. Short, highly predictable selections that are meant to be read aloud and with expression, such as rhyming poetry, are ideal, Rasinski suggests, for developing fluency.

Topping (1987) found that paired reading could significantly accelerate students' reading fluency and overall proficiency. Rasinski used this approach to good effect. He asked parents of struggling readers to engage in a form of paired reading with their children for 10 to 15 minutes each evening. Parents read a brief poem or passage to their children. This was followed by the parent and child reading the text together several times and, finally, the child reading the text to the parent.

Laura Huxford also suggested a 'buddy system' for improving Stephen's fluency and Teresa Grainger called the same idea 'reading partnerships'. Research has shown that 'buddy reading' is an excellent way to promote fluency (Rasinski *et al.* 1994). In this the benefits of repeated readings and paired reading are linked. Let's take a Year 3 child like Stephen who lacks reading fluency. This child is paired with a Year 2 child who is also having difficulty in reading. The Y3 child meets the Y2 child twice a week and reads with her or him a passage from one of the Y2 child's books for about 20 minutes. To plan for the encounter, the Y3 child needs to practise the assigned passage (which will be somewhat easier for her/him to read because it is at a difficulty level appropriate for Y2 child) so that he/she can read it with accuracy and expression with his/her partner. This may require several readings of the passage. The Y3 child does this with enthusiasm since it has a real purpose. Rasinski suggests the Y3 child first reads the passage to the partner, then they read it together once or twice, and then, if time allows, the Y2 child reads it while the partner follows along and provides support and encouragement. His evidence shows that both children gain from this experience as readers.

Finally, a 'Readers Theatre' performance (Tompkins 1997) is a dramatic reading of a script by a group of pupils. Teresa Grainger also recommended

ach for Stephen. Pupils assume roles and rehearse reading the
ring rehearsals the pupils practise reading a particular character's
... ..ıc script. They convey the mood and theme by using their voices
and facial expressions. Then the pupils give a performance of the script for
a group of children or another audience.

Should children be taught the alphabetic system early?

In an earlier section I mentioned Cunningham's critique of the conclusions
drawn by the National Reading Panel, and in particular his critique of the
NRP's claim that children should be taught the alphabetic system early.
The question is: how important is it that children are able to use the alphabetic system early? In the light of the evidence discussed here, you should be
in no doubt about the thinking of those who take a cognitive-psychological
perspective on reading in relation to the significance of early word recognition
skill. It is seen as vitally important.

This is so, they argue, because early attainment of decoding skill very
accurately predicts later reading comprehension (e.g. Clay 1979; Lesgold
and Resnick 1982; Juel 1988). The conclusion from this body of literature
seems to be that a child who does poorly in reading in the first year of school
(after kindergarten or nursery/reception) is likely to continue to do poorly.
There is also evidence that good 9-year-old readers from previous assessments
are likely to remain good readers through secondary school (Juel 1991).

This is not surprising when you consider that research has found that
good decoders in Grade/Year 1 are exposed to about twice as many words
as poor decoders. Juel (1988) found that the in-school differences in exposure to print continue in subsequent years. These in-school differences in
exposure to print are then further compounded when you consider out-of-
school differences in reading. Interviews with the older, poor readers showed
that they read little because by now they had grown to dislike reading.
Also other research, cited in Juel (1991), suggests that in about middle
primary the major determinant of vocabulary growth is the amount of free
reading. In interpreting this downward spiral and labelling it the 'Matthew
effect', Stanovich (1986: 381) says 'the rich get richer':

> The effect of reading volume on vocabulary growth, combined with
> the large skill difference in reading volume, could mean a 'rich get
> richer', or cumulative advantage, phenomenon is almost inextric-
> ably embedded within the developmental course of reading progress.
> The very children who are reading well and who have good vocabul-
> aries will read more, learn more word meanings, and hence read even
> better. Children with inadequate vocabularies – who read slowly and
> without enjoyment – read less, and as a result have slower development

of vocabulary knowledge, which inhibits further growth in reading ability.

The message we need to take from this is that acquiring the alphabetic principle early is important. However, we need to bear in mind that the best way of achieving this in the classroom is by building meaningfully on what the learner already knows. This would require the integration of print knowledge with real reading for meaning, as I have emphasized at various points above.

Developing comprehension strategies in the classroom

There is one other important aspect of reading to which this school of thought made a significant contribution and here David Wray's own research is especially important in England. This is comprehension. In discussing Stephen's needs David Wray emphasized the importance of having a wider choice of reading material available to him. He talked about the importance of non-fiction texts, especially for boys, and he mentioned the tendency on the part of some teachers to privilege story or fiction. In addition he talked about the importance of silent reading and finding ways (other than oral reading) for Stephen to demonstrate what he can do with text. He would encourage Stephen's teacher to use silent reading and to foster his comprehension strategies.

Comprehension has not typically been taught well in schools, often being relegated to subjects other than English or reading lessons and, as I mentioned in Part One, studies of practice by Her Majesty's Inspectors in England highlighted the need for more effective ways of promoting children's comprehension and information-seeking skills. Indeed it is likely that you cannot recall any time when you were taught comprehension in an explicit way. It is most likely that you experienced lessons where comprehension was tested i.e. where a typical comprehension lesson consisted of reading a piece of prose and then answering mostly literal questions and possibly some inferential questions about its content. In the past teachers typically did not show pupils strategies they could use in reading to comprehend what they read.

The idea behind more explicit teaching of comprehension is that it can be improved by teaching pupils to use specific cognitive strategies. Such strategies are designed to guide pupils to become aware of how they are understanding as they read, and ultimately to read demanding text independently of the teacher. Our better understanding of cognition, i.e. of how people come to know and understand things, has led to the development of practical strategies for improving comprehension. Furthermore, the research evidence (see NRP 2000) demonstrates that pupils at all skill levels benefit from being taught comprehension strategies.

Comprehension is complicated and it requires a correspondingly complicated set of educational strategies to foster it effectively in the classroom
(Pressley 2000). Rather surprisingly, in view of its significance, how children
learn to comprehend text only began to be studied scientifically in the past
thirty years. Although the cognitive-psychological school designed and
tested theoretically based strategies for the development of comprehension
in the classroom and demonstrated the need to teach comprehension, you
will see how the psycho-linguistic perspective also informed this line of
enquiry. Much of the research that has been conducted conceptualizes reading as a purposeful, active, meaning-seeking process. According to this
view, a reader reads a text to take a message from what is read, to construct
memory representations of what is understood, and to put all that to some
use (NRP 2000: 4–39). First, I will briefly describe some concepts that
underpin the pedagogical approaches detailed in this section, the first of
which owes much to the psycho-linguistic school. Most of this section,
however, will be devoted to strategies for the promotion of comprehension in the classroom.

Schema theory: the significance of prior knowledge

Schema theory is a theory about the way knowledge is structured and
stored in memory (Rumelhart 1980; Pearson and Stephens 1994; Pressley
2000). A central tenet of schema theory is that much of what we know is
stored in complex relational structures known as schemata (i.e. the plural
for schema). Schemata are like containers into which we store particular
experiences we have. The schema for chair is stored in our chair schema.
The schema for a wedding ceremony is stored in our wedding ceremony
schema. Thus, the schema for wedding includes its purpose – so two people can get married – where it happens – in a church or a registry office –
who attends – bride and groom, guests etc. Schema theory explains not
only how and where we store information in memory but also how we
establish relations between one schema and another, and this enables us to
understand events easily. So for example, once you encounter a small part
of the wedding ceremony schema, like the bride's dress, this activated
schema causes reasonable inferences to be made about other possible details
of the event – the groom, the bridesmaid and so on. Schematic processing
is top-down in that the higher order process is triggered first and this
triggers attention to the details.

Schematic processing influences comprehension of events around us from
early in life and it is this knowledge that allows readers to draw inferences
from text that includes information related to their schematic knowledge.
Thus the richer a child's world experiences (whether real or vicarious i.e.
via reading, TV, etc.) the stronger the schematic knowledge base (Pressley

2000). Clearly, another term for schematic knowledge is prior knowledge –
something the psycho-linguists greatly stressed. Schema theory fits well
with the constructivist notion of learning, that all learners build their own
meanings. In terms of comprehending written language, this means that
the prior knowledge the reader brings to the text is crucially important and
the implication is that the location of meaning is problematic. Where is
meaning actually located? How can meaning now reside in the text? Does it
reside in the reader who constructs her or his unique interpretation of the
text based on her or his prior experiences? Or is it somewhere in between,
in the interaction between the reader and the text?

But, for now, you can appreciate the situation where a reader's interpretation may be too text-based or too reader-based (Tierney and Pearson
1994). In the former case it may be that certain conditions of schooling
predispose the reader to give such independent status to the text it is
entirely divorced from the reader's prior knowledge. The task of reading
is seen as having little to do with the person's personal life or lived experiences. What can a teacher do in such circumstances? Cloze procedure
exercises that require exact word replacements would obviously encourage
such thinking. Cloze procedure exercises are used to develop and assess
text comprehension. The teacher selects an excerpt of say 300 words from
a text – informational book, textbook or storybook. Then s/he deletes
say every fifth word in the passage and the task for the pupils is to use
their knowledge of the topic or narrative, of word order in English, and of
the meaning of words within sentences to decide on the missing words
in the passage. Variations on this procedure include deleting the content
words, deleting phrases or even whole sentences. Cloze procedure exercises that invite discussion of plausible words, phrases and full sentences
would suggest a more personally creative and individual response demanding more integration with the reader's previous knowledge and experiences. Pupils work in groups or individually and they discuss and justify
their selections. Another technique is to ask pupils to say what they think
of when they hear the word x (the topic of the text they are about to read),
jotting down all the suggestions and perhaps categorizing them in some
way. Then they read the passage or the chapter to learn more about x.
They return to their own original categories and now they add to them
on the basis of their new knowledge. What this kind of activity offers is
a demonstration of pupils' pre-existing schema, new learnings from the
text, and the link between new and old knowledge (Tierney and Pearson
1994).

The reader who tends to be too reader-based needs to attend more carefully to the text, to self-monitor (see below), perhaps to take notes, and to
underline key ideas.

Unsurprisingly, good readers use their relevant prior knowledge to
make sense of what they read and weak readers frequently undermine their

comprehension by bringing in irrelevant prior knowledge and linking it to the text. But comprehension does not always occur via schematic knowledge. Sometimes comprehension occurs from the bottom up with the reader working through many separate ideas or propositions in the text so you end up with networks of ideas or propositions. In either case – whether through schematic processing or developing a network of propositions – the process is automatic and largely unconscious.

Conscious comprehension processing: what do readers do?

We now know that sophisticated readers use a range of strategies as they read texts. David Wray and Maureen Lewis (1997) offer a very useful description, based on their own research with teachers, of the kind of mental activities that go on as we interact with texts, specifically non-fiction texts. They called their project *Extending Interactions with Texts* (EXIT). Here are the mental activities involved:

1 Eliciting previous knowledge (the use of KWL grids are helpful here – see below).
2 Establishing a purpose (they suggest the purpose should be precise so for example 'to find out about dinosaurs' may be too vague; it might be better to have a purpose such as 'find out about the size of dinosaurs so I can draw scale pictures of them on the wall chart').
3 Locating information.
4 Adopting an appropriate strategy (here modelling might be useful, see below).
5 Interacting with text (e.g. underlining, highlighting, numbering, cloze procedure).
6 Monitoring understanding.
7 Making a record (e.g. notetaking).
8 Evaluating information (e.g recognizing when information might be dated, wrong).
9 Assisting memory.
10 Communicating information.

Teaching strategies for fostering some of these specific mental activities are described below.

Duffy, another researcher in this field, argues that comprehension strategies are not skills that can simply be taught by drill methods, rather they are plans for constructing meaning (Duffy *et al.* 1998). Being strategic is not simply about knowing the strategies – like summarizing, self-questioning, predicting based on prior knowledge – but about knowing how and when to apply them. It is not surprising therefore that comprehension development is a long-term project. Pupils need more than mere practice in the application of these strategies; they need opportunities to see the value of them and to apply them flexibly.

Pressley (2000) suggests that unless the reader can recognize most words in the text automatically, it will be impossible to apply reading comprehension strategies effectively. His first piece of advice, therefore, is to teach decoding skills and encourage the development of sight words. He also suggests the teaching of vocabulary. The NRP's review of effective vocabulary instruction recommends that vocabulary should be taught directly and indirectly. There is a need for direct teaching of vocabulary that is required for a specific text to be read as part of a lesson. The more connections that can be made to a specific word or term, the better that word or term is learned. Pre-teaching of vocabulary in reading lessons has been shown to have a significant effect on learning outcomes (NRP 2000: 4–25).

Ways of developing comprehension in the classroom

There are two key elements of comprehension: first, knowing the strategies and second, knowing when to use them. Drawing mostly on the work of Pressley (2000), Gaskins and Gaskins (1997), Wray and Lewis (1997) and the work of the National Reading Panel (2000), I will begin by outlining some important tried and tested strategies and then I will describe 'reciprocal teaching' or 'multiple strategy teaching' which is designed to promote the coordination of several cognitive strategies. The latter is about adapting cognitive strategies and using them flexibly according to the demands of the situation.

Teaching that is explicit and informed: summarizing

All readers benefit from explicit teaching but it is even more important for poor readers like Stephen who may not discover concepts, skills and strategies on their own as good readers often do. Teaching that is explicit and informed means explaining clearly what the concept or skill is that you are trying to develop in your pupils, how and when they could use it, and why it is important. Having pupils informed about its usefulness has been found to be important for their ability to transfer what has been learned to new situations. Here is how Gaskins and Gaskins (1997: 151–2) imagine the dialogue for explicitly introducing a new strategy:

– 'What': Today we are going to learn . . . What this means is . . .
– 'Why': This is an important strategy because . . .
– 'When': You can use this strategy when . . . Tomorrow I want you to tell me a time during reading when you applied the strategy we are learning today.

- 'How': The teacher next tells the students exactly how to do the strategy, being very explicit about the self-talk (what students should say to themselves as they employ the strategy) and usually illustrating the use of the strategy with a personal experience.

They go on to describe how one teacher introduced summarizing as a way to self-monitor.

Teacher: Today we are going to learn a strategy for self-monitoring. What this means is we are going to learn one way to figure out whether we understand what we are reading. Why do you think it is important to self-monitor as you read?

Student: Because reading has got to make sense and, if it doesn't, you've got to fix it.

Student: Because if you don't think about what you're reading, you won't know what you're read when you get through.

Student: Strategies keep you actively involved.

Teacher: Those are fine reasons. You seem to be saying that it is important that you take some kind of strategic mental action while you are reading to be sure that you are making meaning. Self-monitoring is a strategy you can use whenever you read . . . One way I self-monitor is to read a portion of text, then stop and try to say in my own words what the important points were that I just read . . . I find when I just say the summary to myself, I sometimes kid myself into thinking that I understand when I don't. Therefore, when the information is new to me and it is important that I understand what I am reading, I usually not only say the summary to myself, but, after I say it, I write the summary. When I can't write a summary of what I read in my own words, then it usually means I didn't understand it . . . I photocopied one of the chapters so we could work on it together. Follow along as I read the first page and think aloud about the main point in each paragraph, then I'll try to pull these main points together to check my understanding.

These researchers have trained teachers to *walk* pupils through how to use the strategies. The teachers trained in this way do not expect that their pupils already know how to do such things as summarize, predict, infer and self-monitor.

Question generation and asking 'why' questions

Without guidance young readers are unlikely to question themselves as they read. The purpose of helping pupils to generate questions as they read is to enable them to construct better memory representations of the text contents. If you encourage, and model for pupils, self-questioning while reading, you help them to integrate parts of the text and gain a deeper understanding of the text. There is strong scientific evidence that teaching pupils to question as they read promotes reading comprehension in terms of memory, answering questions based on the text, grasping the main idea, and summarizing the text. Pupils can be encouraged to ask themselves why, how, when, where, which, and who kinds of questions as they read.

Expository text or non-fiction or fact-filled text can be made much more memorable by encouraging pupils to 'why question' and answer themselves about why the facts in the text are sensible. This approach is especially beneficial for pupils in middle and upper primary grades. The reason this approach is so successful is because it taps pupils' relevant prior knowledge or existing schema and encourages them to link what they read in the text with their previous experiences and understandings.

One particularly successful question-generating strategy, developed by Ogle (1986), is the K-W-L strategy, or Know, Want-to-Know, Learned. This has since been recommended by several reading theorists including David Wray. It can be used with the whole class, small groups or by a single individual. Before a non-fiction text is read the pupils brainstorm all they know about the topic, and list these facts as bullet points in a chart that is ruled into three column headings as follows:

What we know	What we want to know	What we learned

The first column is about activating prior knowledge. Under the second column the pupils generate some questions they think the text might address. This part requires them to think about questions, to predict and to reflect on the information that is needed. Following their reading of the text (either silently or as a shared activity) they summarize, using bullet points again, the main points they have learned from the text. Here they have to reflect, consolidate, evaluate and summarize. Some writers (Yopp and Yopp 2001) have added a fourth column to the chart requesting pupils to record how they felt about the material in the text and how they plan to use the information they have learned.

Mental imagery

Visualization is often recommended by psychologists as a means of preparing to cope in a new situation. For example, if your new experience is to attend what you suspect will be a challenging interview or to teach a difficult class, it is suggested that the act of visualizing yourself successfully operating in that situation helps you to adapt to its demands. Mental imagery in comprehension is not unlike that. In imagery training for comprehension, the pupils are taught to construct a visual image to represent the text as they read it. To do this requires an interpretation of the text. This is especially suited to a situation where what is to be read is a short passage or even a sentence. Imagery training improves memory and assists connection making as well as supporting inferential reasoning. The idea is that the constructed image serves to embed the text's meaning in memory.

Graphic organizer

This is a diagram of the concepts and their relationships in the text which can be either fiction or non-fiction – often referred to as a story map, if fiction. The graphic aid or diagram helps pupils to focus on text structure while reading and assists them in writing summaries. You show your learners how to create a graphic organization of their ideas. For example, you could provide a graphic metaphor like a picture of an umbrella for the main ideas. Another might be a circle where the centre of the circle has the main idea of the story or passage with other ideas written in around the main idea.

Story structure and story mapping

Story structure and mapping are ways of helping the reader identify the content of the story and the way it is organized into a plot structure. Understanding that a story is organized as a set of episodes with a setting, a series of events, reactions, goals, attempts, and outcomes, helps the reader understand the who, what, where, when, and why of stories as well as what happened (NRP 2000: 4–88). Essentially you teach pupils how to ask and answer five main questions:

1 Who is the main character?
2 Where and when did the story occur?
3 What did the main characters do?
4 How did the story end?
5 How did the main character feel?

Pupils are helped to construct a story map by recording the setting, noting the problem, identifying the goal and the action that was taken, and stating the outcome of the events. This strategy proved to be especially helpful with less able readers. More able readers may not need such explicit teaching.

Multiple strategy teaching: reciprocal teaching

Reciprocal teaching is intended to help pupils adopt a flexible approach to comprehension strategy use. It is designed to help them understand how to study and learn from text (Palinscar and Brown 1984). The job of the teacher here is to show and give practice to pupils in the use of four strategies: prediction, questioning, seeking clarification when confused, and summarizing. It is best to ensure that the pupils know and can use each of these strategies on their own first. You can do this through teacher modelling, thinking out loud, direct explanation, and giving plenty of guided practice in the use of the strategies (see above example about summarizing). If, for example, the strategy is predicting, you might model the process of predicting – you think out loud about what clues are being used to make a prediction, why you (or some pupils) selected a particular clue, and how you or they put the clues together to make a prediction. What this involves is making the mental processes, that are usually hidden from view, overt.

Reciprocal teaching is most suited to a small group situation. For convenience a reciprocal teaching lesson can be described in six steps (Herrmann 1988: 27–8):

1 Read the text title and invite the pupils to say what they expect to learn from the text. Summarize the group's predictions.
2 Read a few paragraphs of the text aloud.
3 Ask a question about the content. Discuss the answers. Invite the group to pose their own questions.
4 Summarize what has been read by noting the gist of the section and explain how you arrived at this summary. Invite comments on your summary from the group.
5 Lead a discussion to clarify any words or ideas that are unclear or confusing.
6 Signal preparation to move on to the next section of the text by eliciting predictions regarding upcoming content. Select a pupil to be the next 'teacher'.

The cognitive-psychological perspective and the National Literacy Strategy

Current literacy policy in England is hugely influenced by the cognitive-psychological perspective discussed above. In this section, I will refer to the nature of that influence.

Where is the influence of a cognitive-psychological perspective? It is evident in two key respects that bear on the content of the literacy curriculum. First, the emphasis on word recognition, and within that on phonological awareness, and second, the emphasis on comprehension in the text–level work. The evidence discussed in this Part would support the status that the NLS accords to word recognition. The development of the beginner reader's spelling–sound knowledge by engaging in activities and with texts that lay bare the alphabetic principle is a key message of the cognitive-psychological school. In the NLS, there are 14 precise objectives associated with word-level work to be achieved by children in their first year of school; a further 14 in term one of their second year; and a total of 87 up to the end of the year in which they reach seven years of age – all to be addressed in the specified sequence. Further sets of objectives are prescribed for these children in sentence-level and text-level work.

What teachers have to do during the 15 minutes of word-level work, which the Strategy says is to take place in a whole-class setting, bears on content, sequence and objectives:

> There must be a systematic, regular and frequent teaching of phonological awareness, phonics and spelling throughout Key Stage 1. Teachers should follow the progression set out in the word level objectives carefully. It sets out both an order of teaching and the expectations for what pupils should achieve by the end of each term.
>
> (DfEE 1998a: 11)

While there is a strong emphasis in the NLS on the systematic teaching of word recognition via phonics, there are also several references to the importance of the application of this knowledge so it is meaningful to the learner. All of this fits with the research reviewed above.

What is less easy to justify in the Strategy is the prescriptive nature of the pedagogy designed to achieve that content. The NLS seems to be more prescriptive about sequence and organization of learning than the evidence reviewed in this Part of the book would sustain (and as we noted in Part One it is out of step with the principles of whole language). For example, the NRP suggests the evidence supports the teaching of phonemic awareness to small groups of learners whereas the NLS tends to place more emphasis on large groups i.e. whole-class work (DfES 2001). To be fair it also emphasizes the use of small-group work but the strong emphasis on whole-class teaching might be considered questionable given that all children in the class may not have the same phonological learning needs. I should point out though that the evidence from the NRP in relation to the development of phonic knowledge, unlike that of phonemic knowledge, is that there appears to be no significant difference between different organizational arrangements i.e. the review found no effectiveness difference between small-group and whole-class organizational strategies.

The sequence of phonological development specified by the NLS could be problematic insofar as the evidence currently available is neither definitive about the best sequence nor the amount. There is some evidence to suggest that a little phonological awareness goes a long way and it may be that, with the emphasis on delivery in a whole-class setting, the NLS over-emphasizes it, at least for some children. Finally in relation to this particular aspect, you could question the balance between the part-to-whole and the whole-to-part nature of the activities and games, or, to use the language of much of the literature reviewed above, the bottom-up versus top-down emphasis. There is a very strong emphasis on part-to-whole or synthetic phonics and considerably less on whole-to-part or analytic phonics. There is evidence now that both are needed. However, this evidence was not available at the time the Strategy was being developed.

The NLS places considerable emphasis on comprehension and on reading for information. Leaving aside the prescriptive nature of the pedagogy, the emphasis on text comprehension is entirely consistent with the evidence from this perspective on reading.

PART THREE
A SOCIO-CULTURAL
PERSPECTIVE

INTRODUCTION TO PART THREE: A SOCIO-CULTURAL PERSPECTIVE ON READING

This part of the book should make you begin to question some of the assumptions of Parts One and Two, particularly some assumptions of the cognitive-psychological perspective, and encourage you to be more aware of the complexity of issues associated with how a child learns to read and how a child reads for a variety of purposes. In taking on board a socio-cultural stance on reading, you are likely to be more critical of the simplistic accounts of reading and literacy that we so frequently encounter, say in the media, and become more sophisticated in your thinking about what words like 'literacy' and 'illiteracy' signify.

Some of the ideas discussed by the scholars who feature here were also flagged by our first two scholars. However, both Henrietta Dombey and Mary Hilton are very explicit in their references to themes associated with socio-cultural aspects of reading and much of what they had to say about Stephen and about their own underlying philosophy of reading can be linked directly to socio-cultural theory. This part of the book begins with transcripts of the interviews conducted with both these scholars. This will be followed by a detailed discussion of some of the issues raised in their interviews and will consider, in particular, the implications of this perspective for literacy teaching.

HENRIETTA DOMBEY'S OBSERVATIONS, SUGGESTIONS AND THEORETICAL PERSPECTIVES

This section briefly profiles Henrietta Dombey and her work. It then presents her interpretation of Stephen and her recommendations for taking him forward. The theory of reading underpinning her suggestions is signalled throughout her comments, suggestions and ideas. Like several others whose perspectives on Stephen are presented in this book, Henrietta participated in a symposium on this theme at the United Kingdom Reading Association's annual conference in Oxford 2000. What follows is based on that presentation and an interview I conducted with her in November 2001. Her responses below are entirely her own words as recorded in a face-to-face interview. The final part draws more directly on her conference paper.

Brief profile of Henrietta Dombey

Initially educated as a secondary English teacher, Henrietta swiftly moved into primary teaching where she felt children's encounters with words could more easily be enriched by visual images, concrete materials and move-ment. This kindled a long fascination with the processes involved as chil-dren develop a command of literacy, enlarged by her experiences in teacher education. Her research has focused on the kinds of classroom interactions between children, teachers and texts that seem productive of important literacy lessons. Henrietta is Professor of Literacy Education at the Univer-sity of Brighton.

Interpreting the visual evidence

First I would like to say that to use videotape for an enquiry of this sort is an excellent idea as you get all sorts of visual indications that amplify the sound track. We see the teacher looking at Stephen in a supportive and encouraging way, taking account of how he seems and giving him space – that's very evident in the video. What we also see is an uncomfortable and dutiful boy who is conscious that the camera is on him – he flicks his eye towards the camera at times, but I think he's more dominated by some obligation to his teacher whom he obviously respects. His eyes follow the text when his teacher is reading, and he does what she asks of him. But there is no clear sense from the visual evidence of his involvement in the text. (I don't think that comes through either when we look closely at his words and the way he speaks them.) Although he looks amused at points, he also seems tense and nervous and his arms are held very rigidly. At the very beginning he doesn't choose a book to read with much eagerness. And at the very end he tries to get away as soon as he can. He makes one little comment, 'funny', which doesn't show much involvement.

His retelling

Stephen's intonation patterns support my interpretation of the visual evidence in that he reads with flat intonation, and while this shouldn't always be taken as an incontrovertible indicator of lack of interest or commitment, in this case it merely reinforces the view gained from the visual evidence.

On other evidence you could say his retelling is largely implicit, and that it lacks any sense of dynamic. You don't get a feeling of the inherent movement of the story. It doesn't come through at all in his retelling and what he does produce only comes after lots of prompting from his teacher. So he really is not retelling in any significant way. He's certainly not creating any sort of interesting experience for a listener. He's responding to a test situation. The whole thing is for him a test. It's a test that is, as it were, kindly delivered by the teacher but it's not a task that he takes on and makes his own. The retelling is not something that he rises to and enriches with his own experience of life and text and, I mean, he doesn't put all his energies into this.

His reading

Stephen makes very little use of picture cues unless he's prompted. He makes very little use of context cues and some of his miscues show he's really going off the semantic rails. So what we have here is some-one who is in a test situation who is not bringing in information from outside, whether of life or of other texts, to any significant degree. There are some minor things that indicate some familiarity with book language – looked/look, for instance, indicates a certain familiarity with book language.

Yet he's not got to grips with the story. If you get down to the phonic level he appears to have a bit of phonic knowledge. He isn't actively engaged with this task of reading. He is perfunctorily re-sponding to a teacher-set task. But he is doing it with good grace.

Henrietta's hunches about Stephen and what she'd like to know

I'd like to know quite a bit more about Stephen. Maybe I've chanced my arm too far anyway. I'd suspect that he's not generally engaged with the written word. I'd suspect that he would have great difficulty with writing, seeing it as a task or sort of test to be completed, and not as a means of communication, much less as a means of ordering and systematizing and developing his thinking. The chances of him being like that are very slight indeed. That's a hunch. All of these literacy activities I think he would see as tasks to be completed before you go out to play.

But to get a fuller picture of him I'd like to know a range of things, some of them are to do with what Myra Barrs calls small shapes and some are to do with big shapes. Some are to do with the overall significance of literacy in his life.

Significance of reading in Stephen's life

I'd like to know whether he has a favourite book, what books he has at home, whether he's a member of a public library or book club, whether he readily goes to any written text, for example, a timetable for infor-mation or whether he's one of the many children still who actually conduct a large part of their lives through oral encounters, only resort-ing to the written word when they absolutely have to.

I'd like to know whether he reads frequently with or to a parent at home, and if so, which gender. I suspect that, like the very many boys in Gemma Moss's study, Stephen does not see reading or writing as a central part of his social identity. I suspect that (and I think the video recording was made when Pokémon cards were in vogue) he may well collect the Pokémon cards but is unlikely to engage with any written text. I'd be interested to see whether computers are of any interest to him, and if so, whether computer games or computer magazines would feature at all.

In general, I would like to find out what meaning literacy holds for Stephen. What kind of active dynamic is he calling up when he confronts a text? I suspect that he's operating at a rather limited, word identification level and with some access to literal meaning but without any kind of, as it were, determination to construct a more coherent and complex meaning. To him, it seems, that is not the name of the game. However, to state this with any degree of certainty, I would have to observe Stephen in a range of different situations.

The nature of Stephen's involvement with literacy in and out of school

In other words, I suspect that the culture in which he moves for much of his life, out of school and in the playground, is not one in which literacy figures large. But I suspect that also he doesn't seem to be a kind of active rebel. I suspect that he might be susceptible to concerted attempts to interest him and involve him in literacy. But I'm jumping ahead here; what I should be saying, at this point, is that I think that all these things would need to be looked at quite closely.

What does he do with books in school?

How does he actually interpret and approach reading and writing tasks?

Is there any point in the day when he's actively engaged in constructing or interpreting text? Also, how much is he read to in school?

And it would be very interesting to see, if and when his teacher does read to the class, what he makes of these literacy events.

What kinds of texts does he steer himself towards?

Are these information texts, stories, poems, or comics or just Pokémon cards?

And if they are information texts, is he just pretending to read as Gemma Moss found some boys do?

Teachers in busy classrooms with upward of twenty-five children can't observe every child's encounter with the written word, desirable though that might be.

Does he pull the wool?

Is he evading print?

Is he actively entering into some kind of subterfuge?

I also think it's worth looking at whether he reads collaboratively with others, whether, like the children studied in Croydon by Linda Graham, he can become more engaged with texts as a collaborative activity, whether it is that lone encounter that he finds constricting, difficult, unrewarding, threatening. In general, how he goes about his reading during the school day would repay investigation.

Also I would suggest looking to see what phonic knowledge he has, how he draws on this in making sense of a whole text.

Kid watching

What I'm recommending I suppose, really, is kid watching, but it's kid watching, not just on an individual basis, but looking at how he relates to other kids. And also what goes on at home, in and out of school situations in which literacy plays a part because we may find that actually there may be quite significant literacy events in his home but somehow they are disengaged from what is going on in school.

Underneath these questions, underlying all of this, my concerns would be to do with matters such as: does he show a capacity for independent problem solving in other contexts? I think the Bussis study showed us so convincingly that children approach reading much like they approach other tasks. I think there's something about the necessity for problem solving and the necessity for persistence which may well relate to other situations. But on the other hand, it may be that there are areas in his life where he does actively solve problems, in which case these might be good contexts in which he could engage with the written word.

What does Stephen think reading is good for?

I suppose ultimately that the question I've been hinting at all along is, to use Margaret Meek Spencer's phrase, What does he think reading is good for? I think this comes up in the work of Gemma Moss, and Judith Solsken, who show us that young children do develop very significant ideas about what literacy can and cannot do for them and how it relates to their social identity and their family. So I'd also like to know the family's pattern of literacy.

And related to this is the notion of what part he sees reading and writing playing in his present and future life. I remember a child who I taught many years ago, George, who had a Schonell Reading age of 5.4 (that was a test commonly used then) at the age of just 7. At the end of the year he had a reading age of 12.5 years – he was a very bright little boy from a Caribbean family. I remember asking him 'How come you never learned to read downstairs?' He said 'What, Miss, with them books downstairs? You're joking Miss.' But at the end of the year he said 'It's good to read.' When I asked him 'Why?', he said 'Well Miss you might be in the country . . . you might . . . there might be a sign in a field saying "danger" and if you couldn't read you might be in danger.' In a sense this notion of what reading can do is laughably limited – much more limited than the notion of a technically much less proficient reader in the same class as George. This was a boy called Lloyd who came in one day asking me to find him a poem about a cat, saying 'Miss, me cat died and when you read about something, it helps you to sort it out in your mind.' But George's notion was none the less very strongly held – the notion that literacy could keep you safe – so I feel that I would like to know what part Stephen sees literacy playing in his present and future life and in connection with that I'd like to know who his heroes are. Who would he look up to? Superman?

What's the family pattern of literacy? As I've hinted before, he seems a dutiful boy. But I'd want to know what enthuses him so we know what might really engage him. But meanwhile, what can his teacher do?

What Stephen's teacher might do

Depending on what answers emerge to the questions set out above, what follows may well need to be modified. But it seems that Graham Frater's recent work on effective classrooms, on classrooms where boys don't lag behind the girls in literacy, is relevant here. You look at school level to create a positive climate for literacy work and to create a more involving culture of reading. I would suggest that within the class the teacher could work to create a more involving culture of reading. I say more involving; I don't know a great deal about what that teacher does.

There needs to be 'hospitality' to reading material reflecting popular culture. The classroom shouldn't just reflect the community children come from and do no more than this. But there should be hospitality and respect for the culture that the children bring to the school, which means including Disney comics as well as award-winning picture books.

I would suggest more collaborative activities to engage him in a social way; and also story readings that invite active participation – that invite, not just a rehearsal of what's happening, but active engagement regarding what's going to happen and speculation about the attitudes of people involved, this sort of thing.

Henrietta puts forward the following more specific suggestions of ways in which Stephen's teacher might create a positive climate for his literacy development:

Create a more involving 'culture of reading' in the class

She could focus on:

- displays and collections of comics – for study as well as enjoyable reading;
- author displays;
- league tables of popular books;
- writing frames for reviews, which are then placed in a public place and used by children to guide what they choose to read;
- quizzes on books, perhaps with mini-prizes – this kind of competitive approach is especially good for involving boys;
- involvement in a book club, and it's good to see the books before buying them;
- inviting in an author of some interest to Stephen;
- poetry might well be an avenue in; some studies show that boys can get into reading through poetry.

Show him what literacy can do

She could:

- make evident, perhaps through drama, the role literacy plays in some situations (medical? sporting?) and roles which are of real interest to Stephen and others in the class who may be like him; and
- regular teacher demonstration of how reading helps you through the day, in and out of school.

Engagement in class story-readings

Initially the teacher herself could do this through:

- choosing herself texts she thinks might be of interest;
- developing an interactive approach to reading aloud, in which the children, particularly Stephen, are encouraged to speculate about the events etc.; and
- setting up role play activities related to the text.

Motivating Stephen and enhancing his reading strategies

His teacher could:

- introduce him to texts that he will want to read again and again, because of their themes and their language, from jokes and comic rhymes to haunting stories;
- engage him in purposeful information reading on a topic of real pressing interest, with a public outcome (e.g. a visual display of different types of fish and the most effective ways of catching them, a multimedia presentation on the history of the local football team);

- tackle his fluency problems and help him develop the 'tune' of the text through making available taped readings of texts for use with headphones, to accompany his own reading of interesting texts at a level of difficulty just beyond those he is comfortable with;
- engage him in Literacy Circle work, where a portion of the text is read before the session, and the group time is used to discuss responses to the text;
- involve him in big book or 'guided' reading in a way that invites and encourages independent problem solving – in terms both of how the text will go and of word identification;
- in individual reading, get him to focus on what might happen in a story and to act 'like a detective' in finding out if he is right;
- encourage him to use context cues through:
  - re-reading the previous phrase/s with an expectant intonation;
  - asking him to leave the word out and go back to it at the end of the sentence;
  - encouraging him to reflect on relevant aspects of the text thus far;
- help him to tackle more unknown words independently, through being tuned in to their morphemic and phonic patterning, perhaps through:
  - pointing out morphemic units (e.g. the 'ed' on 'wanted', the 'one' in 'anyone');
  - pointing out families of words sharing rime patterns (e.g. 's/ound', 'f/ound' etc., 'sh/out', '/out' etc.);
  - pointing out larger phonic patterns (e.g. 'scribble', 'wobble' etc.);
  - getting him to attend to key letters of misread 'known' words (e.g. 'she', 'it', 'the' etc.) through pointing to them silently.

  Displays of 'word families', referred to at relevant points might help here.
- when she judges that the time is right, the teacher might help him into Harry Potter, perhaps through:
  - a collaborative Harry Potter display, made with all the children;
  - a role play exercise, with some key props;
  - reading part of one of the earlier books;
  - making available taped reading of subsequent short extracts for use with headphones to accompany his own reading of the text;
- invite one or both of his parents to work with her in school, to help them see and experience a meaning-focused approach to reading.

The reading theory underpinning these suggestions

- the power of home learning and how it can be harnessed (Hannon 1995);
- that different communities have different uses for literacy and different sets of social practices involving literacy (Heath 1983);

- that all young children have ideas about what are the uses of literacy and how it relates to their current and future identities (Solsken 1993);
- that fluent reading is not a bottom-up, synthetic process in which we first recognize letters, then build them into words, but a highly complex process involving many kinds of knowledge in the initial perception of words (Cattell 1886; Clay 1972; Rumelhart 1976; Goodman and Goodman 1977);
- that children use fundamentally different processes to recognize words as they make progress in learning to read (Bussis *et al*. 1985; Frith 1985);
- that analogy is a powerful learning strategy for young children generally, and in particular for their learning of phonics (Goswami 1992);
- that powerful reading lessons can only be taught through powerful texts (Meek 1988);
- the importance of reflection and metacognition in children's literacy learning (Clay 1972);
- that brief teacher–child interactions, where the teacher acts as 'consciousness for two', can significantly advance children's learning (Geekie *et al*. 1999);
- the importance of social learning in large and small groups (King and Robinson 1995);
- that effective teachers of literacy have developed a coherent philosophy towards it, involving substantial attention to meaning (Poulson *et al*. 1997; Medwell *et al*. 1998).

MARY HILTON'S OBSERVATIONS, SUGGESTIONS AND THEORETICAL PERSPECTIVES

Brief profile of Mary Hilton

Mary Hilton is a university lecturer in Primary English in the Faculty of Education, University of Cambridge. She has written and researched on a range of aspects of children's learning in literature and literacy. She has edited *Potent Fictions: Children's Literacy and the Challenge of Popular Culture* (1996) and, together with Morag Styles and Victor Watson, *Opening the Nursery Door: Reading, Writing and Childhood 1600–1900* (1997). Alongside her interests in literature for children, media education and community practices, she has recently focused her research on the history of education. She has edited, together with Pam Hirsch, *Practical Visionaries: Women, Education and Social Progress 1790–1930* (2000). Mary is currently working on a book which explores the writings of leading women educators in the century 1750–1850.

Mary Hilton participated in the symposium on this theme at the United Kingdom Reading Association's annual conference in Oxford 2000. What follows is an edited transcript of an interview I conducted with her in January 2002.

KATHY HALL (KH): *What do we know about Stephen as a reader?*

MARY HILTON (MH): I only know him from the video and miscue so my knowledge is quite limited but he did seem to be typical – he seemed to be a boy with reading problems and they didn't seem to be unusual ones.

In fact I thought he was typical of a lot of children of that age so I thought the exercise was really interesting in that way.

I also thought things were revealed from the video about his interactions with books which helped me come to certain conclusions.

I didn't think that the books that were on offer were particularly related to him as a reader. In a nominal way he was given a choice – he picked one but I think his teacher said 'You don't have to take that one'. He then just picked up the next one, he was anxious about that, he wasn't really choosing. She asked him why he chose it and he didn't really know why, he said he thought he might like some of the pictures. So the kind of processes of choice were pretty narrow and artificial really. I think he's failing at some level.

I thought what he was actually doing was going through the motions of reading to his teacher without any real commitment, autonomy or any of those things that might take him forward. In terms of the miscue he could read off certain words at a literal level, but the kind of inferential structures of the text, he wasn't really engaging with those at any level. Can I bring my research to bear on this?

KH: *I'd be delighted if you would.*

MH: Well, I've done quite a lot of examination of the national reading tests. One of the first bits of evidence was the government-commissioned study of 45 schools in Inner London – the present government drew lots of erroneous conclusions based on this rather facile report – but what the report did seem to show was that large numbers of children do learn to read at a very basic level. They called it 'reading age of 8' in that Report, and this would seem to have been backed up subsequently by the national curriculum testing. That is that we can teach almost all children to read up to the level that Stephen was almost operating at. Let's say a reading age of about 8. He was learning to read the words on the page but what he wasn't able to do was to understand the text at a deeper level, and understand inference, deduction, pleasure, prediction and all that kind of thing. He just wasn't operating at that kind of level and it didn't look like he was going to get there. We now know that huge numbers of children do pass through the school system without ever doing any more than read at a very basic level. So I think he's a really interesting case study because of his sheer typicality – we now know statistically that he is one of many.

KH: *Thanks for that Mary. What would you like to know about him as a reader?*

MH: I would like to know a lot more about him than the evidence from the video and miscue. I would like to know what he reads – and I'm taking reading in a very broad sense. I would like to know what he reads for pleasure, and if that's video text. Does he play computer games? Does he watch videos? What other texts does he approach? What does he genuinely choose for himself? What are his real likes and dislikes? This might take a lot of working with him to determine that, and indeed watching him and talking to his parents.

I would like to know a lot more socio-cultural information. I would like to know who he plays with, what the reading practices at home are, who reads what and who gets pleasure from what, what the kind of literacy practices are, who writes what and so on – information that could be gleaned from his parents, possibly not. I'd like to have a much wider frame than the evidence of him performing on a miscue or a taped thing like that. I'd like to know what he writes too. I'd like to see examples of his writing, right from the early stages, and to see developmentally how he's going along with writing.

I'd really like to know from him as well what he thinks it means to read, what he sees reading is for, if you like, and what he understands about the nature of reading. And I'd like to know how that's contextualized within the culture of home and the community. And so I'd also like to know what his friends get up to, what they read, and what they talk about as I just don't see how you can move him onwards with reading in any way without having a lot of that information to hand. You can then get him stimulated and I think that's what I was very worried about when I watched the video. I've called it a pathology of school. What was happening was that there seemed to be a school-level definition of reading that he was attempting to come up to but it wasn't a real level, no personal autonomy involved in any sense. His own sense of his personhood if you like wasn't there and my worry is there will come a widening gap between those two things – school literacy and a literacy that is personally meaningful to him.

KH: *Many thanks for that Mary. What do you think his teacher should do to advance him as a reader?*

MH: I think there were a lot of things his teacher could do. It sounds a bit bossy but I think she does need to review her whole classroom practice. I think she is caught into a paradigm that she would need to break out of which involves certain kinds of rather rigid definitions of what reading is. I think she's got to have a wider and more imaginative classroom literacy practice. She needs to bring in more texts that those children, who are failing, are interested in. I think she needs to introduce more media and more popular culture into her work – so that's taking a wide-angle look. In more detail, she needs to talk in depth to his parents about his reading habits – when he does read, who to, what he reads, through to how the family view reading so she can work her practice in more culturally sympathetic kinds of ways.

Then there are also important facets to getting him to write as well as to read, so getting him to write about things that give him pleasure, getting him to re-engage with the processes of literacy along pleasurable lines. It seemed as if he was doing it for her, and probably because his parents were anxious; it wasn't engaging for him though. I think she needs to work very hard at re-engaging his interests, and his imagination, through following his interests. She needs to bring to the classroom those kinds of texts that interest him. She needs to engage him in ways that he finds meaningful. That might well mean making overheads for a little media production or writing texts for his friends, or setting down to write a fantasy story that he really can deeply engage with through play and through his imagination. And so I think there are quite a lot of things she could do.

I'm sorry to go on at quite a general level as I'm not sure what she really does do but those are the kinds of things that I would do.

And my absolute aim would be to get that child hooked on books and I wouldn't really care too much what those books were at this stage; I'd want him to come to literacy as a meaningful activity.

It seems the teacher does have comics in the classroom but clearly that's not quite enough and I don't blame any teacher, particularly inexperienced ones, as they've been trained to disengage with more imaginative approaches to the teaching of reading. I have the impression that his teacher may be of the view that you can train pupils through phonics, exercises, and instruction. Of course you only do learn to read at a very basic level with those kinds of techniques, and if you want children to read at a deeper level, you must bring back in practices which promote autonomy and pleasure. If you want children to understand inference for example, you must do this to engage with texts in an intense and meaningful way.

I've jotted down things like computer games, what stories turned him on, what reading does he do for pleasure, home–school links and all the kinds of changes in classroom practice that that might incur. To re-engage this child with meaningful literate practice is key.

KH: *As you were speaking there I was thinking of the National Literacy Strategy and whether some teachers would find inconsistency between the Literacy Hour and the suggestions you are advancing?*

MH: The whole idea that literacy just happens in an hour is a quite frightening one, an idea we've got to get rid of. Literacy in the primary school happens all the time, and must happen all the time, and somehow this idea that you can stand up and instruct children for an hour and you've done your literacy work is a terrible mistake and will lead to lower standards. I'm engaged in an argument with the government as to whether standards are going up and I don't think they are going up. The teaching profession is caught in a kind of contradictory discourse around these things and I think it's not doing them any good really, and it's certainly not doing children any good.

One of the problems as I see it centres on this reading age of 8 idea – I do actually think that there is a place for phonics, word recognition games, rhyming games and all the rest of it but this only takes you up, as it were, to around a reading age of 8. There's a kind of cut off at this point, and the government has to become aware that we can teach large numbers of children to do this quite well using the kinds of techniques they are advocating. Indeed if the early stages of reading had been the problem then all these kinds of techniques and initiatives would have been worthwhile, but the point about it is that it wasn't the problem. Even in the 45 schools report it said large numbers of children learn to read up to this point so it's not really a phonics or a word recognition problem. The real problem is inference. Many children are failing to understand what's not there in a text, to read between the lines. Things like that which we call 'higher order' skills. Children are learning all the lower order skills, and teachers have always taught those well, but what's not happening is the development of the higher order skills. And I think that's where media education comes in. Many children are actually learning higher order inferential skills from media texts, from film more than they are from print text, so it does bring back media texts firmly into the Key Stage 2 classroom.

KH: *And into the Key Stage 1 classroom also?*

MH: Yes; as I say, I don't want to get into a paradigm that says all the mechanical things happen when they're younger and all the interesting reading happens when they're older, because that would be very wrong. Clearly you have to talk about how stories are made and how they work, and all that sort of thing from the very beginning. But I think there is some argument that you do need lots more instructional support for a very early reader. It's a symbolic system and you have got to show children how it works. I've never really had any objection to that. What I do object to is the idea that this will carry them into Key Stage 2, when they've mastered the basics. What many primary pupils are failing to do is to understand text, and genre and inference. And they never gain it – they go on to secondary school still reading at a very basic literal level. So to me there is a big problem with reading in Britain and one they ought to address – but it's not the early stages.

KH: *Is Stephen beyond the instructional support level, do you think?*

MH: Yes, I think he is. When you look at his miscues and the things that he can work out, he had some familiar words that he could get right. It seems to me he had some fairly substantial knowledge of how the symbolic code works. I'm not saying that you would totally remove all that support, but it's dangerous at this level to assume that this is all he needs. He needs a lot more; he needs to see the text as doing much more clever things than merely being literal. And indeed this is the problem that is being shown up by the national tests, that 90 per cent of kids can answer the literal questions but when you ask 'Why was Laura unhappy on the way to the postbox?' and it doesn't actually say it in the text, the numbers actually drop down dramatically – often to lower than 20 per cent, so that they're completely failing with higher order questions and responses. And large numbers of children won't even attempt questions like that. So Stephen is a child who is just at this watershed. He has had a lot of phonic, word-level training; he now needs to see that texts are actually clever, and interesting, and put himself into them.

And on this I'm probably an old-fashioned teacher in some respects, but I would work very much on his writing at this point because I think if he took off as a writer he might begin to have more understanding of what he reads. As a teacher myself I did a lot on writing, and reading was encouraged to support pupils' writing, but that's just me; I liked them to be creative. Close attention to texts was used to spur their imaginations.

KH: *What theoretical perspectives inform all those suggestions?*

MH: I have done two higher degrees with The Open University which I loved very much, and I think as a result of that work – a lot of it was empirical work here on a council estate where I worked – I definitely take a socio-cultural and anthropological view on literacy. My gurus are probably Shirley Brice Heath and Brian Street. Heath's work I think is absolutely outstanding. *Ways with Words* is probably the most important text for me. She was the first person that showed how deeply enculturated, even within a general American culture, different communities of readers and writers are. And we all live in that world now where different ethnic communities and classes and genders actually come to reading and writing in deeply enculturated ways. I think the only way you can teach children from all different cultures is, yes, to have a generalized school system but the school needs to have an ear out into the particular community that it serves. Until we do that we're not going to reach the Stephens of this world. Many children are going to have two completely different discourses going on: they're going to have the school's definitions – where they're going to fail before long – and they're going to have home where the reading and writing practices are quite different. Home literacy practices are for different purposes and children come to them in different ways, and until teachers, new teachers, go out into the profession looking outward to the community I don't think we are going to raise standards.

Here I think Stephen is a paradigmatic example of the current failure to appreciate the child's culture.

I feel I'm an anthropologist, a social anthropologist, on literacy itself. I think the work of Street is very interesting as he has worked on breaking down any monocultural idea about what literacy is, and has said it depends on people and what they want to say to each other and the way they take meaning from text. And I think that's absolutely true and it's terribly important with young children to use anthropological concepts in order to get them talking about the kinds of things that frame their everyday lives, their kinship patterns, the family myths and stories, the things that are important to them; this is straight social anthropology really. And I think reading and writing fit into that anthropological pattern, particularly when we are young. Before you are locked into what you might call a generalized intellectual culture of the West, all you know, all you bring to school as a 5-year-old, is your family culture. Teachers need to acquaint themselves with the way that culture works and then I think they would be more effective as teachers. I think I've been fairly consistent all the way through. I think that's what that young teacher ought to do: talk to families, see what reading actually means to them, what they think it's for, how they perceive it and then adjust the classroom practice to that, and to appropriate texts.

Now that doesn't mean that teachers haven't got an agenda for themselves, a perfectly legitimate one. For example, it's our job to introduce children to great literature, powerful fiction and classics, such as Shakespeare, but I think again it's got to be done with a sensitive knowledge of the child's home culture. This knowledge makes you a more sophisticated teacher and a better teacher of literacy. I can't think of anybody else's work I admire as much as Heath's. Sadly the government here thinks teachers were wasting their time by familiarizing themselves with children's culture and it's going to take a long time for that to change.

KH: *Some of the things we're talking about here are probably beyond numerical measurement and in the current climate that is an issue?*

MH: I do think it's quite important to have national literacy tests if they're well constructed. I actually think there should be a national literacy test at 9 and children and schools that are aren't doing very well should be allocated more resources. It shouldn't happen at the end of the primary school phase as it's too late to do anything about it then. I think they should get rid of the tests for 7-year-olds and 11-year-olds, and make a proper test for 9-year-olds, as until we do start to measure we don't really know what's going on. As a progressive teacher I've never been frightened of my pupils' progress being measured. It's very easy to get cornered if you're someone who is defined as progressive and creative, to get labelled as someone who just 'loves children' and who doesn't really care whether they are doing any better, and I never want to get cornered in that position. I wanted the children in my class to do well and the methods that I'm suggesting are not as easily measured in small units of discrete work but I claim they are important to progress. This progress can, I believe, be carefully assessed and evaluated in a summative way on an annual basis. The government has so far failed to do this satisfactorily. In fact I think the current national curriculum tests are being rigged; I think they're dishonest the way they are changing them at the moment and that is maddening. They have decreased the number of inference questions and increased the number of literal questions in the reading comprehension tests to make them easier since 1998. This has enabled government to claim a rise in standards – not true! But I'd never like to be positioned as someone who doesn't believe in testing at all because I do believe in it. And I think it's very important for progressive teachers to keep that national picture of results in our heads. Even if you can only measure certain very basic things, I still think you need to measure them. It reassures the public at large and gives teachers a sense of progress. What we desperately need are accurate and honest national literacy figures. This is because I believe school is failing large numbers of mainly working-class children and the current situation is not helping – it's making it worse. The kind of rigid practices that student teachers are now seeing in schools is dreadful. And yet it was Britain which a few years ago was leading the way in so many imaginative and progressive educational ways. Media education now, for example, is so marginalized – it has been written out of the curriculum, yet very recently we have found that children who watch films and television are often the best readers and writers. But as a result of this neglect I also think what children do when they produce and react to media texts is under-theorized at the moment. All the same this is a topic that will continue to be important as films are the central cultural texts that children 'read'. Certainly the current climate of English teaching with its narrow 'standards agenda' and the heavy emphasis on linguistic features of texts is self-defeating. We will soon be left behind by more enterprising nations with more sophisticated education systems.

KH: *Thanks very much for agreeing to participate in this project, for studying the video of Stephen and for giving me this interview. Many thanks, Mary, for such a full response to all the questions.*

READING AND COMMUNITIES OF PRACTICE

What is reading for?

Both Henrietta Dombey and Mary Hilton referred very directly to what Stephen thinks the purpose of reading is. They both asked 'What does he think reading is for?' They were keen to emphasize the significance of reading to Stephen's life, how he himself rated it in his life. Ann Browne and Teresa Grainger also posed this question directly; all the scholars did in some way, and as we shall see later, our final two participants similarly emphasized this in their responses to the evidence. The question 'What is reading for?' raises a host of other issues about reading that we have not addressed so far in the book. It raises other questions about what we mean by reading, and about its links with writing and other language modes. We are beginning to get a sense of a broader notion of reading and of literacy now and in a way that raises issues about learning more generally. The question 'What is reading for?' raises a crucial question about context and how people are enculturated into what is called 'communities of practice'.

It is opportune to consider in more detail some of the themes highlighted by the two scholars whose transcripts feature in this Part. First I will discuss the notion of communities of practice and identify the implications of this for what we mean by a socio-cultural notion of literacy. Recent developments of Vygotskian thinking will be used to do this, especially Bruner's theory of cultural psychology because I think these perspectives get at the heart of a socio-cultural interpretation of what it is to become a (better) reader. The significance of home and school literacies will get special attention and some ground-breaking research admired by our scholars about the meaning and role of context in literacy learning will be explained. Throughout, I will exemplify these perspectives with reference to practice and to a rationale for a socio-cultural perspective at the level of the classroom. You will be directed back to our participants' suggestions frequently. Finally, this part of the book will discuss the fit between the ideas presented here and the model of literacy learning currently endorsed by official policy in England.

Communities of practice: literacy is about ways of being in the world

In Parts One and Two we became familiar with various definitions of, or assumptions about, literacy. We encountered Goodman's notion of reading as a psycho-linguistic guessing game while the cognitive-psychological school implied that reading is a cognitive skill and that it is the ability to decode and comprehend written language. Highlighted in both these accounts is a notion of the individual possessing or lacking certain knowledge and skills about reading. What the psycho-linguistic and cognitive-psychological schools have in common is an exclusive focus on the child-as-individual, on pedagogy, and on school literacy. Both perspectives emphasize the individual nature of the construction of meaning: the individual is seen as the centre of all thought. Both perspectives also prioritize the primacy of mind over social or contextual dimensions, and cognitive-psychology, in particular, treats culture as merely a variable that influences how meaning is made. The socio-cultural perspective, exemplified in the writings of Luis Moll (2000), sees culture as a set of practices such that the study of culture is the study of the way people live culturally – rather than the study of static cultural traits. This section explains this point.

In presenting the ideas of the four scholars who featured in Parts One and Two of the book, I chose to single out particular aspects of reading for detailed discussion (e.g. response to literature, phonemic awareness etc.). As I have said several times now, some of these same scholars also subscribe to the perspectives discussed here in Part Three. On the other hand, the thinking of both Henrietta Dombey and Mary Hilton is explicitly informed by the ideas of this part, hence their inclusion at this point.

A socio-cultural perspective on reading shifts the emphasis from the individual *per se* to the social and cultural context in which literacy occurs. We shift our perspective now from personal skill to cultural practice or towards the study of the social group and its history. This means that the social dimensions of learning are brought to the fore. It means that literacy is discussed in relation to culture, to context and to authentic activity. And it means that culture is treated, not merely as a variable contributing to meaning-construction, but as *the* key to meaning making. Several sections will focus directly on the classroom practices associated with this line of thinking.

The socio-cultural perspective, sometimes described as socio-constructivism, stresses the symbolic nature of knowledge and thought – it implies that knowledge is based on agreed-upon beliefs about the world, based in turn on human beings' interactions within that world (Hiebert and Raphael 1998). Meaning emerges from social interactions. These ideas originated in the writings of the Soviet psychologist, Lev Vygotsky (1978) but have been taken up and developed by several others (e.g. Bruner 1996 and Lee and Smagorinsky 2000) over recent decades. Vygotsky talks about socio-constructivism and Bruner describes his theory as cultural psychology. Vygotsky's followers don't necessarily always agree on all the finer points but I'm not concerned with those details here (for some debates see Lee and Smagorinsky 2000). I'm more interested in the overarching perspective itself. For convenience, but especially because I think his development of Vygotskian thinking over recent decades is especially insightful and brimming with implications for the promotion of literacy, I take Bruner's research as my main theoretical base for the moment.

Bruner's cultural psychology

Culture itself is about the way we make meanings, the way we assign meanings to things in different settings in particular situations. Culture is an outcome of people's histories, experiences and efforts and it also shapes those histories, experiences and efforts. A socio-cultural position on reading draws attention to how readers' negotiation of meaning is bound up with the context in which reading occurs. In this perspective the mind is seen, not as a computational device, but as something more subtle, as something constituted by culture, shaped by culture. Bruner says mind could not exist without culture (1996: 2). He makes the point that although meanings are in the mind, meanings originate in the culture in which they are created.

This is a crucial idea for its major implication, from the point of view of this perspective on reading, is that learning and thinking are always situated, always in a context, and always dependent on the use of person-made tools or resources. And the tool of all person-made tools is surely language. Language is the primary symbol system that allows us to shape meaning – it gives our thoughts shape and expression, yet it also shapes our very thoughts in the process. As literacy educators we are hugely interested in improving our learners' human capacity to use that symbol system. But we must recognize that symbol system as constructed historically and culturally. People, tools, and culturally created ways of using tools are inseparable.

This leads to the important conclusion that learning is inherently social, even when others are not physically present. Even reading a book alone involves the reader in a written code developed through long periods of use by other people and of course what the reader brings to the book has been influenced by the thinking of others and the previous social contexts in which the reader has been (Au 1997; Lee and Smagorinsky 2000). That learning literacy is social and cultural is inescapable.

Bruner makes the important point that while nothing is culture-free, neither are individuals mere reflections of their culture. The interaction between the individual and the culture gives rise to human thought having 'a communal cast' on the one hand and having an 'unpredictable richness' on the other (Bruner 1996: 14). This gives rise to subjectivity – one's personal take on a situation or event – which in turn gives rise to the need to negotiate, share and communicate our meanings to others in the community. But as he observes, humans have a sophisticated gift for coming to know the minds of others in their community – he calls this intersubjectivity – whether through language or other signs like gestures. He says 'It is not just words that make this [intersubjectivity] possible, but our capacity to grasp the role of settings in which words, acts, and gestures occur. We are the inter-subjective species par excellence. It is this that permits us to negotiate meanings when words go astray' (Bruner 1996: 20).

So children, Bruner argues, are especially good at tuning in to what he calls the 'folkways' they see around them. They are predisposed to assimilate the practices and activities of their parents and peers around them in their community. They appear to be willing apprentices to their more adept peers. On the other hand, adults, and arguably any knowledgeable people in the culture, appear to have a disposition to demonstrate performance for the benefit of the novice. They appear to be willing mentors. Knowledgeable members of the culture assist others in learning. The notion of apprenticeship becomes important. It flags the learner as active, not passive, in a community of people who support, challenge, and guide development.

On the grounds that children are active learners, Bruner suggests that teachers have to be interested in determining what learners think they are doing and their reasons for doing it. He also says '. . . a cultural approach emphasises that the child only gradually comes to appreciate that she is acting not directly on the world but on beliefs about that world' (Bruner 1996: 49). The first premise of his culturalist approach is that 'education is not an island, but part of the continent of culture. It asks what function does education serve in the culture and what role does it play in the lives of those who operate within it?' (Bruner 1996: 11). As I see it this gets at the essence of our scholars' question, 'What does Stephen think reading is for?' What beliefs about literacy is he acting on? What role does reading play in his life? Henrietta and Mary wanted to understand this and both wanted lots more evidence about Stephen in this regard.

Significant others and multiliteracies

Where is all this getting us in terms of reading development and the teaching of reading? It's getting us towards an appreciation that reading, including learning to read, cannot be separated from the context in which it happens, which includes why it happens, and how it is valued by significant others in the culture. Learning to read is concerned with how reading is done. One's experience of reading is first of other people reading – it is in experiencing other people's reading, and in experiencing one's own attempts in certain structured settings (like school) that one learns what counts as reading. Henrietta Dombey and Mary Hilton wanted to know much more about the wider literacy contexts Stephen experienced and gravitated towards, including collaboration with peers and parents about all kinds of texts, especially popular media.

As socio-linguists put it, becoming literate involves learning a specific discourse, that is it involves learning particular ways of thinking, acting and valuing (Michaels and O'Connor, cited in Hiebert and Raphael 1998). Reading, like any social activity, involves a set of cultural practices that are embedded within webs of relationships. Henrietta and Mary both wanted to know about Stephen's web of relationships around texts. This is a stance that sees the learner as a thinker, as knowledgeable, and as having agency. A stance that sees learning to be a better reader as social as well as cognitive; that it involves motivational and emotional dimensions as well as intellectual and academic ones.

It also sees the classroom itself as a context and a culture in its own right – that is that it has its own system of socially made beliefs, values and ways of doing things and that these in turn guide people's thoughts, feelings and behaviours (Au 1997). The classroom or school or home or community is a community of practice with, say in the case of literacy, its own ways of being literate and demonstrating literacy.

It is important to understand incidentally that the idea of community in this context does not refer to harmonious living. Rather it refers to a shared set of social practices and goals, to the patterns and habits of behaviour and thinking on the part of groups of people – it refers to ways of being in the world. Some call this 'discourse' (e.g. Gee 1999a). Different groups or communities of course may have different patterns, habits and ways of dealing with the world; for example they may have different literacy practices, different discourses – there are different communities of practice. Importantly, a single individual is likely to be a member of several different communities of practice.

It logically follows from the above that there are many literacies, just as there are many communities of practice. To exemplify, with some diverse examples. Learning to read the Koran involves rote memorization and people are not usually expected to decode the written passages or interpret what they say – the latter being the job of the 'learned scholars'. The religious purpose of prayer does not necessitate comprehension. Literacy is used in a specific way here and the context promotes particular skills (Rassool 1999). On the other hand graffiti artists operating in the underground or the subway are expected to devise their own trademark logos. A third example pertains to information technology. Over the past twenty years or so technology has allowed us to communicate across time and space and to link a wide range of textual information into our communications – visual, audio, and behavioural. All of this gives rise to the notion of multiliteracies (Cope and Kalantzis 2000; Kress 2000a, 2000b). So being literate depends on the context of interaction, and depends, not so much on being right, as about knowing the rules and conventions of the particular discourse or language register.

The upshot of this line of thinking for reading is that its study has shifted from psychology, especially experimental psychology and the ways of the 'hard' sciences, to having a greater involvement with disciplines that are about the way people behave in groups, like sociology, anthropology, and socio-linguistics. Literacy is now a multidisciplinary field. One way that researchers have sought to explore literacy learning in this perspective is through ethnographic studies of situated literacies, of literacies in the context of their occurrence. Researchers have used open-ended styles of interviewing and observation over very long periods (often years) to try to understand literacy from the perspectives of those inside a particular community or culture. And reports of such work are quite different to the style of reporting used by, say, cognitive psychologists. Some researchers working in the field of education have presented their findings in the form of individual learning biographies of the children studied (e.g. Bussis *et al.* 1985; Solsken 1993; Hicks 2001).

One message of this line of enquiry is that understanding the nature of literacy interactions and practices in the home is critical for maximizing literacy learning opportunities in school. When the ordinary events of the home and print in the environment are integrated into school contexts or, put another way, when there is continuity between school and out-of-school literacy, meaningful participation in literacy is greatly enriched for learners. The lesson we need to learn from this is that when the literacies of the community, home and school are viewed as complementary, when these literacies are used to build on one another, connections are made for pupils. In practice this may mean that the literacies of the home be adapted to become more school-like as children come closer to school entry. In this way transition to the new community of school literacy practice becomes smoother. By the same token, school literacy may need to approximate more closely the literacy practices of the home (Cole 1990; Hiebert and Raphael 1998). As Cole (1990) suggests, the problems that some children encounter in schools lie not so much in the acquisition of cognitive skills, but in becoming accustomed to the specific tasks and activities required by the school. In the case of becoming a better reader then the issue is not just a matter of acquiring skills (like decoding) but coming to know how to be like a reader in the context of the literacy demands of the school. In the next section we will look more closely at this theme in relation to home and school literacies.

If you see literacy as social practice, then you are likely to see literacy teaching as apprenticing children into the discourses and social practices of literate communities. It is important to consider our frameworks and this is what this book is all about. The scholars whose transcripts are included in this and the next part of this book look beyond texts to what people do with literacy and to how, when and where they do it. They are interested in different uses of literacy in different contexts, from print to visual literacy, and from computer to oral ways of communicating. Literacy is what literacy does. Literacy can only be understood from knowledge of the conditions under which it occurs. Mary Hilton and Henrietta Dombey are interested in informal learning and everyday, home practices, as well as school practices. They go beyond classrooms and pedagogical methods. Above all, they see home, school and community as complementary sites of literacy learning.

Below I will describe some examples that seek to align home and school literacies. I will outline a school literacy programme as an example of a curriculum devised along socio-cultural principles. But first I will refer to school literacies and the potential variation across the experiences of different groups.

Definitions of literacy: school literacies

In a recent issue of the *Journal of Research in Reading*, devoted to socio-cultural perspectives on literacy, Freebody and Freiberg (2001) claim that school literacies have dominated the field to the extent that they have come to determine what is recognized as reading and writing, not just in schools but in homes as well. School literacies, they argue, act like 'evaluative filters' defining certain practices as 'adequate', 'appropriate', 'effective', 'efficient', 'warranted'. The result is that for many people school literacies define reading as 'a portable capability' (Freebody and Freiberg 2001: 223) rather than something which is distributed or shared among groups for different purposes. They also argue that school literacies set limits on what can be taken to mean effective reading. Other writers argue along similar lines. For instance, Kathy Au's work in the United States (1980) and Eve Gregory's work in this country (Gregory 1998 and Gregory and Williams 2000) shows that literacy practices outside school often require pupils to use skills and strategies more complex than those required in school. Bilingual children, for example, frequently translate for their parents whose first language is not English. Allan and Carmen Luke (2001) talk about the complex skills required to navigate the world wide web or play video games – skills that are not part of the formal school curriculum and that most adults lack. As Ann Haas Dyson (2000) reminds us, many children are now forming a social childhood that we adults have not experienced and they are in need of a language to talk about that world.

Freebody and Freiberg criticize those taking a cognitive-psychological stance (like Adams; Burns *et al.*; NRP) on the grounds that they make prescriptive statements about preferable literacies rather than basing research on actual reading practices in homes and in schools. In other words, in relation to school literacy, a normative version of how teachers should act is presented as a research-based, accurate description of how teachers do act.

Different classroom literacies for different pupils?

Some brief examples of socio-cultural studies of literacy demonstrate how even within the same classroom different literacies are experienced. First, one from this country, then three from the US to demonstrate this point.

Henrietta Dombey referred to Gemma Moss's work in the context of Stephen's orientation to reading. Moss's case study of school reading practice showed how 'boys and girls gender reading for themselves . . . and how reading is gendered for them through their interactions' (Moss and Attar 1999: 133) with others. Proficiency in reading was deemed important in the classes observed and pupils themselves were as aware of where they and their peers were on the 'proficiency ladder' as were the teachers. Children who were 'free readers' or who could read independently could select whatever books they liked from the class library but those who were not so defined could not, being confined instead to the reading scheme. Girls, the observational evidence of their behaviour showed, were much more willing to go along with their teachers' judgements of them than were boys. Boys resisted teacher definitions of their proficiency. They typically sought ways of avoiding having their proficiency labelled. They sometimes refused to read the book allotted to them on the grounds that it was babyish or they argued that the books from which they could select were all boring and dull.

Henrietta's own account in interview of 'George' fits this kind of scenario. Moss and Attar concluded that low proficiency rankings seem to cause boys more problems. What their study and those of others begin to highlight is that the conditions for underachievement are at least partially created by the actual reading curriculum within the classroom.

Over twenty years ago Allington (1980; 1983) analysed how teachers in twenty primary, ethnically and socio-economically mixed, classrooms in New York responded to children's oral reading errors. In most of the classrooms studied those in the top and bottom reading groups varied along social class and ethnic lines. He found dramatic interactional differences according to ability group. Teachers were more likely to correct errors that poor readers made and to correct them more rapidly at the point of error. There were also differences in the prompts offered, with poor readers being more likely to be given graphophonic cues and good readers being more likely to be offered semantic/syntactic cues.

In similar vein, a study by McDermott and Gospodinoff (1981) compared the lessons on offer to three different ability groups in an early years classroom. Striking differences were found between the top and bottom groups. The researchers described how the attention of the members of the top group and their teacher was on the text – they called this positioning 'looking at the book'. In the bottom group, attention of the pupils and the teacher wandered and much time was spent on positionings described as 'getting a turn to read' and 'waiting for the teacher'. This happened because the teacher frequently did other things while teaching this group; she was frequently interrupted by children outside the group and attended to their needs. And this happened because children outside the group knew they could get the teacher's attention while she worked with the bottom group, but not when she worked with the top group. As a result, of course, the bottom group got less teaching and attention than the top group – the researchers described this situation as a case of the rich getting richer and the poor getting poorer. The researchers also noted that the children in the top group were of middle-class, mainstream backgrounds while those in the bottom group were mainly of diverse cultural backgrounds. They pointed out that the interactions negotiated by the children and their teacher during reading lessons reflected the school's function as a sorting mechanism for the broader society, dividing each generation into 'haves' and 'have nots'. In their analysis the teacher and the children unwittingly collaborated in this process.

Much more recently Duke (2000) confirmed this line of thinking through an analysis of quantitative data in US schools. Her evidence led her to conclude that socio-economic differences in both print environments and print experiences 'run wide and deep' (Duke 2000: 470). Although she found that there were fewer books and magazines available to pupils in low socio-economic-status classrooms, there were other differences that could not be explained with reference to resources. For example, there were significant differences in the opportunities to write for audiences beyond the teacher, favouring high-SES groups. She concluded that school may contribute to relatively lower levels of literacy achievement among low-SES children. She suggests that the widening gaps in literacy achievement between low- and high-SES children in the middle of elementary schooling may be explained with reference to the way schools themselves offer relatively poorer print experiences to low-SES children.

These examples demonstrate two important things: first, that schooling and more specifically pedagogy is implicated in the creation of privilege and disadvantage, and second, that, as Bruner (1996: 63) reminds us, 'pedagogy is never innocent. It is a medium that carries its own message.'

According to socio-cultural theory, one way to stop this happening is to ensure the starting point of reading is meaning and interpreting the world rather than going straight for decoding and reading aloud. This is not to deny the importance of basic skills, but simply to recognize that skills are always part of activities and settings and that they take on meanings in terms of how they are organized. Kathy Au's work, described below, provides an example of such a literacy programme in practice.

Ways with words

Before considering Au's curriculum it is worth demonstrating why we should link home and school literacies. A brief account of the ground-breaking work of Shirley Brice Heath, who was mentioned by several of interviewees as having influenced their thinking is relevant here.

Heath spent over a decade studying the interactional patterns and 'ways with words' (Heath 1983) used by two working-class communities in the south eastern part of the United States. Roadville was a white, rural, hard-working community with a strong tradition of church life. Trackton was a Black, Afro-American community with a strong oral and literate tradition. Children here had lower levels of educational achievement than their peers in Roadville. Parents at Trackton were optimistic about the role of school in their children's lives while Roadville too wanted the best for their children educationally. In Roadville, babies were immersed in communication and talk was modified to enable understanding and communication. Their early utterances were acknowledged directly. Adult ways of naming and defining the world were paramount – for instance children were not allowed to tell stories unless they were true; adults intervened a great deal in children's language with lots of correcting and encouragement to 'say it right'. In Trackton the expectation was that children would acquire language through exposure, through observation of what was going on around them, not through direct verbal interaction. Children were not incorporated into adult conversation until they were 'old enough' to become active participants. On the other hand children here were expected to give public performances to peers and sometimes elders – in the form of songs, stories and rhymes. The use of language was highly contextual; verbal cues and gestures were important and people had, therefore, to intuit motivations and intentions on the part of others. Referring to the different discourse patterns in both these communities, Heath concluded that '. . . the different ways children learned to use language were dependent on the ways in which each community structured their families, defined the roles that community members could assume, and played out their concepts of childhood that guided child socialisation' (Heath 1983: 11).

The question Heath poses in relation to this evidence is: what will children from each community be looking for in terms of feedback in school? Clearly Roadville children will expect adult intervention to correct and reward right answers while children from Trackton will expect their teachers to offer highly contextualized, non-verbal as well as verbal cues of adult approval and disapproval. What her evidence makes clear is that all communities do not rely on the same set of language socializing procedures – procedures like expanding children's utterances, using leading questions, or using simplified language. Her research signals the dangers of assuming universal, 'natural', cross-cultural language learning conditions in communities. Understanding the nature of literacy interactions in the home is critical for the design of literacy contexts in schools. This becomes especially significant in the case of those children who come from non-mainstream cultural and ethnic backgrounds.

Mary Hilton's advice that teachers should go out into the community to become aware of out-of-school literacy practices is offered in the context of this kind of evidence. Teachers are clearly in a better position to support literacy in their classrooms if they recognize and build on their pupils' use of literacy patterns in their homes and communities.

But what exactly is being asked of teachers here? The socio-cultural perspective asks teachers to use information or insights gained in one context (the home or the community) to inform the activities and routines in the classroom. Teachers are being asked to create a different kind of classroom dynamic in which these activities would make a difference to pupils' learning. It would be naïve to believe that this is a simple matter. Proponents, practitioners and researchers of this approach (e.g. Moll 2000) acknowledge the challenge involved in doing this and it seems teachers need to be well supported through study groups involving themselves and teacher educators. It is in this context that scholars such as Florio-Ruane have argued that until teachers (usually white, female and middle-class) can understand personally the role of culture in their own lives as literacy learners, they will struggle to understand it in the learning of their pupils. At another level, Janet Maybin (1999) points out that the appropriation by the school of typically out-of-school texts or activities runs the risk of removing the very meanings and functions that gave them their power and attraction in the first place. This is so because, as we have been pointing out, literacy activity is made meaningful to such a large extent through the ways in which it is intertwined with particular situated practices and relationships. Maybin advises that out-of-school activities require very skilful recontextualization to become effective resources for learning.

This section can no more than illustrate some of the ideas that others have sought to implement in their particular settings – it cannot prescribe or mandate the pedagogical details since these will depend on the specific contexts of each classroom and school.

Funds of knowledge and culturally responsive literacy: an example

One of the most powerful notions emerging from the socio-cultural perspective on literacy is Moll's notion of 'funds of knowledge'. I think this idea is not unlike Mary Hilton's notion of 'culturally sympathetic kinds of ways' or Kathy Au's 'culturally sensitive' approach (Au *et al.* 1997). Moll (2000: 260) suggests that teachers create what he calls 'household analogs' where the aim is not so much to reproduce the household in the classroom but 'to recreate strategically those aspects of household life (e.g. social networks, funds of knowledge) that may lead to productive academic activities in the classroom'. What he calls 'funds of knowledge' are the bodies of knowledge that underlie household activities. In documenting and using them in classroom activities Moll seeks to make obvious the wealth of resources available within any single household or local community – resources that may not be so obvious to teachers or even pupils themselves.

So instead of attending to a community's deficits, attention shifts to the possibilities represented in the 'funds of knowledge'. Many of the teachers Moll has worked with do not live or initially know people within the communities in which they teach. He suggests that such teachers are often the most prone to holding normative notions about, say, the working-class school's community. They are frequently the most likely to assume that parents and pupils don't care about education. As they become more involved in the community their ideas change. The work of Moll and his teacher colleagues sets out to develop 'intentional educational communities . . . grounded in social relationships with families, and intentionally defined by the knowledge and resources found in local households' (Moll 2000: 264). A sample of this knowledge from Moll is offered in the following table.

Moll prefers the concept of 'funds of knowledge' to the term 'culture' or 'culture-sensitive curriculum' on the grounds that the latter in his view overly relies on storytelling, dance, arts and crafts, what he calls 'folkloric displays' (Moll 2000: 261). He says:

> Although the term 'funds of knowledge' is not meant to replace the anthropological concept of culture, it is more precise for our purposes because of its emphasis on strategic knowledge and related activities essential in household functioning, development, and well-being. It is the specific funds of knowledge pertaining to the social, economic,

Table 4 Examples of household funds of knowledge

Agriculture	*Economics*
Ranching and farming	Renting and selling
Gardening	Loans
Hunting, tracking, dressing	Accounting
Animal husbandry	Trade/finance
Construction	*Repair*
Labour laws/construction codes	Automobiles
Carpentry	Airplanes
Roofing	Household appliances
Masonry	Tractors
Design and architecture	Fences
Arts	*Religion*
Music	Bible studies
Lyrics	Catechism
Painting	Sunday school
Sculpture	Liturgy

Source: Moll (2000)

and productive activities of people in a local region, not 'culture' in its broader anthropological sense, that we seek to incorporate strategically into classrooms.

(Moll 2000: 262–3)

Among the people who set about bridging the gap between school and community literacies, drawing on Vygotskian theory and on Moll's notion of 'funds of knowledge', was Kathy Au who since 1989 has researched the Kamehameha Elementary Education Program (KEEP) in Hawaii. Despite its proven success (e.g. Tharp 1982), this work is not so well known in this country. I will present an account of some of the aspects of it here to illustrate a socio-cultural stance on literacy that is relevant to English education. However, space prevents a comprehensive account (but see Au 1980, 1992, 1993, 1997).

The project is targeted at pupils of native Hawaiian ancestry attending elementary schools in low-income communities throughout Hawaii. The purpose of it is to help native Hawaiians achieve high levels of literacy in school. Making up almost one-fifth of the state's population, these pupils tend to underachieve in English literacy as indicated by standardized tests, compared to other ethnic groups. Their first language is Hawaii Creole English (HCE) which is a non-mainstream version of English and which tends to be viewed generally as a form of broken English and not a language in its own right. Standard American English is the language of power in the state. As Au (1997) observes, the situation of native Hawaiians mirrors that of other diverse cultural groups in the US who have subordinate status with respect to the mainstream American culture. Au suggests that because the school tends to reflect the ways of the dominant, mainstream culture, it should not be surprising that the pattern of academic achievement is as it is. In recent years in England a considerable body evidence has accumulated which similarly demonstrates the underachievement of ethnic minority groups (e.g. Gillborn and Gipps 1996; Gillborn and Youdell 2000).

The principles on which the project is based are as relevant in this country as they are in the States. These are:

1 that ownership of literacy (i.e. that pupils value literacy and are willing to make it a part of their everyday lives) as well as the acquisition of meaning-making strategies and skills of literacy are important; and
2 that higher levels of literacy follow if literacy teaching happens in a culturally responsive manner.

In justifying the first of these Au claims that people who experience ownership of literacy in school get the immediate rewards of schooling. The immediate, as opposed to the delayed, rewards of schooling are especially important for pupils from non-mainstream backgrounds since their families may not typically show connections among schooling, jobs and general life chances. As we have seen above, a socio-cultural perspective on literacy does not separate intellectual from emotional aspects. The status attributed here to ownership is in line with socio-cultural theory in taking account of the relationship between motivation for schooling and family and community background.

While the overall curriculum goal is ownership, the project focuses on five aspects of literacy, namely the writing process (writers' workshop), reading comprehension (readers' workshop), language and vocabulary knowledge, word reading/spelling strategies, and voluntary reading. The writing process includes the range of activities associated with writing: planning, drafting, revising, and publishing, and pupils engage in all these aspects in the 'writers' workshop' (Graves 1983). Mini-lessons on the various aspects of writing are provided but such lessons occur in the context of drafting and revising self-chosen topics. A socio-cultural perspective on literacy is highly consistent with explicit instruction. Pupils also help each other and they come together as a community of learners to share their writing in discussion groups and conferences.

Reading comprehension involves the ability to interpret text, respond to literature, and link what is read to one's own life. The teacher's role is considered crucial in supporting pupils' reading development – the emphasis being on the Vygotskian notion of moving gradually from assisted to independent performance. A key feature of the reading workshop is the coming together of small groups of pupils to participate in teacher-led, and, in the case of older pupils, also pupil-led, literature discussions. Language knowledge is about learning and using appropriate language terminology and structures. Word reading strategies covers all the cueing systems, and voluntary reading refers to pupils' willingness to read books independently. Achievement in literacy is assessed in a variety of ways through continuous teacher assessment using conferences, portfolios and tasks.

Three ways are worth highlighting in relation to how Au sought to apply the second principle – the notion of a culturally responsive approach. First, she devised what she calls the 'experience-text-relationship' (ETR, see Au 1997: 191). Before any text is read the KEEP teacher engages her small group in a discussion that is labelled 'experience' – the reference to 'experience' signifies what is important in the content of the lesson. Discussion is focused directly on children's experiences relevant to what the teacher knows the content of the story to be. The payoff here is twofold: for the children it evokes those concepts that will be most useful in comprehending the text to come; and for the teacher, it displays the children's ideas so misconceptions can be discussed and missing ideas introduced. The teacher then moves to the text and together they read and discuss parts of it. Finally, the R-phase involves the pupils in making links between the text and their own background experiences. This phase is considered vital since it allows for the Vygotskian idea of the weaving together of abstract and everyday concepts.

The second noteworthy point about how a culturally responsive curriculum is applied bears on the interactional patterns. In most Western classrooms, interaction continues to be dominated by what is known as the Initiation Response Feedback (IRF) pattern. The teacher initiates an interaction with a question to the pupils, a pupil is selected to respond and the teacher follows the pupil's response with some kind of feedback comment. This interactional pattern is especially evident in whole-class settings but also in small group work (e.g. Hall 2002). This style of interaction encourages pupils to be competitive and to perform as individuals, possibly reflecting Western values.

In the small group discussions of the literature they have read or shared, interaction in the KEEP classrooms gradually takes on an overlapping-turn structure similar to the overlapping speech that is common in ordinary Hawaiian conversations. A particular style of interaction known as 'talk-story' (Au 1997: 197) emerges and is permitted to emerge in these discussions. In talk-story in the community, a story is co-narrated by more than one person, and the speech of the narrators is also overlapped by others in the group. In this setting the skilled speaker is one who knows how to involve others in the conversation – this person does not dominate the conversation. Since they are familiar with this kind of speech event outside school, the pupils introduce it into their story discussions in school. So the pupils work together to answer the teacher's questions. The KEEP teacher, appreciative and knowledgeable of the children's family and community culture, is willing to relax her control of turn-taking and allow more than one child to speak at a time as long as what is being said is relevant to the discussion.

Au explains that in many Hawaiian families cooperation rather than competition is seen as important for the well-being of the extended family. Individual achievement is less highly prized than group contributions that benefit the family. In school lessons talk-story appears to be successful as it reflects this family emphasis on cooperation. Interestingly, as they get into the upper grades of the primary school, Hawaiian children do not like to be singled out in front of their peers, even to be praised.

A third feature of practice in this programme is teaching and learning from siblings and peers. In addition to teacher-led lessons, pupils benefit from assisting and being assisted by peers. Again their home culture prepares them to participate in teaching and learning interactions with peers. Hawaiian children are used to caring for siblings, being cared for by siblings and seeking help from siblings as well as from adults. It seems teaching–learning interactions with adults are less common in Hawaiian families than in mainstream households where adults may provide children with almost constant companionship. Friendship groups are also important, although the dynamics of such groups seem far from simple and teachers are trained to be sensitive to the roles and dynamics that can operate in peer groups. The implication for classrooms is that, because they respond so well in situations where they can work cooperatively, much learning can be carried out in pairs, triads and small groups. Almost all the scholars interviewed for this book talked about 'paired reading' or 'partner reading' or 'buddy reading' – such practices are common and highly successful in this programme.

This example suggests to me that programmes based on socio-cultural principles are promising for improving literacy among pupils who do not come from middle-class backgrounds – pupils whose home and community culture may not align with the traditional school culture of literacy. The underlying premise of this statement is that education must be concerned about equity and fairness.

Influence of the socio-cultural perspective

What this perspective has given us are richer and more nuanced ways of conceptualizing, teaching, and studying reading. The research explored in this part of the book has made us appreciate the significance of the question 'What is reading for?' to the learner. For example, Moss's recent work in the UK (2000) and Solsken's in the US (1993) has shown that, unlike girls, some boys associate reading more negatively as children's business rather than adults' business, and as work rather than as play. Such findings give insights into the factors that hinder (or enhance) people becoming enthusiastic readers.

There is evidence over the past decade or so that those working in the whole-language tradition are increasingly embracing socio-cultural principles into their practice (e.g. Cazden 1992). However, it is reasonable to conclude that the ideas enshrined in this perspective are not prioritized in current literacy policy in England. Having said that, however, elements like partner reading, cooperative group work and reciprocal teaching, strategies described more fully in Part Two, are encouraged in the *National Literacy Strategy*. Such collaborative approaches are highly consistent with socio-constructivist perspectives on learning and as such acknowledge the significance of context and the learner's meaning in literacy events.

PART FOUR
A SOCIO-POLITICAL
PERSPECTIVE

INTRODUCTION TO PART FOUR: A SOCIO-POLITICAL PERSPECTIVE ON READING

Part Four is not an abrupt departure from the ideas presented in Part Three for all the assumptions and principles that apply to a socio-cultural take on literacy also apply to a socio-political one. However, a socio-political position on literacy or a commitment to critical literacy merits separate discussion on the grounds that it is more politically aware and more tuned into issues of power and equity. Vygotsky, hugely influential in informing the socio-cultural stance, did not foreground power relations within the social context of learning. However, scholars who took up Vygotsky's ideas and developed socio-constructivism (e.g. Bruner 1996) are more explicit in this regard.

The two scholars whose literacy philosophies appear in this part of the book not only express a socio-political perspective but are energetically developing its theory and practice in their own work. In interview Jackie Marsh said that 'literacy is embedded within discourses of power'. She said the question that exercises her as a researcher is: 'How are children's interests excluded from the curriculum and what are the processes involved in that?'. Socio-cultural studies of school literacy practice discussed in the previous part of the book shed light on some of those processes – they demonstrated that classroom literacy is actually implicated in the creation of difference. The work of Carolyn Baker, Allan Luke and Peter Freebody (e.g. Baker and Luke 1991; Baker and Freebody 2001) to which Barbara Comber refers also shows how classroom practices produce advantage and disadvantage, distinction and indistinction. Barbara Comber said 'I want to be engaged with kids in questions about language and power, and this partly comes from my own history about being concerned about kids who don't have an easy time in school'. She says 'literacy is always political'. Part Four explores literacy as a political construct.

We begin this part with transcripts from our final two scholars, Barbara Comber and Jackie Marsh. This will be followed by a discussion of some of the major ideas raised by these interviews.

BARBARA COMBER'S OBSERVATIONS, SUGGESTIONS AND THEORETICAL PERSPECTIVES

Brief profile of Barbara Comber

Barbara Comber is Director of the Centre for Studies in Literacy, Policy and Learning Cultures at the University of South Australia. Her research interests include literacy development, poverty and education, teachers' work and critical literacies. She was a researcher in the '100 children go to school' longitudinal study of children's literacy development from pre-school through the first four years of schooling and also a project with the Department of Education, Training and Employment, South Australia, which documented the literacy development of socio-economically disadvantaged students in the middle primary years. She recently co-edited two books: *Negotiating Critical Literacies in Classrooms* (Falmer, 1999) with Ann Simpson and *Critiquing Whole Language and Classroom Inquiry* (NCTE, 2001) with Sibel Boran. She has an ongoing commitment to fostering teacher research and collaborative inquiries.

What follows is an edited version of the recorded telephone interview I did with Barbara in January 2002.

BARBARA COMBER (BC): This is a general response to begin with and this gives a context for what I say later. One of the things that I ask myself is 'What can be judged from one reading event and one that is a staged performance at that?' I think quite a lot can be inferred in terms of performance in that practice, and it suggests hunches about what Stephen knows and can do as a reader in those circumstances with that kind of a text. So even though we should be very aware of the limits of looking at one event like this, it does actually tell us quite a bit about what he can do in that kind of event.

My own view is that we would need multiple instances to confirm or disconfirm any hypotheses so the things that I say later are really hypotheses. Also, in my view, we would need different literacy practices so first, we would need multiple instances of that kind of event to confirm or disconfirm any hypotheses we might make about him as a reader in that kind of situation and second, we would also need to see him in different literacy practices to tell us more. The dominance of this one kind of event in early childhood education means ultimately that we tend to see only one kind of learner reader; that there is a dominant normative reader. And Stephen has had a very good go at this in my view.

The thoughts that I have now are not necessarily in any order so I will go quickly through them.

I think that who is holding the book as an indicator of who is responsible for producing the text is a really interesting thing to think about – because you intervened and I noticed it myself before that and wanted to do something about it myself. Certainly this is worth thinking about. Part of the training of Reading Recovery teachers involves them in thinking about who is responsible for producing the text and doing the reading. Holding the book is quite interesting in that regard.

It seemed to me that the teacher was concerned to maintain enjoyment of the story as a whole plus support Stephen as a student reader. I like in your proposal that what you want to do here is to think about the realities and the complexities of teaching and I wholeheartedly support that. And I think in this instance we see some of this going on. We see the tension between these twin agendas: he must orally and 'independently' perform in order to be analysed, in order to improve as a student reader and at the same time the teacher tries to make it a pleasurable event. So you can feel for her in trying to do that.

One of the other things I noticed is the shift in Stephen's body (and the teacher's) at various stages of the event, and in Stephen's case we see lots of indications – from pleasure and relaxation when he takes on the role of listener to wriggling and some discomfort as he moves to the work of the task of reading. You see some shifts in the whole body there.

His focus is very much on the operational aspects of reading – I'm using Bill Green's term now and we can come back to this later. He's focusing on what Alan Luke and Peter Freebody would call decoding and text use and to some degree the cultural (in Bill Green's terms) and what Alan Luke and Peter Freebody would call meaning making. There's little that we can see in this particular event that focuses on the critical or analytical in this instance. But then, having said that, this is also where the teacher's focus is.

I suspect he could do some analytical work. And the evidence I would point to on this is that he was looking for more at the end and I'll come back to this a little later – he was looking for more at the end of the book. And also his sense of humour showed that he had quite an understanding of the plot and in particular the role of Sophie in the story. So it seems to me he has the potential to do some analytical work.

And another thing that interested me and this is interesting for teachers and student teachers to think about – that is that dialect affects what can be heard (what I could hear). Stephen's pronunciation affected what I could hear and I was glad I had your transcript and I read it three times. I couldn't actually hear and it wasn't because it wasn't loud enough. I think this is always going on in classrooms and we're not always aware of it even when students are using their first language, and when they don't, of course, there is even more going on that we may miss. This always makes a difference but often we are unaware of it. Also his cold and the tape-recording mean that I missed some stuff and that must make a difference to teachers in classrooms, especially in ones that are highly culturally and linguistically diverse. The other thing I thought, with regard to that, and this is a top-of-the-head response – this is the whole question of health concerns in early childhood. Children often have colds and ear infections and, given that reading tends to be an oral performance and the strategies that children have tend to be phonetic, I think that this raises questions about hearing and health more broadly. This is something we looked at in our longitudinal study.

I thought the teacher interventions were interesting, her whole style, and I know the focus is not very much on her. I've been very influenced by the work of Carolyn Baker and Peter Freebody who have taken an ethno-methodological look at classroom literacy events, particularly at shared book experience. I had students who used their kind of approach and one, in particular, studied parents hearing reading. The whole time I was watching the teacher I was thinking of the ethnomethodological question – what is being accomplished here? In particular I observed that when the teacher intervenes – she points, she offers words, she whispers, and she collaborates in the sounding out process. And Stephen, well he is able to incorporate this fairly smoothly into his performance. You can tell the two of them have done this before. And Stephen knows this classroom routine as a performative event. They bring the reading off together. She scaffolds his performance to both maintain the event itself and to achieve a reading that has satisfaction pedagogically and as a pleasurable event. That whole way of seeing familiar literacy events is quite powerful.

One of the other things I thought about, and this might be as much a comment about the teacher as about Stephen, but we can only see Stephen in relation to what his teacher invites him to do. The retelling doesn't invite any analysis or interpretive work. It was reading as remembering what happened.

Just a final comment on this question about the ending of the story – there is a sense that this is a cop out/adult ending. The ending could have been discussed. There is potential for critical text analysis in this reading event. It seems to me that when Stephen turns over and they've finished that last page and he's looking for more, there were some questions that could have been asked there: what was he looking for? What did he expect at that point?

These are just the things that I wrote down having viewed the video.

KH: *What do we know about Stephen as a reader?*

BC: I think he wants to please his teacher and I think that's important. The whole reading performance is quite a lot of hard work for him. He does, nevertheless, want to please his teacher by his reading performance. In terms of the children I've watched I think we can predict that on that particular performance Stephen is going to get there without any long-term difficulty. He has difficulties but it seems he's got it sussed. Pretty soon he's not going to need much help with that kind of performance.

Some minor observations: he uses pictures to help him select the text. I would guess that he has a preference for humour (on the basis of the limited evidence available). He likes being read to: he physically involves himself as a listener, and hearer; his enjoyment is obvious, he's smiling at the humour. He is settling back in terms of the body, yet at the same time as he relaxes he attends incredibly closely to what the teacher is doing.

I thought the teacher's finger pointing was interesting. This suggests that she believes that Stephen still needs to read word by word and finger point. Now interestingly, he doesn't actually finger point, he does what Marie Clay calls voice pointing. So the teacher is still doing something that she thinks will be helpful to him and maybe that does help him but he doesn't actually finger point himself when he's holding the book. Teacher finger and voice points to encourage him to join in; she does both of those. It seems to me that this is how she is expecting him to read; she's expecting him to word-read, word by word, which in fact some of the time he does. She's also expecting him to need the crutch of the finger pointing which he doesn't, he echo reads at first – he repeats her words as she tries to get him into it.

In terms of the cueing systems, he uses the whole range of cueing systems, not always successfully. He's got a whole lot of things happening so he uses visual, semantic, picture cues, not always attending to syntactic cues. If things don't sound right he's not always correcting on that basis. When things don't make sense grammatically he tends to proceed. He also uses syllabic chunking (e.g. for the words lunches, feeding, middle, peeped) and does some sounding out. But it does seem to be more letter by letter than by syllables. He has some memory for whole words – has some sight vocabulary. For example, he knows the words 'friends', 'school', 'wouldn't', and 'elephant'.

Interestingly he is aware of the camera, and questions of appropriateness and what is awkward to say – he gets to potty, for instance, and words that are not always said – in the presence of two female educators while being videotaped! He actually looks up to the camera when he is retelling before saying the word toilet. He gives a sideways glance to the camera and actually looks uncomfortable before he gets to say the word.

Back to his actual decoding: he has problems, like many children of his age, with common words e.g. 'she', 'where', 'the', 'behind', 'with', those kinds of function words. He's better on the content words; he has more trouble with the prepositions and pronouns, indefinite articles etc., which is not unusual. One of the things that is interesting I think is that he's reasonably confident with his strategies – words like 'deliberately' he spent quite a lot of time on and persisted, so he's got quite a lot of faith in his ability to work these out. He uses some good miscues e.g. 'track' for 'tunnel' and a few others like that where he comes up with a word that makes sense.

He sometimes gets let down by his combination of visual and phonetic approach i.e. 'birda' for 'bridge'. He got stuck around that as his strategies don't work for some words and he doesn't do what some teachers here would encourage children to do which is read that again and see if you can work it out, he doesn't read on and he doesn't read back yet. He tends to stay with the word which again is what his teacher is encouraging. She's encouraging him to go to the picture cues rather than to use a more seman-tic or even syntactic approach. 'Does that make sense or does that sound right?' 'You wouldn't say that, would you?' So he's not doing that yet or not in that particular episode anyway.

One of the other things – and this relates back again to the work of Carolyn Baker and Peter Freebody – one of the things I found fascinating about the teacher is the kind of whispered decoding that went on, the two of them in cohoots together, the private negotiation of the decoding. As if to say 'We're going to get this right and then we'll say it more loudly', and I think that's really interesting. That goes on in classrooms all the time and I think it's worth thinking about. What is accomplished by this practice? 'It's our job to perform the reading of this book and we might have a few hiccups along the way but that's between us – here are some clues, and together we will make sure that you can do it.' I have seen other teachers doing something similar but never quite seen it like this – the whispering and the volume shutting you out, 'just between the two of us'. In class-rooms teachers probably do this to protect children from their peers, read-ing aloud involves a hell of a lot of peer judgement. There's a lot of social work going on in classrooms. Of course this is all on the basis of just one short episode, I would really need to see him again, with other teachers, with friends etc.

One of the things about the approach that I would take is that so much is produced by the social cultural context of a literacy event and it would be interesting to see Stephen in different circumstances and this is getting us to the next question.

KH: *What else would you want to know about him?*

BC: Now I could go on for days on that question. I would like to know what his preferred texts are, what he would choose to read at home and in school, and in different situations in school, and how he'd go about doing that. What other genres he'd go to in school, what kinds of books, and other texts that he might prefer to be looking at, and it may be that he would choose similar sorts of texts that he chose from that small selection that were available to him there in that event.

How does he go about reading when there's time to read in the classroom? How is he when there is time to read in the classroom? For example, does he ever volunteer to read in front of his peers?

I guess I would want to see more oral readings on different kinds of texts and different levels of difficulty. What kind of level of difficulty does this book represent for him? How might he have performed on easier and more difficult texts? I was interested in what he can do when he reads a known text, and what he might have done had he had the opportunity to reread that text or to have rehearsed reading that text silently or orally before reading it as a performance.

I would also be interested in what he can do when he reads with his peers/on his own. I found it interesting that in this particular event we didn't get a sense of what he made of this story at all, apart from the retelling in the middle. And I'm not criticizing at all as I thought that was a good idea to do that. What has he made of this story? While the performance and the completion of the text were achieved, we have no idea about what he thought was going on there.

In order to be able to say more about him as a reader I would like to see him in a whole lot more reading events. I'd want to know whether he chooses to read to his parents at home, whether they read to him, or whether reading for him is largely a school-based activity.

I would also want to look at his writing to see what he can write.

And I'm wondering about what he thinks of his reading and writing now? Whether he has some kind of self-awareness and self-assessment, whether that's something he'd be able to articulate or not I don't know. What he'd like to get better at if he was able to participate. He couldn't wait to get out the door when it was over.

Also, there's a whole lot of other things as well that I'd like to know. Having done these longitudinal studies of children, we are now kind of swimming in data, and trying to make sense of it all and obviously building up hypotheses about children as literate people over time. So I guess this is where I'm coming from and even then we think we hardly know anything about those children, having watched them for years. We know quite a lot but there's a lot we don't know as well, I guess there are so many questions, we could go on and on.

KH: *What should his teacher do?*

BC: This is always a hard question in a way. I think it's important to start with what already has been accomplished, and really a lot has already been accomplished. He's a very willing participant in school-based reading practices as far as we can tell. He obviously likes to hear reading and she obviously reads to the class a lot. She's a good oral reader, very engaging, she'd want to keep doing some of the things that are obviously working.

She would want to continue providing him with opportunities to gain satisfaction from his reading. Some of the things she could add, and again I feel quite awkward about saying this as of course there will be lots going on that I don't know about, and these comments are based obviously on what you can see. I think opportunities to reread and rehearse reading are important. I wanted her to stop occasionally, she was so focused on getting that book read – that's partly the research as well, of course. I would like her to get him to reread sections and I wondered if she gave him opportunities to rehearse reading – he came to this very cold. There was no prediction, you know, 'I wonder what could this be about' – she probably does those kinds of things in the classroom but we didn't get to see it in that context.

I think once again there is something about that reading to the teacher, reading to the mother event that shuts out other kinds of social practices that would typically occur around reading the text, very much on the performative aspects. And there's something about miscue too, it makes visible particular kinds of reading; other kinds of reading practices become invisible. And again she may already do this but you would want him to have opportunities to read across genres and text types, to encourage more talk about what is going on in the story. I wanted to intervene myself and give him an opportunity to talk about what's happening and particularly to invite him to ask questions, to comment, to analyse. As it is it's all very unproblematic.

Because her emphasis is on appreciation and decoding – she's got those two things going together, let's appreciate the story and let's decode it – it means that interpretive work, prediction, evaluation, intertextual referencing and comparative work like 'Have we read any other books like this?' 'Have we seen any cartoons like this?' 'Have we seen any movies like this?' – none of that happened, either before, during, or after, because that's not what she's trying to accomplish in that particular event.

So, again, to go back to your question, I would want the teacher to worry less, on some occasions, about the performative aspects of the literacy event and work more on depth, what's he learning to do, what's he learning to understand. There were so many questions that could have been asked, and he might have had questions too. The obvious ones are: 'What else could have happened in this story?' 'Why might the author have finished it this way?' 'Why are books for children so often about teddy bears?' I think that the literary twist left him a bit flat really, he wanted more at the end.

These ideas are not in any particular order.

KH: *What theoretical perspectives underpin your suggestions?*

BC: One of the first things to say, having been in this game for a long time, is why I take the view that I have taken. I began as a secondary English teacher and very quickly found that many of my children couldn't read – that's how I got into the world of literacy and reading. And so I hadn't always come from the position that I come from now. It's about teachers assembling repertoires of theories and practices over time. It's a historical kind of thing, so when I discovered that a number of the children in my Year 8, Year 9 and Year 10 classes were really struggling to read their school texts, I actually went back to study myself. The kind of place I started was very much with a psycho-linguistic perspective, reading the work of Marie Clay, the Goodmans, and Margaret Meek Spencer, and many people like that. One of the things that I could have done here is to look at that event using just that knowledge. The psycho-linguistic perspective is quite helpful as you do get a sense of how it is that individual children in particular circumstances are trying to make sense, how they try to make meaning, the kind of strategies they have. I certainly don't want to throw that out.

But what that didn't do for me was give me some kind of social and political analysis of what was going on. Because I've always been concerned with the kids that don't do well in school, I've been looking for theoretical perspectives that help me understand what's going on in the case of the children who seem to be failed by schooling. I came to socio-cultural theories of literacies and more critical and political analyses of progressive literacy in the middle of my own career. I came to those perspectives almost kicking and screaming as I had wanted to believe that we could fix things for all kids by a very progressive, liberal kind of approach with a focus on individuals.

So eventually I came to think of literacy as social and cultural practice; I came to think of literacy events as accomplishments of teachers and children; of literacies as multiple and, more recently over the last decade or so, to really focus on what we could do with critical literacy which embeds those views of literacy as social and cultural practices; the non-neutrality, non-innocence of textual practices, right from the beginning of school. I want to be engaged with kids in questions about language and power, and this partly comes from my own history about being concerned about kids who don't have an easy time in school and who don't just naturally join the literacy club, who don't become what you see Stephen in the process of becoming.

I was very influenced, and still am influenced, by the work of Shirley Brice Heath and Ann Haas Dyson – people working as ethnographers of literacy in communities and schools who were trying to work out how cultural difference makes a difference to kids in classrooms, how cultural difference might be considered a resource, not a problem. And because my own work is concerned with children who are growing up in poverty, poverty by Australian standards, I've been really interested in the work of people like Alan Luke, and the New Literacy Studies (NLS). But in a sense the NLS is kind of a bit arrogant in a way as people have been doing this work for a long time. I understand why people do this kind of naming and claiming, but many, many others have been working with these hard questions for a long time.

I know I'm circling around a bit here. I guess for me the theoretical perspectives that I've come to, which are aligned with what people would now call the New Literacy Studies, come out of my own history as a school teacher in disadvantaged schools, and as a researcher working with children growing up in poverty, and in culturally and linguistically diverse communities. It seems to me that the explanations we had for how children acquire language and literacy were unhelpful for many teachers working with many children. We felt like we were doing a bad job, or not doing it properly, or that the parents weren't doing a good enough job. These explanations didn't help us to teach better; they only helped us work out what the kid wasn't doing, what should have been happening at home.

So my own work now is overtly political in the sense that most of what we do is about trying to tell complex stories about teachers' work in disadvantaged schools. I know this is leading away from reading. I come back to stories of teachers' work in disadvantaged schools, stories of actual children growing up in actual places, with real lives that they don't leave at the gate when they go into school.

So to really work against the developmental view that is extremely normative, exclusionary and elitist – that is where I am, I guess. My own view is that there are multiple literacies across a range of domains; some of them allow you to do some things and some of them don't and the irony in all this is that early childhood is still dominated by picture book literacies. Meanwhile there are little kids with their own websites so the extremes between what children are doing seem to me to be getting greater. So the kind of work that we are doing recently suggests that a kind of linear model of literacy development is quite dangerous because while we have all the kids and all the teachers focusing on getting all the kids through a linear model, some children are learning incredibly sophisticated literacies, that don't necessarily involve these kind of sacrosanct approaches to literacy at all. Children do not have to learn with picture books, for example. So my own view of literacy is that it is always political, it always involves socio-cultural practices and particular events, and that it is extremely possible, and, in my view, desirable, to start having conversations with very young children about representation, about author's choices and decisions about how things could have been written differently. I have written about these things in my own research.

I'm profoundly interested in what individual children are making of a situation. I love watching Stephen, and what teachers do. It is absolutely fascinating, it always is to watch kids. I'm interested in the kinds of learners that schools are producing and the kinds of textual practices and repres-entations that children are acquiring, so it's always about that; it's about which kids are getting which literacy, and then what can they do with that.

KH: *And in turn this goes back to your interest in social justice and the notion that a major of aim of education is social justice and democracy?*

BC: Most literacy educators would say that they are committed to social justice, and most literacy policy, worldwide, has that as part of its rhetoric; most government ministers would say we need everybody to be more literate so there's not an awful lot of disagreement on that front.

KH: *Yes, but isn't it the case that for very many of those people matters of social justice and democracy follow once you become literate in a traditional sense?*

BC: Yes; we'll give you a good dose of school literacy and then you'll be able to learn about democratic processes, ethics, the political system and power. Well the thing for me is that we must not postpone that as what you can end up having – and I'm not suggesting for one minute that that is what's happening in the video – is so much routine, going through the motions of literacy events day in and day out, whether it's the Literacy Hour or shared book reading. The kids learn to perform; they may not be barking at print, they are doing something else, that need not involve a great deal of thinking. Even when they are thinking, and Stephen is thinking, his face is changing you know. What is he thinking? We have no idea. What can he articulate about that story? We have a minimal idea about that because his job is to produce the words as they are written. I find the work of Carolyn Baker and Peter Freebody on children's school books really helpful on this, about disrupting these very familiar early childhood classroom events.

I'm not unaware of the inertia and the conservatism in schools, not only in classrooms but in universities as well. We try to work with teachers who are interested in these questions. A lot of the work is with teachers who are not comfortable because their kids are not doing well by traditional standards. One of the things happening here and in many Western countries is the realization that very few teachers can take for granted that the children sitting in front of them are going to speak English as a first language, that they will come from comfortable middle-class families with a mother and a father. Because teachers' work is changing, because the people who are sitting in front of them are changing, teachers in the schools that I work in – and they're not all receptive, I don't want to give the wrong impression – teachers are looking for ways of doing it better. They are no longer able to consider that the children in front of them are just like they were, and I think that that fundamental challenge means that some teachers are much more receptive to doing things differently.

There are two other major things that we've worked on – one is the kinds of debate between the media and popular culture and the other is the move to new technologies. What we try to do in our work is to say that we need to think differently about popular culture and that popular culture is part of what all children have access to, and about how we can work with it as a resource. So rather than believing that we can fix everything with a good dose of children's literature, we really need to think about what it is that children have as part of their cultural repertoires and cultural representations. And that's why I find Ann Dyson's work and Jackie Marsh's in the UK very, very helpful. We've worked with teachers around that and I guess what we've tried to do is think about what are the problems and challenges that teachers are facing anyway, and to think about what critical literacy or critical language awareness might offer. What extra resources it might offer them for their work? We're not denying the importance of what they're already doing.

The other space that has been quite productive is the emphasis on the new technologies. This means that teachers are having to rethink what they know, what they can do, their own competencies. Whether they like it or not, it's changing and we see this as an opportunity. These are all challenges that are not going to go away. So the changing political, social, cultural and media environments that teachers are living in mean that their nostalgia for the kind of traditional literary literacy must be challenged – I think they can see that no matter how much nostalgia there might be, it's on the way out. They have to work with multilingualism, multiculturalism, global migration, global economies, and you know they're not going to do it with *Bear*. There's nothing wrong with *Bear* but it's a question of what else you would bring to that early literacy curriculum. Reading that book to his teacher is one among many things he might be doing.

I'd be lying to you if I said we have it all sussed. There is a high level of energy amongst teachers here about working with children to study language, to consider questions of language and power, to have kids working as researchers, to have kids producing multimedia texts, and I know this is happening in the UK and other places as well. We try, as part of our agenda, to tell good news stories as well as doing the critique. While I'm committed to critical sociology and the importance of this for disrupting the taken-for-granted, I'm equally committed to critical and innovative practice so that we have images of how it might be different. We have documentaries of teachers because we believe that teachers need to be able to imagine asking different questions, having kids produce different kinds of texts.

KH: *Thank you very much, Barbara, for participating in this project, for being so generous with your time and for your detailed responses to the questions.*

JACKIE MARSH'S
OBSERVATIONS, SUGGESTIONS AND
THEORETICAL PERSPECTIVES

Brief profile of Jackie Marsh

Jackie Marsh is a lecturer in Education at the University of Sheffield, where she teaches on the MEd in Literacy and the MA in Early Childhood Education and is involved in research degree supervision. Her research interests are focused upon the use of popular culture and media texts in the early years and primary literacy curriculum. Jackie has published a book, co-written with Elaine Millard, on this topic: *Literacy and Popular Culture: Using Children's Texts in the Classroom* (Paul Chapman/Sage, 2000). She is currently co-editing a *Handbook of Early Childhood Literacy Research.*

What follows is an edited version of the interview I did with Jackie towards the end of 2001.

KATHY HALL (KH): *What do we know about Stephen as a reader?*

JACKIE MARSH (JM): As you say, it is limited evidence, but I saw that here was a child who knew how to engage in school literacy practices and was willing to engage in those school literacy practices. He knew how books worked. He obviously responded to humour in stories. In terms of his reading skills, he was able to identify key events, he could use context cues. There's some evidence of self-monitoring in his comprehension; he knows when he doesn't get a word right at times – 'bridge' and so on. He has developed a sight vocabulary; he uses a range of cues, although not consistently. He does use semantic, graphophonic, morpho-syntactic cues, but not in a consistent manner.

He brings his experiences or lack of experiences to the text, like any reader. So as he read peanut butter, for example, you could almost see that on his breakfast table, he was so familiar with it, whereas as he struggled with rucksack, I wondered – could he have come across a rucksack, did he know what one was?

He obviously had some difficulty with the structure of this particular narrative text in terms of the use of first person and past tense and I could see the teacher would probably perceive him as a struggling reader, someone who lacked confidence.

But I primarily saw him as a child who lacked motivation in this particular instance. I know he had a cold that day and that might have impacted on his performance, but he did not bring any enthusiasm to that task. It was a performance and, in terms of expectations, he met them. He wasn't challenging those expectations. And that's why I thought that he was a boy who conforms to school literacy practices. A number of boys give resistant readings to that sort of discourse with teachers, whereas Stephen was very compliant. There were times when he did respond to the text, particularly to the onomatopoeic words and the humour around the text. But I never really got the sense that he was fully engaged with the story.

So that's what I feel I could tell about Stephen as a reader from that evidence: someone who, I assume, would not gravitate towards the kind of picture books that were on offer to him. It was interesting to observe the way he responded at first. He looked around as if to say 'Is this all that's on offer?' And he gravitated towards the book *Funny Bones* first. I noticed that and, again, I think that's understandable in terms of what we know about young children's attraction to popular culture – *Funny Bones* looks like a comic. And then the teacher redirected him. I think she said 'What about something else?', and then because of that compliance I mentioned earlier, I think maybe he thought 'I ought to look at some of the others', and he moved on to Bear. But I think that was just because it was the nearest book to him. I don't feel that it was a considered choice, although he did spend some time looking at it; he flicked through it. He's obviously able to grasp the elements of a narrative pictorially and again I'll talk later about how I feel that may link in with his televisual literacy practices. So there are lots of positive things there and lots of skills to build on.

KH: *Thank you, Jackie. Tell me what you would like to know about Stephen.*

JM: Obviously what I'd like to know about him is what he likes to read outside the classroom and what his self-perceptions are as a reader. Indeed, does he enjoy reading? What does he read at home? Who with? How is that reading linked to his other interests, so, for example, does he play computer games like Nintendo, watch TV and so on? How does his reading fit in with those other patterns? I'd like to know how his reading is linked to socio-cultural patterns within the home and his community. I'd like to know much more about Stephen as a reader in terms of how he perceives reading within his world, what he perceives are the meanings attached to the prac-tices of reading. We got one view of Stephen – seeing reading as a school practice, in which he did certain things and responded in certain ways to the teacher. I'd like to know much more about how he engages with reading outside those schooled literacy practices. I think that they're the key things that I'd like to know about Stephen.

I'd like to know about his reading history as well – whether he was more oriented towards those school texts in the past and whether he became less so as he went through school. I'd like to know what he was offered in terms of texts throughout his early schooling and what the affordances of those texts were for him, whether any of those texts reflected his own socio-cultural literacy practices and, if they didn't, whether that contrib-uted to his alienation from school literacy practices. I'm only talking about alienation in terms of what I observed, which was this tendency towards conformity and not enthusiasm. I know I'm making huge assumptions here; it could be that he just wasn't in great form that day. But it seemed to me that here was a boy who perhaps had not seen himself reflected in the texts on offer and that this had contributed to his disengagement with reading as a pleasurable activity.

I'd also like to know about his reading within the classroom: when he chooses to read, if indeed he does; whether it is a social practice; whether it involves sharing texts with other children, and particularly boys. I'd like to know whether he engages with gendered structures of literacy practices within the classroom, and how far he has developed a community of readers with other children in the class; whether they talk about and share texts. Those are the kinds of things I'd like to know more about.

KH: *Can I ask you to explain a little more about gendered structures of literacy practices.*

JM: It is based on the work of people like Elaine Millard and others who have demonstrated how literacy is a differently gendered practice. So within a classroom, often girls are more oriented towards the teacherly texts that teachers present through shared reading – 'quality' picture books and so on. And it has been demonstrated that some boys are not as oriented towards those kinds of texts and prefer non-fiction texts, comics and magazines. That's in terms of reading. And obviously in terms of writing, evidence shows that again boys are less likely to be motivated and oriented towards writing practices within the classroom, and that they find it more of a struggle and less of an incentive in terms of what they get out of school. I would like to know how far Stephen fitted some of those patterns.

However, critiquing that discourse, it's not all boys who underachieve; there are some boys who are heavily oriented towards school literacy practices. I actually think that, although we need to incorporate the interests of boys within the curriculum, it shouldn't be at the expense of some of those other texts which we know have lots to offer and can orientate them towards the discourses of power that they need to access in order to achieve success. I don't think I would be suggesting that we should flood the classroom with football texts, for example. I think that we should have a more balanced approach and use the cultural interests of all children, both boys and girls, as I think girls' out-of-school practices are often as much excluded as boys' are. So we need to find a way that these texts can be appropriated – what Deborah Hicks, Kris Gutierrez and others call the development of 'hybrid pedagogical discourses'. When I recently read a paper by Deborah Hicks, *Literacies and Masculinities in the Life of a Young Working-Class Boy*, which describes how an American working-class boy's home literacy experiences are not reflected in the school curriculum, I thought of Stephen.

KH: *Are you happy to move on now, Jackie? Can we move on to talk about what his teacher might do to advance him as a reader?*

JM: The teacher should develop his motivation and confidence in reading and I think that can be done primarily by finding out what he enjoys, what his literacy practices are outside school, what he does in those hidden gaps in the classroom, times when he's not observed, like break-times and wet play times. What texts is he oriented towards then? What books does he have at home?

One of the first things his teacher could do is ask him to keep a literacy diary of his reading, so getting a sense of what his reading practices are over a number of weeks, establishing what he reads, who he reads with and how he reads, to ascertain how Stephen situates reading within his life. Then, I would suggest that his teacher should incorporate those texts as far as possible into the literacy curriculum. Let him bring texts from home to read for and with other children, make tapes of those particular texts. Also the teacher should provide books within the classroom environment that resonate with Stephen's interests.

Within the literacy diary, Stephen should document his reading of televisual texts, not just print-based texts, but also televisual and computer games, as they make a contribution to the reading diet. The classroom could then start to reflect some of those wider interests, so computer games, magazines and so on could be part of his reading in school.

A school that I worked with had a very good home–school comic library. As well as taking home a reading book on a weekly basis, children took home comics and that was really successful in orientating boys like Stephen, who were demotivated by the literacy diet on offer, towards reading. It did have spin-offs in that the children began to read more widely across the curriculum.

So, his teacher could enhance his motivation towards school literacy practices by opening out some of the areas away from school discourses towards popular discourses. For example, the teacher could have a book corner based on a theme from Star Wars. One school has used a successful 'boy zone' reading area. Again, I would be wary of that. I would like to see a 'boy zone' and a 'girl zone', but I wouldn't want to have children just gravitate towards those gendered discourses without challenging them. Barbara Comber's work on critical literacy shows that we need to get children to critically analyse those discourses of power in the texts that they encounter.

And so whilst I think practices that are aimed at specific genders are useful as a starting point, I think that's all they should be – a starting point – and then they should be moved on to challenge those discourses.

So, those are the strategies I would suggest – for this particular child, basically, bring popular culture and media into the curriculum. Also, don't just make those choices on offer throughout the classroom, but have them centrally embedded within the delivery of the curriculum. This gives those texts agency and it lets children know they have some value within the school and the school literacy curriculum. It gives the texts power if the teacher uses them. For example, in shared reading and writing, comics could be used and teachers could draw from the children's knowledge of televisual discourses in discussions. However, I don't mean this should just take place within the context of a session which focuses on comparing a book to a film, as often happens. I think that is very valuable and is very safe for teachers who are not very confident with televisual texts. But all that does is to emphasize the primacy of the written text and I think there are times when we should move towards just focusing on those televisual practices that the children encounter outside school. For example, you can use the latest game on Playstation within a shared reading session and you can talk about the narrative structure of that game – what is the narrative structure, how do you move from one level to the next, what is the role of the central character within that computer game and so on. So it's a two-pronged strategy – providing those opportunities in the classroom, but also embedding them in the curriculum.

Another thing that the teacher should do is become familiar with the texts that children encounter outside school. We often make assumptions about those comics and magazines and yet they are very challenging as reading texts. If you look at the range of visual cues children have to navigate, at the page layout and so on, they are actually very complex texts. We need to look at the affordances of those popular culture and media texts and understand what the pleasures are for children. Teachers might also want to challenge the gendered, the sexist and racist nature of some of the texts, but spending time on what children are actually engaged with, rather than making assumptions about those texts, would be profitable.

KH: *Did the project you mentioned, Jackie, promote their self-confidence and sense of engagement?*

JM: Yes, with certain children – mainly boys, although I haven't reported on that element of the project. Boys within that project did improve in that classroom, they became more motivated. Teachers talked about it having a big impact on motivating children towards reading. It definitely facilitated their entrance into the literacy club that Smith talks about, when there might have been many barriers to that entrance previously.

KH: *The final question I'd like to explore with you concerns your own theoretical perspective on reading. You've been alluding to it all along really, but can we talk about that more specifically now.*

JM: Primarily, I base my work on a theoretical perspective that sees literacy as a socially situated practice. Barton and Hamilton's work or Street's work outline how literacy is not a set of discrete skills; it is not autonomous. It's powerfully situated within social contexts and is socially constructed. The critical literacy discourse has also been very important – the work of Luke and Lankshear demonstrates that literacy is embedded within discourses of power; it's not a neutral technology. So that has been very important to me in tracing how that works and operates within early years classrooms. How are children's interests excluded from the curriculum and what are the processes involved in that? That's really been a key thrust of my work so far.

Also central to it is Bourdieu's concept of 'cultural capital' – that notion that it is only some children's cultural capital that is reflected within the curriculum, generally middle-class children's cultural capital. A lot of my work has been predicated on the notion that, by recognizing the texts that are embedded within children's daily lives, you are providing them with some recognition of the cultural capital within their world. And that's not a simplistic notion that suggests that process will suddenly empower them to succeed within the education system. But I do think that self-esteem is at the root of our learning. Self-esteem is built on how far we can see ourselves reflected in the eyes of others, and on the walls of the environments we inhabit. I do think that Bourdieu's work has been important in that respect.

In terms of looking at how a curriculum is framed, Bernstein's work on classification and framing has been important. Again I'd want to critique a simplistic cultural reproduction model. I think, for me, his concepts are important, especially if we think of the NLS – his notion that once you have strong classification of what counts as knowledge and strong framing in terms of how that knowledge is delivered, there is less chance for those literacy practices that are situated outside school to embed themselves within the curriculum.

In terms of looking at the importance of media texts in children's lives, Anne Haas Dyson's work has been key to that. She examines how children recontextualize and reconfigure the cultural worlds in school to develop those hybrid literacy practices that are meaningful to them, but do take on some of the school literacy discourse. I think her work is central in developing our understanding of that process. I think Muriel Robinson's book on children's reading of televisual narratives has also been influential and has developed our understanding of how reading practices, in terms of reading printed and televisual texts, are very similar in some ways, for example in developing understanding of narrative and narrative structures, the role of characters within those narratives and so on. David Buckingham's work on the place of media texts within children's lives, how those texts create meaning for children and create communities of readers around media texts, has also been influential.

I think the work of Kress is very important. What Kress has done is show how the changing landscape of communication impacts on the literacy curriculum. His work has developed our sense of how the visual and iconic have become central to the literacy texts that children encounter through the medium of popular culture and outlines how schools have been rather slow to recognize that changing landscape of communication. The school still hangs onto the printed text as the primary form of communication.

And looking at the work on gendered literacy practices, the work of Elaine Millard, Pam Gilbert, Nora Allaway – that has given us insights into how literacy practices are situated within gendered discourses and how girls and boys often have different trajectories in relation to literacy development. There are difficulties too around that discourse, as it has often been taken over by people who have wanted to trumpet boys' underachievement, without looking in more complex ways at what's going on.

KH: *To what extent do you think teachers could incorporate critical literacy including work with televisual texts within the current policy of the National Literacy Strategy?*

JM: Well I think it's easy if certain conditions are in place. It really depends on school culture and teacher confidence. But I think that if a school is willing to look more broadly at notions of literacy and is willing to engage with children's out of school literacy practices in order to see how they can motivate children, then that can facilitate a movement into the use of televisual texts. I think that if teachers can have guidance and information about children's televisual texts, it can develop their confidence. I have lots of examples of teachers embedding popular culture and televisual texts within the National Literacy Strategy – at shared reading level, shared writing level, group work level, plenary session and so on, so it obviously can be done.

KH: *Can you give me an example of what you mean there?*

JM: Yes, Elaine Millard and I documented that in the book *Literacy and Popular Culture*. For example, some classes have used a big comic in shared reading sessions – that is, an enlarged text comic. Teachers have also used pop songs and rhymes to develop children's phonological awareness. They have looked at the patterned rhymes within those pop songs, or rap, within the classroom.

A very successful session that I saw involved a teacher sharing a Pokemon game in a shared reading session and they looked at it on the screen, they talked about the game, the rules of the game, the narrative structure of the game, the characters in it, and then the children developed and planned their own game on paper – they hadn't the software at the time to develop a computer game using the computer – but they planned a computer game. This particular teacher was looking at the genre of instructional texts and focused mainly on children developing instructions for that Pokemon game. This is a very simple example of how the instructional genre can be embedded into children's popular cultural interests. It motivated them towards that particular task. The work of Dyson has been important for showing us how it is this kind of activity that can provide a bridge to canonized literacy practices – so work on Batman can lead to work on Greek myths and legends, for example.

Part of my PhD work is about looking at what prevents student teachers from using popular culture in the classroom and the key thing that prevents them is a discourse within a school that suggests that 'Oh, that's taboo, we don't do that sort of thing here, it's so full of sexism and racism', so instead of finding ways of working round that, that is the biggest thing that's stopping them. The other factors are a lack of confidence and lack of knowledge of those texts. Teachers are very busy and it's easier to work with texts that you are familiar with and that are part of your training and maybe your own experience of growing up, but it's less easy to draw from texts that you are less familiar with.

KH: *Many thanks, Jackie. I very much appreciate your contribution.*

READING THE WORD
AND THE WORLD

Introduction

This part of the book explains and discusses some issues in a socio-political approach to literacy, drawing on the suggestions and theoretical issues identified by our two scholars, not only in the transcripts here, but also in their extensive publications. Much of this part consists of illustrative classroom examples of critical literacy – from Australia, the US, and England. These examples facilitate an exploration of several themes, namely, the connection between literacy and power, being a text critic, the use of popular culture in the classroom, and the status of critical literacy in practice.

What has literacy got to do with power?

There is no neat consensus about what critical literacy is although there is broad agreement about its aims. Critical literacy challenges inequities in society and it promotes social justice and a strong or participatory democracy, the kind of democracy where power is with, not just some people (like special interest groups or the wealthy) but all people. As Powell *et al.* (2001) point out, though, equity does not mean the realization of individual personal interest; rather it means that everyone has a role in deciding what is best for the common good. A strong democracy on these terms involves collaboration and compromise. Barbara Comber says in interview that 'most literacy educators would say that they are committed to social justice, and most literacy policy, worldwide, has that as part of its rhetoric'.

A socio-political view of literacy takes it that no knowledge is neutral but rather is always based on some group's perception of reality and on some group's perspective of what is important to know. On this basis those subscribing to a socio-political view of literacy, or a critical literacy, hold that learning to read includes being able to determine underlying assumptions and hidden biases in texts. This is how literacy and power connect. Taking a critical stance requires that issues of equity come to the fore, so questions like the following become prominent in classrooms that foster critical literacy:

- What images of and ideas about, say, race, gender, ethnicity, socio-economic class, disability are on offer in the text?
- Whose interests are being served by the text?
- Whose voices are included and excluded?

What this approach does is to help learners understand how texts have power, how that power is exercised in a given text, how it works to privilege particular knowledges, beliefs, attitudes and values, and to marginalize or silence others. It is an approach that asks learners to question taken-for-granted or 'natural' assumptions about the world. It is based on the assumption that language reflects the way the world is and the world is to some extent the way it is because of the way our language is. As Morgan *et al.* (1996: 9) note, the word and the world 'each shapes and constrains the other'. So reading involves not just reading the words but reading the world as well (Freire and Macedo 1987). Critical literacy is about making explicit the relationship between 'the word' as in language and 'the world' as in the reality we live and how we understand that world to be. This is how Morgan *et al.* (1996: 9) explain what critical literacy is about: 'Critical literacy is concerned with enabling us to take particular texts and explore the ways in which these texts are implicated in making the world the way it is; in helping us to keep the world the way it is; and in 'coercing' us to see the world in certain ways rather than others.'

With reference to the text–reader relationship earlier in the book I raised the question of where meaning lies. This was in a discussion in Part Two bearing on what the reader brings to the text in terms of preconceptions, prior experience and so on. I want to elaborate now on more implicit meanings that texts and literacy events carry in order to highlight further the relationship between literacy and power. An insight made available through socio-linguistics and through the notion that reading is a social process is helpful here (and is relevant to the discussion below about readers as text analysts). This is a dimension of reading that Bloome (1993) calls 'author–reader interaction'. In any text, he suggests, the author sets up a social relationship with the reader and structures identities for him or herself and for the reader. To do this the author may use particular linguistic devices like commands ('Stop and read the previous section'), pronouns signifying inclusion or exclusion ('we', 'I', 'you', 'them'), as well as linguistic tactics bearing on sentence structure, dialect, tone and genre. The author also establishes an identity for her or himself, perhaps as storyteller, expert, friend, fan, reporter. There may be indications of the author's gender, age, ethnicity, socio-economic status etc. The author's social identity inscribed in the text is known as the 'author-in-the-text' (Bloome 1993). The 'reader-in-the-text' is also positioned, perhaps as child, colleague, adult, expert etc. The 'reader-in-the-text' may be assumed to be a particular gender, from a particular ethnic group or from a particular social class background class background and so on. Bloome notes that such positionings are not givens; they depend on the reader's interpretation of the linguistic features used and on the reading event itself. Such positionings, in other words, can be disrupted, challenged, accepted or resisted. There are other assumptions too – assumptions about the way the world is which may not be shared by all groups in society. All these assumptions can be made explicit and challenged.

A second important insight is that social relationships are always established during a reading event and this point has already been made in Part Three of the book but it is worth emphasizing here. Bloome explains how participation may include ascribing social identities and status to oneself and to others, allocating rights and privileges to talk, to engage in other activities. Through their social interactions with each other and with the text, teachers and pupils in a classroom define each other as 'teacher', 'pupil', and allocate rights and obligations for how they are to behave and how they are to interpret the text. Through a close examination of classroom interaction, my own work in a multi-ethnic literacy class documents how teacher and pupils defined each other in various ways (Hall 2002). It shows how one pupil managed occasionally to subvert the teacher's strong positioning of him and of others in the class by using a variety of linguistic devices to change the conventional pattern of identities available to learners. Like other work in this tradition, the study illuminates how pedagogical discourse shapes learning opportunities in literacy, how there is scope for individual children to make an impact, to shape events, to negotiate roles and expectations so that pupils and teacher jointly construct the contexts in which they work.

Critical literacy seeks to make explicit the various positionings and identities that are on offer in texts but that are mostly left implicit and taken for granted. Learning literacy then is about understanding how attitudes and beliefs about the world are manipulated by language. Understanding how one writes to position oneself and others and how one is positioned by a text to view the world is a prerequisite to developing other possibilities or opposing interpretations. It is worth noting here, however, that the purpose of a critical literacy orientation is not merely to help learners appreciate that texts can be manipulative or stereotype people. While this is part of the process, critical literacy is essentially about understanding how texts work to achieve certain effects. A critical literacy classroom involves teachers and pupils working together to see how texts construct their worlds, their cultures and their communities. In addition, it involves reworking or using those texts to reconstruct different worlds, worlds that are more equitable and fair (Comber 2001).

Learning to read in this perspective is as much about learning identities and values as it is about learning skills and codes. Powell *et al.* say that literacy teachers can either teach literacy as a series of skills and codes or they can teach it 'as if the words matter' (2001: 780). The point here is that it's not a matter of some methods working and others not working since they all work to create different literacies and different literate repertoires in classrooms. Rather, literacy teaching is ultimately about the kind of literate person that is, could and should be constructed. Unlike, say, the stance on reading discussed in the first two parts of the book, critical literacy goes beyond providing authentic purposes and audiences for literacy. Its emphasis on the power–literacy relationship and on raising awareness about equity and social justice often leads to social action – in other words, literacy has transformative potential in a democratic society. Good examples of such work can be found in Comber *et al.* (2001) and Powell *et al.* (2001).

The kind of literate persons that are envisaged are citizens who

- are able to analyse texts for their implicit, taken-for-granted assumptions about the way the world is and ought to be;
- challenge the identities that texts offer when they run counter to principles of fairness and equity; and
- use their literacy to make a difference to their world.

Is literacy empowering? Why critical literacy?

In interview, Barbara Comber said that earlier in her career she had wanted to believe that we could 'fix things for all kids by a very progressive, liberal kind of approach with a focus on individuals' – much like the approach discussed in Part One above. She said she came 'kicking and screaming' to socio-cultural and socio-political perspectives on literacy. In mid-career her thinking on literacy shifted to take account of the way power and literacy are intertwined. And as she observes herself (Comber 1999), in the 1980s and 1990s some critical educators began to argue that progressive literacy pedagogies (the kind described in Part One of this book) were actually (re)producing injustices by privileging particular forms of texts, language practices and tastes and, at the same time, excluding others. For me one of the most salient ideas underlying my own recognition of this is that literacy is indeed a 'double-edged sword' (Green 2001: 8). This is so in the sense that literacy can be liberating or dominating.

The double-sided nature of literacy is a theme that crops up in socio-political accounts. According to Pam Green (2001) there is a duality about literacy. If, for instance, school texts are limited to portrayals of the world from a mainstream perspective or if school literacy is reduced to the completion of worksheets or copying, then literacy cannot be considered liberating. Drawing on Alan Luke, she suggests that while being able to construct meaning from print may seem empowering, it may open up the potential for one's exploitation – 'You may just become literate enough to get yourself badly in debt, exploited and locked out' (Luke, cited in Green 2001: 8).

The point is that literacy is not necessarily empowering or liberating and it could be exploitative. Whether or not literacy is empowering depends on many factors. Pam Green claims that while taking a critical stance on liter-acy may unpack the power base of society, it may not necessarily provide the learner with access to that power base. However, she says that while achieving literacy does not earn one access to the power base of society, those who are powerful are usually literate. Being critically literate does not give any guarantees of empowerment either. As Luke (cited in Green 2001: 11) says, 'Having it [literacy] doesn't guarantee anything, but not having it systematically excludes one from cultural and economic power'. It is reason-able to conclude, however, that a teaching practice that makes explicit the workings of power and ideology has a much better chance of empowering people than a literacy which does not do this (Kempe 2001).

This is a crucial point, I think, as it reminds us that it is not so much what literacy *is* that is so important but what literacy *does* that is key. Margaret Meek has argued that the great divide in literacy is not between those who can and can't read but between those who have and haven't worked out what kinds of literacy society really values and how to show literacy competencies in ways that gain affirmation and recognition. The work of Scribner and Cole (1981), for example, demonstrated that literacy *per se* does not necessarily lead to cognitive growth and development; that what matters is not literacy as an isolated skill, but the social practices into which people are enculturated or apprenticed as members of a specific social group.

And the social practices into which different children are apprenticed probably varies more now than ever in the past. Barbara Comber remarked that 'there are little kids with their own websites so the extremes between what children are doing seem to me to be getting greater'. Some of the research reviewed in Part Three showed that even within the same class different children are offered vastly different literacy and learning experi-ences, some of which could not be described as liberating.

Critical text analysis: classroom practice

What does a socio-political perspective on literacy entail in terms of classroom practice? Jackie Marsh said Stephen probably didn't see himself reflected in the texts on offer and that this had contributed to his probable disengagement with reading as a pleasurable activity. Barbara Comber would encourage a lot more analysis of texts, and in her view this one event of Stephen reading and retelling to his teacher had the potential for critical text analysis. This, she suggests, might have been encouraged in the observed event through questions like the following:

- Have we read any other books like this?
- Have we seen any cartoons like this?
- Have we seen any movies like this?
- What else could have happened in this story?
- Why might the author have finished it this way?
- Why are books for children so often about teddy bears?

Barbara (and Teresa Grainger) observed that the retelling didn't encourage any textual analysis. What was important was remembering what happened and being able to retell it to the teacher. Left unanswered for Barbara was the key question, 'What has he made of this story?'. Now it is important to emphasize that the scholars recognized that this was but one event, and a very artificial one at that, one that was highly constrained by the context of video-recording and the demands of the miscue itself. As Barbara said '[A miscue activity] makes visible particular kinds of reading; other kinds of reading practices become invisible'. Similarly, David Wray said a miscue analysis gives only a partial picture of reading.

In this section I will describe what critical text analysis means and outline some examples from classroom practice.

Luke and Freebody (1999; and Luke 2000) talk about 'families of practices' involving four types of reading competence. Learners can be described as:

1 *Code breakers* (How do I crack this text? How does it work? What are its patterns and conventions? How do the sounds and the marks relate, singly and in combinations?).

2 *Meaning makers* (How do the ideas represented in the text string together? What cultural resources can be brought to bear on the text? What are the cultural meanings and possible readings that can be constructed from this text?).

3 *Text users* (How do the uses of this text shape its composition? What do I do with this text, here and now? What will others do with it? What are my options and alternatives?).

4 *Text critics* (What kind of person, with what interests and values, could both write and read this naively and unproblematically? What is this text

trying to do to me? In whose interests? Which positions, voices, and interests are at play? Which are silent and absent?).

Each one, they suggest, is best thought of as a family of practices to emphasize their dynamic, fluid and changing nature as well as to stress the fact that they are undertaken by people in social contexts. For example, constructing meaning of a particular text might count for different things in different settings – it might count for something in the classroom and for something far more or less in a given workplace. They add that this point becomes more of an issue each day, as we encounter unprecedented hybrid multimedia texts.

They argue that, while each family of practices is necessary for literacy in new conditions (cf. technological literacies), none on its own is sufficient for literate citizens. Luke and Freebody (1999) advise that they should be seen as 'inclusive . . . with each being necessary but not sufficient for the achievement of the others'.

Alan Luke suggests that this model provides a useful framework for weighing up and questioning the emphases of current classroom literacy curricula. Perhaps there is an exclusive emphasis on the code aspect with virtually no attention devoted to critical aspects or that the literature-rich programme which is on offer in a classroom neglects the user aspect – the application and pragmatic aspect. Or it could be that the emphasis on the critical work is such that acquisition of the basic textual codes is neglected. In my view this is an extremely helpful model to interrogate literacy policy and practice, at both the level of the school/classroom and a national or regional level.

It is in the fourth family of practices that the scope for critical literacy particularly lies. The role of text analyst or text critic entails pupils coming up with alternative readings of a text through considering such questions as:

- What is being portrayed as natural?
- Who is in power?
- What emotions are attached to the participants?
- Who or what is left out of the text?
- Who plays an active role? Who doesn't?

Pupils in a critical literacy class are encouraged to reread and rewrite texts from different and multiple perspectives.

Illustrative examples: teaching strategies

Barbara Comber's research features many examples of critical literacy in action. I will describe just one of her examples, based on the ideas discussed above, to illustrate how very young children (ranging in age from 5 to 8 years old) can engage in text analysis. This example is based on the work of

Jennifer O'Brien, a primary teacher in a suburban, disadvantaged school in South Australia (Comber 2001). This teacher typically problematizes the fiction and non-fiction texts that she reads to her pupils and the texts that they read themselves. This means that she encourages her pupils to consider the versions of reality that are presented in the texts and to construct other possible versions of reality, i.e. other possible types of mothers, fathers, boys, girls, foxes, pigs etc. So the children in Jennifer O'Brien's class, some of whom were not yet able to decode, were already beginning to question taken-for-granted or 'natural' representations of the world. They were asked to 'disrupt' the realities presented to them by doing such tasks as the following (Comber 2001: 94):

> Draw a witch like the one in the story.
> Draw a different witch.

> Draw the mean characters in the story.
> Draw different mean characters.

They similarly scrutinized non-fiction texts. For example, they examined junk mail and Mother's Day catalogues. Their teacher encouraged them to record and reflect on their reading through the following:

> Draw and label six presents for mothers you expect to see in Mother's Day catalogues.

> Draw and label some presents you wouldn't expect to find in Mother's Day catalogues.

> What groups of people get the most out of Mother's Day?

Having studied the catalogues they were asked to:

> Draw and label six kinds of presents you can find in Mother's Day catalogues.

> Make two lists: how the mothers in the catalogues are like real mothers; how the mothers in the catalogues aren't like real mothers.

> Make a new Mother's Day catalogue full of fun things.

These children were learning what the purpose of the junk mail was, that it was designed to sell products, and that this in turn influenced the way people and things were presented in those particular texts. They were learning that a text is constructed to represent a particular reality, one that may differ from their experience of the world, one that could be different.

An example from an upper primary context used gender as a vehicle for introducing pupils to the non-neutral nature of texts. An Australian primary teacher collaborated with a researcher, Ann Kempe (detailed in Kempe 2001), and together they devised a range of literacy teaching strategies to explore gender issues. They selected gender for two reasons – first because they reckoned it was an issue primary children can readily relate to and second, because gender is so often considered merely a peripheral issue in the curriculum rather than integrated into it.

They wanted pupils to compare and contrast texts in order to highlight them as crafted pieces. Hence they chose conventional and unconventional texts across a range of genres, from different periods of time and from different ideological perspectives. For example, they compared traditional and modern fairy tales. They compared unconventional and conventional texts to examine how this opens up multiple readings. They examined the roles and relationships given to girls and boys in reading scheme material. They rewrote stories from outdated readers. They constructed alternative endings in order to challenge dominant readings.

In addition, the pupils were encouraged to become aware of their own reading practices through such questions as (Kempe 2001: 45):

- What are you thinking about, or feeling while you are reading? How are those thoughts and feelings influenced by your background, your experiences with other texts you have read?
- What is the text asking you to think or feel? Do you agree with the point of view offered by the text? Why or why not?
- What events or points of view might have been left out of the text? Would you have left them out? Why or why not?

Such strategies assist learners begin to address the question 'Why are things the way they are?', and thus challenge the inequalities of the status quo.

Teachers in this country will be familiar with some of the new versions of old tales where the roles have been reconstructed to ones where the characters themselves are aware of their own social positioning. Excellent examples include *Snow White in New York* (French 1990) and *The True Story of the Three Little Pigs* (Scieszka 1999). These new versions help to expose how identities and roles are socially created. With particular reference to gender roles and identities, fairy tales became the focus of much feminist writing because of its perceived function of acculturating young girls into passive sexual and social roles (Cranny-Francis 1990, 1993). Writers such as Angela Carter and Tanith Lee created different versions of the tales, changing the female roles from ones where their only value was their physical appearance to one where they became active in determining their own fate. *The Bloody Chamber* by Angela Carter offers different versions of 'Bluebeard', 'Red Riding Hood' and 'Beauty and the Beast' while *Red as Blood or Tales from the Sisters Grimmer* retells 'Cinderella', 'Red Riding Hood' and 'The Pied Piper of Hamelin'. The purpose of all these retellings is not to replace the traditional tale but to expose their patriarchal, taken-for-granted assumptions and their particular constructions of femininity (Cranny-Francis 1993).

When should critical literacy start and what about the pleasure of reading?

Barbara Comber's response to the evidence on Stephen clearly testifies to her belief that he is capable of text analysis. Several times she talked about what the story meant to him, what he made of it, how he expected more at the end and so on. In her writings she also argues that children – far younger than Stephen – are capable of critical literacy practices. Her logic here is persuasive. She points to the amazing linguistic achievement of young children, how linguists and developmental psychologists have been fascinated by the way young children acquire not just one language, but often several languages. Therefore, it should not be surprising, she says, that young children can analyse texts critically:

> It is not cognitively, nor linguistically 'beyond them'; text analysis is a dimension of the practice, not an added layer. Just as we have held high expectations for all children to learn language, in the same way we need to credit them with the competence for understanding the specific effects of language use in specific sites.
>
> (Comber, in press)

Moreover, she argues that critical literacy is not 'a developmental milestone, nor an optional extra for gifted students'. Rather she sees it as a diversity of essential practices that can be learned while children are learning, say, the alphabetic code. She says: 'As they come to learn how texts work they can also investigate how texts work in the world.' Furthermore, even very young children are highly aware of fairness, justice and equity and their opposites. It is naïve, she suggests, to consider children as innocent and incapable or unaware of power in the world. They learn about power in everyday contexts and they learn to use language in the context of power relationships with families, peers etc. (Comber, in press).

Several scholars who were interviewed for this book wanted to know what Stephen thought reading was for. Learning what reading is for is an early acquisition and, although home is influential here, learning what reading is for is very much to do with school experience. This is how Barbara Comber puts the case for critical literacy in the early years of school:

> Early childhood is a crucial site of practice because it is during that period that children form initial relationships with schooling and formal learning; it is there where they are first constituted as learners and there where most children are first constituted as readers.

Some years ago, while making the case for critical literacy in the early years of school, I wondered about the extent to which a socio-political approach in the form of problematizing texts might take the joy out of learning (Hall 1998). How, for example, would text analysis of the kind outlined above interfere with children's enjoyment of a story? However, it seems that such fears are unfounded for the available evidence demonstrates that children enjoy sharing different readings of familiar stories, that they are in fact emotionally and intellectually engaged by critical questions that make them deconstruct and reconstruct texts in different ways. Such work connects with their interests not least because they are always motivated by issues of fairness and 'having a go'.

On the basis of her observational evidence of many teachers involving children in critical analysis of texts, Barbara Comber (in press) wrote: 'I have noticed a heightened sense of energy and pleasure [on the part of children].' When she was a class teacher, Barbara used to share and discuss with her pupils cartoons from newspapers, comics, birthday cards, and children's literature with a feminist stance. She used to collect irreverent post cards, jokes and so on and discuss with the class what it was that made these funny. In her experience young people showed a sophisticated understanding of the way language works to make a point (Comber, in press). As already noted above, the purpose of critical literacy is to help pupils understand how texts achieve their effects, not just to spot when a text is or is not politically correct. The work of feminist teacher Jennifer O'Brien (cited in Comber 2001) is especially interesting in this regard since she is careful not to train her pupils in political correctness. Her pupils are encouraged to examine all texts critically and she frequently invites her pupils to disrupt politically correct stories. She does this to emphasize the decision making involved in producing a text.

Funds of knowledge again: popular culture in the classroom

I have already said how socio-cultural and socio-political perspectives on literacy are closely connected. Indeed, the examples of practice discussed in Part Three, e.g. Kathy Au's work in Hawaii, fit equally well within a socio-political perspective. Much of this work emphasizes children's interests and their home and community resources – Moll's notion of 'funds of knowledge' being a good example.

Jackie Marsh talked about some children's and families' 'cultural capital' not being reflected in the curriculum and how her own work with families and classrooms is based on a recognition of the significance of the texts that 'are embedded within the children's daily lives'. For many children, she says, the use of popular culture in the classroom can be a valuable way of recognizing the cultural capital within their world. Jackie's reference to the importance of a child's self-esteem in learning urges teachers to see the social experience the child already possesses as valid and significant. David Wray similarly emphasized this – he talked about the need for school tasks to match 'the kinds of worlds that they mentally inhabit themselves'. These scholars' suggestion is that Stephen's social experience should be reflected back to him as being valid and significant. But it can only be reflected back to him if it is part of the texture of the learning experience created in his classroom.

Given how pervasive popular culture is in the lives of all children, its use in the classroom seems eminently sensible. Some popular texts, e.g. comics, attract greater numbers of boys than girls and greater numbers of working-class children than middle-class children, thus highlighting their potential to extend the literacy skills of groups in society that are often described as underachieving in literacy. Unfortunately teachers are often reluctant to incorporate popular media into the reading material of the classroom, seeing them as inferior and lacking in learning potential. Barbara Comber's reference in her research to the use of popular texts like postcards and newspapers and her comment in interview that 'early childhood is still dominated by picture book literacies' highlight the diversity of texts that are legitimate, but underused, sources in the critical literacy classroom.

Before developing this point further it is worth clarifying what we mean by popular culture. In their recently published book on the topic, Marsh and Millard (2000: 20) defined it as follows:

> Children's popular culture overlaps with that of adults in that the broad fields into which it can be categorized are similar: music, sport, computers and related merchandise, books, magazines, television and film. However, children's popular culture also incorporates such diverse artefacts as toys, games, comics, stickers, cards, clothing, hair accessories, jewellery, sports accessories, oral rhymes, jokes, word play and even food and drink.

So popular culture is not merely texts, it also includes artefacts. Moreover, all these texts and artefacts are often connected by common themes. Marsh and Thompson (2001) demonstrate this with reference to the intertextual world of Pokémon. They point out that children only need to have one feature of the world of Pokémon to participate in the narrative – a packet of Pokémon stickers, for example, will allow the owner to take part in the narrative even though they may not have seen the Pokémon television programme or played the Pokémon computer game. Popular culture's intertextuality and links with children's immediate interests probably explain its appeal to a wide range of ages and classes.

Jackie Marsh argues that children's motivation to engage with texts that connect with their popular cultural interests should be much more fully explored and exploited in the classroom. She outlined the value of comic reading in her discussion of Stephen while her research with Elaine Millard (Milland and Marsh 2001) on a home–school comic lending study showed how such material from popular culture drew in the support of fathers and older brothers in the reading practices of the younger members of the household. The use of popular media to enhance children's literacy skills appears to work because it involves drawing on learners' values, passions and identifications – ones that emerge in home and community life. Jackie likened Stephen to a child described by Deborah Hicks (2001), a boy who became increasingly distanced from school literacy because he saw little or no connection between the literacy practices valued by the school and the things and ways of being he most valued at home.

Apart from the advantages of building generally on out-of-school literacy experiences and resources and of involving family members not traditionally associated with supporting younger family members' literacy development, the use of popular culture to enhance literacy has very specific merits. For example, television and film provide opportunities to enhance understanding of narrative structures while watching and rewatching videos fosters familiarity with the language of books (Marsh and Thompson 2001).

Mary Hilton also emphasized this point in discussing how children increasingly acquire understanding of inference via televisual texts and do not depend solely on print texts for this skill. What these literacy scholars are recommending here is that teachers recognize what print and televisual texts have in common, i.e. both involve meaning making as a central process. And they advocate that classroom practices build on children's already quite sophisticated understanding of televisual texts to promote a wider range of literacy skills.

Critical literacy includes critical media literacy. The latter is about creating communities of active readers and writers who can be expected to exercise some degree of agency in deciding what textual positions they will assume or resist as they interact in complex social and cultural contexts (Alvermann *et al.* 1999). In line with the accounts offered in Comber and Kempe above in relation to fiction and non-fiction texts, Anne Haas Dyson (1997) studied a primary classroom where the teacher encouraged children's knowledge of popular superheroes as contexts for literacy development. In this class, one group of girls responded to the boys' dominance of superhero play by writing new scripts that placed girls in powerful positions. Another primary teacher guided students to compare their perceptions of male and female superhero attributes, discuss reasons for those differences, and identify ways of changing those differences.

Jackie Marsh's study (2000) in an inner-city, north of England classroom of mainly working-class children, most of whom had English as an additional language, provides a fascinating account of the superhero play of 6- and 7-year-olds. In this project Jackie set up a socio-dramatic role-play area in the classroom – 'the Batman and Batwoman HQ'. The aim of her project was to encourage literacy practices in the role-play area and so in collaboration with the teachers a variety of literacy resources were placed within it. She then recorded the children's play in the area. This is how she describes the 'Bat cave' that was set up and the guidance that was given to the children:

The 'Bat cave' shared a space between two classes in an open-plan base. It was a small area, constructed from drapes and screens in order to produce a cavern-like effect . . . The cave contained two desks, a computer, writing materials (notepads, pens, pencils, lined and unlined paper, two blank books labelled 'Batman's Diary' and 'Batwoman's Diary') and reading materials (maps, comics, messages, instructions). There was a dressing-up rack which contained homemade tabards, commercially produced Batman outfits, a cloak and a hat. Part of the way through the project a cardboard 'Batmobile' (the car used by Batman), which was made by the children, was placed in the cave. The children had contributed to the setting up of the cave, suggesting a range of resources for it and throughout the project they continued to produce new items to place in it (e.g. maps, radios).

When the cave was finally ready for its first superheroes, the children spent some time discussing the possibilities it offered. All the resources in the cave were introduced to them and suggestions were made by children, researcher and teachers as to their possible uses . . . Before taking part in the role-play, the children spent some time discussing the Batman character and the types of activity engaged in by the characters in the television programmes and films they had seen. Extracts from a Batman film were watched and discussed. This was important in order to ensure that all children could engage with the discourse when playing in the cave. The 'Bat cave' was firmly introduced to the children as a place where both boys and girls could take on superhero identities and the sexist nature of some of the video extracts seen was discussed by the children. The children were clear that girls could be Batwoman. Throughout the project, the children were introduced to selected images and texts which portrayed women in an active role . . . Apart from this prior groundwork, the children were given no specific instructions about what to do in the cave as it was a place for child-directed play.

Once attired in Batman or Batwoman regalia, all the children either engaged in imaginative play or sat down to write and read in role. Jackie discovered that, given the opportunity and the permission, girls engage in superhero play. They were eager to be superheroes, they resisted passive, onlooker roles. She noted 'The data contain images of girls flying about, jumping off chairs, driving Batmobiles and capturing villains' (2000: 22). She also concluded that for children to feel secure in taking on and experimenting with alternative roles and to challenge stereotypes, teachers need to intervene to create the conditions in which this can happen. This could involve explicit adult modelling for helping children play with given stories and characters.

The publications of the scholars who were interviewed for this part of the book offer teachers strategies for such pedagogical work. Also Zipes'

(1995) *Creative Storytelling* provides suggestions for the critical use of stories. Drawing on the work of Anne Haas Dyson (1998) we can conclude that the children in the classrooms described in this section are being offered opportunities to imagine new possibilities and new identities for themselves and each other as girls and boys, as children of different socio-economic and heritage backgrounds, and of varied bodily strengths.

Whatever teachers' responses, it is likely that media characters will remain a powerful influence on children's imaginative and social lives. Such characters are sustained, argues Dyson (1998), by 'powerful social desires, most especially the desire to belong'. By orchestrating children's diverse desires, teachers can make opportunities for not only developing reading and writing skills, but also for developing children's sense of what they can be and become. As Jackie Marsh's account above shows, teachers can also develop a sense of their own pedagogical power and the transformations they can inspire.

Influence of the socio-political perspective

A socio-political stance sees literacy not as neutral but as bound up with ethnicity, gender, social class, disability and so on. Its purpose is social justice, equality and democracy. It accepts that literacy is ideological so it involves decoding the ideological aspects of texts to establish whose interests are being served.

The history, emergence, and rationale of the National Literacy Strategy together with the highly prescriptive nature of its content and pedagogy (see Hall 2001 for a discussion) would suggest that it would be difficult to incorporate critical literacy practices into the curriculum and still remain true to its spirit. Drawing on the ideas of Bernstein, Jackie Marsh made the point in interview that when the curriculum is strongly classified in terms of content and strongly framed in terms of its delivery, as the NLS is, then opportunities for bringing in out-of-school literacy practices is more difficult. However, even if it does not explicitly encourage the kind of practices described above, it does not preclude them either. The emphasis throughout the Strategy on 'text-level work' and on developing children's interest (as well as skills) in reading suggests the potential for critical text analysis in a way that also includes popular media. Jackie discussed this in interview and talked about teachers who managed to blend popular culture into the requirements of the Strategy. In addition, to the extent that the kind of pedagogy advocated by those adopting a socio-political perspective on literacy encourages explicitness and is not opposed to direct instruction, showing, and strong teacher intervention, it is not inconsistent with the pedagogy of the NLS.

In my view critically aware and conscientious teachers are not likely to ignore the perspectives discussed in this and previous parts of the book.

But they do need support and this needs to occur at the level of pre-service and in-service teacher education. Bearing in mind that critical literacy, in particular, is a relatively recent phenomenon in the primary pedagogical literature, it is not surprising that we do not yet have very many indications that its practice is widespread.

Countries outside the UK, however, have overtly embraced socio-political perspectives into their literacy frameworks. For example, versions of critical literacy are incorporated into the literacy syllabuses in most states in Australia. Alan Luke's four resources model, described above, has been adopted for use in the largest state in the country, New South Wales. In interview and in her research with Alan Luke and others (Luke *et al.* 1999) Barbara Comber expresses concern about the current shift in policy in Australia along more conservative lines. She suggests that official endorsement of critical literacy may not, unfortunately, be guaranteed in the future.

CONCLUSION

I will conclude by considering briefly some implications of the variety of reading perspectives discussed in the book. What the book demonstrates is that reading or literacy is not a simple matter; it is complex and multi-dimensional. Teaching reading is not a simple task and any teacher who thinks that any one model, scheme or programme will simplify this task or will suit all learners is grossly naïve. And even where there is a national framework in operation, such as the National Literacy Strategy, it remains the case that different teachers in different classrooms will mediate this in different ways and different children within the same teacher's classroom may well have very different experiences of what it is to 'do literacy'. Moreover, mandated programmes, no matter what their format, should not and, in some respects, cannot replace (even if they can constrain) the teacher's professional prerogative and intellectual freedom. Teachers need to be able to draw on research-based perspectives and ideas in order to make judicious choices about the particular teaching methods that suit their pupils. This is not to deny the importance of standards against which pupils can be judged at various stages in their schooling.

One explanation for the complexity of reading is the difficulty in re-sponding to the diverse needs of learners in the classroom. This is why it is futile to search for a single right method for literacy development. This book is based on the premise that we should search for 'multiple perspect-ives', guided by the diverse needs of learners.

All eight scholars emphasized the need for Stephen to get better at decod-ing and comprehending text; all of them referred to the importance of the purpose of reading for Stephen; all referred, albeit somewhat differently, to the social context of Stephen's literacy learning. The expert participants in this study all advocated the following: the integration of reading and other language modes; the provision of lifelike contexts and real purposes for reading; the building up of confidence and positive expectations about what literacy can do for his life; and the use of a variety of texts – not just fiction or picture books – so he develops an awareness of different functions of reading. They advocated the explicit teaching of skills within a context of their application for meaningful purposes. They also advocated shifting the focus from oral reading and reading as a performance – with all the stress that that entails for a struggling reader like Stephen – to silent reading and the application of what is read.

I think the term 'principled eclecticism' (Stahl 1997) is applicable to all our scholars in that they described and justified their interpretation of Stephen's literacy needs with reference to evidence and theory. They drew on more than one perspective and advocated the use of more than one instructional approach for the development of Stephen's literacy competence. It is clear that no one teaching approach is 'best'. Reading is not decoding, yet decoding is an integral part of reading and children need to master decoding as part of learning to read. Moreover, some direct teaching is necessary to learn about the different orthographic patterns of the English language. But that's a narrow notion of what literacy is. Adopting a broader notion of reading requires teachers to use a broader range of teaching strategies from direct explanation and explicit teaching which involve high control on the part of the teacher to modelling, scaffolding, facilitating, guided participating, and participating which involves decreasing control by the teacher and increased activity on the part of the learner.

However, there were significant differences in how different scholars emphasized aspects of reading. For example, one could argue that Laura Huxford's analysis of Stephen's needs would suggest that her cognitive-psychological take on reading is one that sees reading as value-free, autonomous and very much about skills. There is the assumption that literacy is a neutral technology that can be applied to different literacy demands in everyday life. On the other hand Laura also drew heavily on psycho-linguistic themes emphasizing Stephen's personal response and expression.

For several other scholars, e.g. Jackie Marsh, Henrietta Dombey and Barbara Comber, 'how' skills are to be learned is what is significant. In other words, the question for them is 'What's going on around literacy?' They operate on the assumption that what is important is that children are learning how to participate in the social activities of their classroom – they form a community of learners. What teachers and children do together is what is important. The quality of the interaction is vital since children are assumed to learn far more than they are taught. Their notion of reading is bound up with the context in which text interactions occur and they are concerned with ways of making meaning with and around texts. Reading for them cannot be separated from writing, listening and speaking or from motivations, purposes, attitudes and ways of acting and interacting.

Socio-cultural and socio-political perspectives on literacy see the acquisition of school literacy practice (or any school practice) as inseparable from learners' motivations to identify with that practice. Both these perspectives hold to the principle that learners must see for themselves the value in what they are being asked to learn. They must believe it is useful to their lives. Young children are not learning to read but they are getting enculturated into a range of literacy practices, where each one is linked to specific forms of language, specific activities and specific identities (Gee 1999b). And as James Gee reminds us, one can easily fail in school by getting any or all of language, activity, and identity 'wrong'. It is for this reason that it is dangerous to assume that by attending to just one, albeit important, aspect of literacy (say phonemic awareness) one can overcome a particular child's literacy difficulties. Knowing literacy or becoming a reader is a matter of being able to participate in a community of literacy practitioners and being able to use the tools and technologies characteristic of that particular community. And learning is a matter of changing and acquiring new patterns of participation with corresponding changes in identity (Barton and Hamilton 2000).

In my view Luke's model (2000) is extremely helpful and provides an excellent summary of all the elements that need to be part of a literacy curriculum. As already noted, he talks about children as

1 *Code breakers* (How do I crack this code?).
2 *Meaning makers* (How do the ideas represented in the text string together?).
3 *Text users* (What do I do with this text, here and now?).
4 *Text critics* (What is this text trying to do to me?).

But what is important is that children do not begin with code breaking and move in a linear way through the four, only becoming a text critic once decoding, comprehension and application have been established. All four aspects are relevant and essential from the beginning of a child's literacy learning – although different ones will be differently emphasized in various lessons and all four can be developed using a range of teaching methods. In my view this model offers an excellent framework for evaluating the emphases of current classroom literacy curricula as well as current policy nationally.

But what use are the various perspectives presented in this book? What is one to do with them? I think their value lies in the fact that while different perspectives can be described as though they are fixed, they can be used – indeed have to be used – as though they are not fixed. The point is that one cannot urge that a particular perspective be followed faithfully in all situations for all learners all of the time. If one were to do this, then the message to professional literacy educators is that power lies with the perspective, not with the teacher (Duffy 1997). Teachers would be expected to abdicate to the perspective, the programme or the model.

In my view the four major perspectives on offer here are valuable because they invite literacy educators to develop their own literacy stance, combining and adapting principles from different literacy positions. Teachers so informed are likely to demonstrate an enlightened or principled eclecticism in their own teaching practices (Duffy 1997). Such teachers are likely to be in control of the models of literacy they apply and are less likely to be controlled by any single version of literacy.

A knowledge of perspectives highlights the fact that it is futile to search for a solution to a fixed problem but, instead, what teachers have to do on a daily basis is design teaching and learning environments that fit the needs of specific children. They have to begin with children, not methods or resources or programmes. But what is inescapable is that how they interpret a given child's needs, how they define and address those needs, is profoundly shot through with ideas about learning, literacy, children, childhood, appropriate ways of behaving and interacting and so on. The extent to which they themselves are aware of this is a measure of their professionalism and sophistication as professionals, and the various reading perspectives analysed in this book attempt to raise that awareness.

There was agreement across the scholars on one point and that is the idea that learners have to understand and believe that reading is important for them in the here and now of their lives. The way they are taught conveys powerful messages to children about the types of learners they are assumed to be, and children tend to accept these judgements unquestioningly. Similarly, the way they are taught reading conveys to them powerful messages about what reading is and what it is good for. Barbara Comber poses an insightful question for class teachers and to me this is a useful thought on which to end. She asks 'If you only knew about literacy from being in this classroom what would you think it was for?'

APPENDIX

Bear by Mick Inkpen, published by Hodder, 1997
A small whoosing sound.
Then a plop!
A bounce.
And a kind of squeak.
That was how the bear landed in my baby sister's playpen.

Have you ever had a bear fall out of the sky, right in front of you?
At first I thought he was a teddy bear.
He just lay there, crumpled on the quilt.
Then he got up and took Sophie's drink.
And her biscuit.
That's when I knew he was real.

The bear climbed out of the playpen and looked at me.
He rolled on his back, lifted his paws and growled.
He seemed to want to play.

I put him in Sophie's baby bouncer.
He was very good at bouncing, much better than Sophie.

I sneaked the bear into the house under the quilt. At bedtime I hid him
among my toys.
'Don't you say anything Sophie!' I said. 'I want to keep this bear.'
Sophie doesn't say much anyway. She isn't even two yet.

In the morning the sound of shouting woke me up.
'Sophie, that's naughty!' It was Mum.
She was looking at the feathers.
'Sophie! That's very naughty!'
She was looking at the scribble.
Then she looked at the potty.

'Sophie!' she said. 'Good girl!'
But I don't think it was Sophie.
I'm sure it wasn't Sophie.
It definitely wasn't Sophie.

I took the bear to school in my rucksack.
Everyone wanted to be my friend.
'Does he bite?' they said.
'He doesn't bite me,' I said.
'What's his name?' they said.
'He doesn't have one.'

We kept him quiet all day feeding him our lunches. He liked the peanut
butter sandwiches best.

After school my friends came to the house.
'Where is he?' they said.
We played with the bear behind the garage.
We made a tunnel . . . a bridge . . . and a jump!
When the car came back the bear had gone. We looked and looked but
there was no bear anywhere.

At bedtime Sophie wouldn't go to sleep.
She didn't want her elephant.
She didn't want her rabbit.
She threw them out of the cot.
I gave her my second best pig.
She threw it out.
'Sophie! That's naughty!', said Mum.
But Sophie just howled.
She wanted the bear.

CRASH! BANG!
It was the middle of the night.
SMASH! CLANG!

The noise was coming from the kitchen. We crept downstairs and peeped
through the door.

It wasn't a burglar.
'Bear! said Sophie. 'Naughty!'
So today a serious man in a serious hat came to look at our bear. He wrote
something in a big black book.
'Will you have to take him away?' I said.
'We nearly always do,' said the man.
He pointed his pen at my bear.
'But,' he said, 'this bear is an Exception.'
'This bear,' he went on, 'has fallen quite unexpectedly into a storybook.
And it is not up to me to say what should happen next.'
'So can we keep him?'
I said.

'Ask them,' he said.
And he pointed straight out of the picture at YOU!

And you thought for a moment.
You looked at the man.
You looked at the bear.
You looked at Sophie.
You looked at me.

And then you said . . .

'YES YOU CAN!'

So we did.

Have you ever had a bear fall out of the sky right in front of you?

REFERENCES

Adams, M.J. (1990) *Beginning to Read: Thinking and Learning about Print.* Cambridge, MA: MIT Press.

Adams, M.J., Foorman, B.R., Lundberg, I. and Beeler, T. (1998) *Phonemic Awareness in Young Children: A Classroom Curriculum.* Baltimore, MD: Brookes.

Allington, R. (1980) Poor readers don't get to read much in reading groups, *Language Arts*, 57: 872–7.

Allington, R.L. (1983) The reading instruction provided readers of differing abilities, *Elementary School Journal*, 85(5): 548–59.

Alvermann, D.E., Moon, J.S. and Hagood, M.C. (1999) *Popular Culture in the Classroom: Teaching and Researching Critical Media Literacy.* Newark, DE: International Reading Association.

Arnold, H. (1982) *Listening to Children Reading.* London: Hodder and Stoughton.

Au, K. (1980) Participation structures in a reading lesson with Hawaiian children: analysis of a culturally-appropriate instructional event, *Anthropology and Education Quarterly*, 11(2): 91–115.

Au, K. (1992) Constructing the theme of a story, *Language Arts*, 69(2): 106–11.

Au, K. (1993) *Literacy Instruction in Multicultural Settings.* Fort Worth, TX: Harcourt Brace.

Au, K. (1997) A sociocultural model of reading instruction: the Kamehameha Elementary Education Program, in S.A. Stahl, *Instructional Models in Reading*, pp. 181–202. Hillsdale, NJ: Erlbaum.

Au, K., Carroll, J.H. and Scheu, J.A. (1997) *Balanced Literacy Instruction: A Teacher's Resource Book.* Norwood, MA: Christopher Gordon.

Baker, C. and Freebody, P. (2001) The crediting of literate competence in classroom talk, in H. Fehring and P. Green (eds) *Critical Literacy: A Collection of Articles from the Australian Literacy Educators' Association*, pp. 58–74. Newark, DE: International Reading Association.

Baker, C. and Luke, A. (eds) (1991) *Towards a Critical Sociology of Reading Pedagogy*. Amsterdam: John Benjamins Publishing Company.

Barnes, D. (1981) Language across the curriculum, *Use of English*, Autumn: 3–14.

Barnes, D., Britton, J. and Rosen, H. (1972) *Language, the Learner and the School*. Middlesex: Penguin.

Barrs, M., Ellis, S., Hester, H. and Thomas, A. (1988) *The Primary Language Record*. London: Centre for Language in Primary Education (CLPE).

Barton, D. and Hamilton, M. (eds) (2000) *Situated Literacies: Reading and Writing in Context*. London: Routledge.

Bergeron, B.S. (1990) What does the term whole language mean? Constructing a definition from the literature, *Journal of Reading Behavior*, 22: 301–29.

Blachman, B.A. (2000) Phonological awareness, in M.L. Kamil, P.B. Mosenthal, P.D. Pearson and R. Barr (eds) *Handbook of Research*, Vol. 3, pp. 483–502. Hillsdale, NJ: Erlbaum.

Black, W. and Paulson, E. (2000) Research implications of retrospective miscue analysis: struggling readers revaluing themselves and their reading. Paper presented at the National Reading Conference, Scottsdale, December.

Bloome, D. (1993) Necessary indeterminacy and the microethnographic study of reading as a social practice, *Journal of Research in Reading*, 16(2): 98–111.

Bloome, D. and Dail, A.R.K. (1997) Toward (re)defining miscue analysis: reading as a social and cultural process, *Language Arts*, 74(8): 610–17.

Britton, J. (1972) *Language and Learning*. Middlesex: Penguin.

Browne, A. (1993) *Helping Children to Write*. London: Sage.

Browne, A. (1996) *Developing Language and Literacy 3–8*. London: Sage.

Browne, A. (1998) *A Practical Guide to Teaching Reading in the Early Years*. London: Sage.

Browne, A. (1999) *Teaching Writing at Key Stage 1 and Before*. London: Nelson Thornes.

Bruner, J. (1996) *The Culture of Education*. Cambridge, MA: Harvard University Press.

Bussis, A., Chittenden, F., Amarel, M. and Klausner, E. (1985) *Inquiry into Meaning: An Investigation of Learning to Read*. Hillsdale, NJ: Erlbaum.

Calkins, L. (1986) *The Art of Teaching Writing*. Portsmouth: Heinemann.

Calkins, L. (1991) Mini-lessons: an overview, and tools to help teachers create their own mini-lessons, in B.M. Power and R. Hubbard (eds) *Literacy in Process*, pp. 149–73. Portsmouth, NH: Heinemann.

Campbell, R. (1990) *Reading Together*. Buckingham: Open University Press.

Campbell, R. (1993) *Miscue Analysis in the Classroom*. Widnes: United Kingdom Reading Association.

Cattell, I. (1886) The time it takes to see and name objects, *Mind*, 11: 63–5.

Cazden, C.B. (1992) *Whole Language Plus: Essays on Literacy in the United States and New Zealand*. New York, NY: Teachers' College Press.

Chall, J. (1992) Whole language and direct instruction models: implications for teaching reading in the schools. Paper presented at the International Reading Association's Annual Convention Orlando, Florida, May.

Chall, J.S. (1983) *Learning to Read: The Great Debate*. New York, NY: McGraw Hill.

Chall, J.S., Jacobs, V. and Baldwin, L. (1990) *The Reading Crisis: Why Poor Children Fall Behind.* Cambridge, MA: Harvard University Press.

Chomsky, N. (1965) *Aspects of the Theory of Syntax.* Cambridge, MA: MIT Press.

Clay, M. (1972) *Reading: The Patterning of Complex Behaviour.* Auckland: Heinemann.

Clay, M. (1979) *Reading: The Patterning of Complex Behaviour.* Auckland, NZ: Heinemann.

Clay, M. (1985) *The Early Detection Reading Difficulties*, 3rd edn. Auckland, NZ: Heinemann.

Clay, M. (1989) *The Early Detection of Reading Difficulties*, 3rd edn. Hong Kong: Heinemann.

Clay, M. (2001) *Change Over Time in Children's Literacy Development.* Auckland: Heinemann.

Cole, M. (1990) Cognitive development and formal schooling, in L. Moll (ed.) *Vygotsky and Education*, pp. 89–110. New York, NY: Cambridge University Press.

Comber, B. (1999) *'IT's Got Power In It': Critical Literacies and Information Technologies in Primary Schools.* Language and Literacy Research Centre, School of Education, University of South Australia.

Comber, B. (2001) Classroom explorations in critical literacy, in H. Fehring and P. Green (eds) *Critical Literacy: A Collection of Articles from the Australian Literacy Educators' Association*, pp. 90–102. Newark, DE: International Reading Association.

Comber, B. (in press) Critical literacy: power and pleasure with language in the early years, *Australian Journal of Language and Literacy*.

Comber, B., Thomson, P., with Wells, M. (2001) Critical literacy finds a 'place': writing and social action in a neighborhood school, *Elementary School Journal*, 101(4): 451–64.

Cope, B. and Kalantzis, M. (eds) (2000) *Multiliteracies: Literary Learning and the Design of Social Futures.* London: Routledge.

Corden, R. (2000) *Literacy and Learning through Talk.* Buckingham: Open University Press.

Cranny-Francis, A. (1990) *Feminist Fiction: Feminist Uses of Generic Fiction.* Cambridge: Polity Press.

Cranny-Francis, A. (1993) Gender and genre: feminist subversion of genre fiction and its implications for critical literacy, in Bill Cope and Mary Kalantzis (eds) *The Power of Literacy: A Genre Approach to Teaching Writing*, pp. 90–115. London: Falmer Press.

Cunningham, J.W. (2001) The National Reading Panel Report, *Reading Research Quarterly*, 36(3): 326–37.

Cunningham, P.M. and Cunningham, J.W. (1992) Making words: enhancing the invented spelling–decoding connection, *The Reading Teacher*, 46(2): 106–15.

Delpit, L. (1995) *Other People's Children: Cultural Conflict in the Classroom.* New York, NY: The New Press.

DES (1975) *A Language for Life: Report of the Committee of Inquiry appointed by the Secretary of State for Education and Science under the Chairmanship of Sir Alan Bullock (Bullock Report).* London: HMSO.

DES (1982) *Education 5–9: An Illustrative Survey of 80 First Schools.* London: HMSO.

DES (1988) *Report of the Committee of Inquiry into the Teaching of English (Kingman Report)*. London: HMSO.

DES (1989) *A Report of the Committee of Inquiry into the Teaching of English (Cox Report)*. London: HMSO.

DES (1990) *English in the National Curriculum*. London: HMSO.

DfE (1995) *English in the National Curriculum*. London: HMSO.

DfEE (1998) *The National Literacy Strategy: A Framework for Teaching*. London: HMSO.

DfES (Department for Education and Skills) (2001) *The National Literacy Strategy: Progression in Phonics: Materials for Whole-Class Teaching*. London: The Stationery Office.

Dombey, H. (1998a) Changing literacy in the early years of school, in B. Cox (ed.) *Literacy is Not Enough: Essays on the Importance of Literacy*, pp. 125–32. Manchester: Manchester University Press.

Dombey, H. (1998b) A totalitarian approach to literacy education, *Forum*, 40(2): 36–41.

Dombey, H., Moustafa, M., Barrs, M. *et al.* (1998) *W(hōle) to Part Phŏn'ĭcs: How Children Learn to Read and Spell*. London: Centre for Language in Primary Education.

Duffy, G.G. (1997) Powerful models or powerful teachers? An argument for teacher – as – entrepreneur in S.A. Stahl and D.A. Hayes (eds) *Instructional Models in Reading*. New Jersey: Lawrence Erlbaum.

Duffy, G.G., Rochler, L.R. and Herrman, B.A. (1998) Modeling mental processes helps poor readers become strategic readers, *The Reading Teacher*, 4(8): 762–7.

Duke, N.K. (2000) For the rich it's richer: print experiences and environments offered to children in very low and very high-socioeconomic status first-grade classrooms, *American Educational Research Journal*, 37(2): 441–78.

Dyson, A.H. (1997) *Writing Superheroes: Contemporary Childhood, Popular Culture, and Classroom Literacy*. New York, NY: Teachers College Press.

Dyson, A.H. (1998) Folk processes and media creatures: reflections on popular culture for literacy educators, *The Reading Teacher*, 51(5): 392–402.

Dyson, A.H. (2000) Linking writing and community development through the Children's Forum, in C.D. Lee and P. Smagorinsky (eds) *Vygotskian Perspectives on Literacy Research*, pp. 127–49. Cambridge: CUP.

Ehri, L., Deffner, N. and Wilce, L. (1984) Pictorial mnemonics for phonics, *Journal of Educational Psychology*, 76: 880–93.

Ehri, L.C. (1987) Learning to read and spell words, *Journal of Reading Behavior*, 19: 5–31.

Ehri, L.C. (1991) Development of the ability to read words, in R. Barr, M. Kamil, P. Mosenthal and D. Pearson (eds) *Handbook of Reading Research*, Vol. 2, pp. 383–417. New York, NY: Longman.

Ehri, L.C. (1995) Phases of development in learning to read words by sight, *Journal of Research in Reading*, 18(2): 116–25.

Ehri, L.C. (1999) Phases of development in learning to read words, in J. Oakhill and R. Beard (eds) *Reading Development and the Teaching of Reading*, pp. 79–108. London: Blackwell.

Ehri, L.C. and Wilce, L.S. (1987) Cipher versus cue reading: an experiment in decoding acquisition, *Journal of Educational Psychology*, 79: 3–13.

Ehri, L.C., Nunes, S.R., Willows, D.M. *et al.* (2001) Phonemic awareness instruction helps children learn to read: evidence from the National Reading Panel's meta-analysis, *Reading Research Quarterly*, 36(3): 250–87.

Florio-Ruane, S. (1994) The future of teachers' autobiography clubs: preparing educators to support literacy learning in culturally diverse classrooms, *English Education*, 26: 52–66.

Fox, M. (2001) *Reading Magic.* Sydney: Pan Macmillan.

Freebody, P. and Freiberg, J. (2001) Re-discovering practical reading activities in homes and schools, *Journal of Research in Reading*, 24(3): 222–34.

Freire, P. and Macedo, D. (1987) *Literacy.* South Hadley, MA: Bergin and Garvey.

French, F. (1990) *Snow White in New York.* Oxford: Oxford University Press.

Frith, U. (1985) Developmental dyslexia, in K.E. Patterson *et al.* (eds) *Surface Dyslexia.* Hove: Erlbaum.

Gaskins, I., Downer, M. and Gaskins, R. (1986) *Introduction to the Benchmark School Word Identification/Vocabulary Development Program.* Media, PA: Benchmark School.

Gaskins, I.W., Ehri, L.C., Cress, C., O'Hara, C. and Donnelly, K. (1996/97) Procedures for word learning: making discoveries about words, *The Reading Teacher*, 50: 312–27.

Gaskins, R.W. and Gaskins, I.W. (1997) Creating readers who read for meaning and love to read: the Benchmark School Reading Program, in S.A. Stahl, *Instructional Models in Reading*, pp. 131–59. Mahwah, NJ: Erlbaum.

Gee, J.P. (1999a) *An Introduction to Discourse Analysis: Theory and Method.* London: Routledge.

Gee, J.P. (1999b) Critical issues: reading and the new literacy studies. Reframing the national academy of sciences report on reading, *Journal of Literacy Research*, 31(3): 355–74.

Geekie, P., Cambourne, B. and Fitzsimmons, P. (1999) *Understanding Literacy Development.* Stoke on Trent: Trentham Books.

Gillborn, D. and Gipps, C. (1996) *Recent Research on the Achievements of Ethnic Minority Pupils.* London: HMSO.

Gillborn, D. and Youdell, D. (2000) *Rationing Education.* Buckingham: Open University Press.

Goldsworthy, C.L. (2001) *Sourcebook for Phonological Awareness Activities.* San Diego, CA: Singular Publishing.

Goodman, K. (ed.) (1973) *Miscue Analysis: Applications to Reading Instruction.* Urbana, IL: ERIC/NCTE.

Goodman, K. (1989) Whole language research: foundations and development, *Elementary School Journal*, 90: 207–21.

Goodman, K. (1992) Whole language and direct instruction models: implications for teaching reading in the schools. Paper presented at the International Reading Association's Annual Convention Orlando, Florida, November.

Goodman, K. and Goodman, Y. (1977) Learning about psycholinguistic processes by analyzing oral reading, *Harvard Educational Review*, 40: 317–33.

Goodman, K.S. (1967) Reading: a psycholinguistic guessing game, *Journal of the Reading Specialist*, 4: 126–35.

Goodman, K.S. (1973) Psycholinguistic universals in the reading process, in Frank Smith (ed.) *Psycholinguistics and Reading.* New York, NY: Holt, Rinehart and Winston.

Goodman, K.S. (1986) *What's Whole in Whole Language?* London: Scholastic.

Goodman, K.S. (1992) Why whole language is today's agenda in education, *Language Arts*, 69: 354–63.

Goodman, K.S. and Goodman, Y.M. (1979) Learning to read is natural, in L.B. Resnick and P.A. Weaver (eds) *Theory and Practice of Early Reading*, Vol. 1, pp. 137–54. Hillsdale, NJ: Erlbaum.

Goodman, Y. (1989) Roots of the whole language movement, *Elementary School Journal*, 90: 113–27.

Goodman, Y. (1998) Listening to Erica read: perceptions and analyses of a reader from multiple perspectives. Symposium at the National Reading Conference, Austin, Texas, November.

Goodman, Y.M. (1980) The roots of literacy, in M.P. Douglas (ed.) *Claremont Reading Conference Forty-Fourth Yearbook* (1–32). Claremont, CA: Claremont Reading Conference.

Goodman, Y.M., Watson, D.J. and Burke, C.L. (1987) *Reading Miscue Inventory Alternative Procedures.* New York, NY: Richard Owens Publishers.

Goswami, U. (1986) Children's use of analogy in learning to read: a developmental study, *Journal of Experimental Child Psychology*, 42: 73–83.

Goswami, U. (1992) *Analogical Reasoning in Children.* Hillsdale, NJ: Erlbaum.

Goswami, U. (2000) Phonological and lexical processes, in M.L. Kamil, P.B. Mosenthal, P.D. Pearson, and R. Barr (eds) *Handbook of Research*, Vol. 3, pp. 251–67. Hillsdale, NJ: Erlbaum.

Goswami, U. and Bryant, P. (1990) *Phonological Skills and Learning to Read.* Hillsdale, NJ: Erlbaum.

Gough, P.B. and Hillinger, M.L. (1980) Learning to read: an unnatural act, *Bulletin of the Orton Society*, 30: 179–96.

Gough, P.B. and Juel, C. (1991) The first stages of word recognition, in L. Rieben and C. Perfetti (eds) *Learning to Read: Basic Research and its Implications*, pp. 47–56. Hillsdale, NJ: Erlbaum.

Grainger, T. (1997) *Traditional Storytelling in the Primary Classroom.* Leamington Spa: Scholastic.

Grainger, T. and Cremin, M. (2001a) *Resourcing Drama 5–8.* London: NATE.

Grainger, T. and Cremin, M. (2001b) *Resourcing Drama 8–14.* London: NATE.

Grainger, T. and Tod, J. (2000) *Inclusive Educational Practice: Literacy.* London: David Fulton.

Graves, D. (1983) *Writers: Teachers and Children at Work.* Porstmouth, NH: Heinemann.

Graves, D.H. and Hansen, J. (1983) The author's chair *Language Arts*, 60: 176–83.

Green, P. (2001) Critical literacy revisited, in H. Fehring and P. Green (eds) *Critical Literacy: A Collection of Articles from the Australian Literacy Educators' Association*, pp. 7–14. Delaware: International Reading Association.

Gregory, E. (1998) Siblings as mediators of literacy in linguistic minority communities, *Language and Education*, 1(12): 33–55.

Gregory, E. and Williams, A. (2000) *City Literacies: Learning to Read across Generations and Cultures.* London: Routledge.

Gunderson, L. (1997) Whole-language approaches to reading and writing, in S.A. Stahl and D.A. Hayes (eds) *Instructional Models in Reading*, pp. 221–47. Hillsdale, NJ: Erlbaum.

Guthrie, J.T., Wigfield, A. and Von Secker, C. (2000) Effects of integrated instruction on motivation and strategy use in reading, *Journal of Educational Psychology*, 92: 331–41.

Hall, K. (1998) Critical literacy and the case for it in the early years of school, *Language, Culture and Curriculum*, 11(2): 183–94.

Hall, K. (2001) An analysis of primary literacy policy in England using Barthes' notion of 'readerly' and 'writerly' texts, *Journal of Early Childhood Literacy*, 1(2): 153–65.

Hall, K. (2002) Co-constructing subjectivities and knowledge in literacy class: an ethnographic-sociocultural perspective, *Language and Education*, 16(3).

Hannon, P. (1995) *Literacy Home and School: Research and Practice in Teaching Literacy with Parents*. London: Falmer Press.

Harrison, C. (1992) The reading process and learning to read: what a teacher using 'real books' needs to know, in C. Harrison and M. Coles (eds) *The Reading for Real Handbook*, pp. 3–28. London: Routledge.

Harste, J. and Short, K. (1991) Literature circles and literature response activities, in B.M. Power and R. Hubbard (eds) *Literacy in Process*, pp. 191–202. Portsmouth, NH: Heinemann.

Harste, J.C. (1989) The future of whole language, *Elementary School Journal*, 90(2): 243–9.

Heath, S.B. (1983) *Ways with Words*. Cambridge: CUP.

Herrmann, B.A. (1988) Two approaches for helping poor readers become more strategic, *The Reading Teacher*, October: 24–8.

Hicks, D. (2001) Literacies and masculinities in the life of a young working-class boy, *Language Arts*, 78(3): 217–26.

Hiebert, E. and Raphael, T. (1998) Psychological perspectives on literacy and extensions to educational practice, in D. Berliner and R. Calfree (eds) *Handbook of Educational Psychology*, Vol. 1, pp. 550–602. New York, NY: Macmillan.

Hiebert, E.H. (1994) Becoming literate through authentic tasks: evidence and adaptations, in R.B. Ruddell, M. Rapp Ruddell and H. Singer (eds) *Theoretical Models and Processes of Reading*, pp. 391–413. Delaware: International Reading Association.

Hilton, M. (ed.) (1996) *Potent Fictions: Children's Literacy and the Challenge of Popular Culture*. London: Routledge.

Hilton, M. and Hirsch, P. (eds) (2000) *Practical Visionaries: Women, Education and Social Progress, 1790–1930*. London: Pearson.

Hilton, M., Styles, M. and Watson, V. (eds) (1997) *Opening the Nursery Door: Reading, Writing and Childhood 1600–1900*. London: Routledge.

Holdaway, D. (1979) *The Foundations of Literacy*. Sydney: Ashton Scholastic.

Juel, L. (1988) Learning to read and write: a longitudinal study of fifty-four children from first through fourth grades, *Journal of Educational Psychology*, 80: 437–47.

Juel, C. (1991) Beginning reading, in R. Barr, M. Kamil, P. Mosenthal and D. Pearson (eds) *Handbook of Reading Research*, Vol. 2, pp. 759–88. New York, NY: Longman.

Juel, C. (1994) *Learning to Read and Write in one Elementary School*. New York, NY: Springer-Verlag.

Juel, C. (1999) The messenger may be wrong, but the message may be right, in J. Oakhill and R. Beard (eds) *Reading Development and the Teaching of Reading*. London: Blackwell.

Juel, C. and Minden-Cupp, C. (2001) Learning to read words: linguistic units and instructional strategies, *Reading Research Quarterly*, 35(4): 458–93.

Kempe, A. (2001) No single meaning: empowering students to construct socially critical readings of the text, in H. Fehring and P. Green (eds) *Critical Literacy: A Collection of Articles from the Australian Literacy Educators' Association*, pp. 40–57. Newark, DE: International Reading Association.

King, C. and Robinson, M. (1995) Creating communities of readers, *English in Education*, 29(2): 46–55.

Kress, G. (2000a) Design and transformation: new theories of meaning, in B. Cope and M. Kalantzis (eds) *Multiliteracies: Literacy Learning and the Design of Social Futures*, pp. 153–61. London: Routledge.

Kress, G. (2000b) Multimodality, in B. Cope and M. Kalantzis (eds) *Multiliteracies: Literacy Learning and the Design of Social Futures* 182–202. London: Routledge.

Lee, C.D. and Smagorinsky, P. (eds) (2000) *Vygotskian Perspectives on Literacy Research*. Cambridge: CUP.

Lesgold, A.M. and Resnick, L.B. (1982) How reading disabilities develop: perspectives from a longitudinal study, in J.P. Das, R. Mulcatry and A.E. Wall (eds) *Theory and Research in Learning Disability*. New York: Plenum.

Lewis, M. and Wray, D. (1996) *Writing Frames*. Reading: University of Reading, Reading and Language Information Centre.

Lewis, M. and Wray, D. (1998) *Writing Across the Curriculum*. Reading: University of Reading, Reading and Language Information Centre.

Lewis, M. and Wray, D. (eds) (1999) *Literacy in the Secondary School*. London: David Fulton.

Lloyd, S. (1993) *The Phonics Handbook*. Chigwell: Jolly Learning.

Luke, A. (2000) Critical literacy in Australia: a matter of context and standpoint, *Journal of Adolescent and Adult Literacy*, 43(5): 448–61.

Luke, A. and Freebody, P. (1999) Further notes on the four resources model, *Reading Online*, readingonline.org/research/lukefreebody.html

Luke, A. and Luke, C. (2001) Adolescence lost/childhood regained: on early intervention and the emergence of the techno-subject, *Journal of Early Childhood Literacy*, 1(1): 91–120.

Luke, A., Lingard, R., Green, B. and Comber, B. (1999) The abuses of literacy: educational policy and the construction of crisis, in J. Marshall and M. Peters (eds) *Educational Policy*, pp. 1–25. London: Edward Elgar.

McDermott, R.P. and Gospodinoff, K. (1981) Social contexts for ethnic borders and school failure, in H.T. Trueba, G.P. Guthrie and K.H. Au (eds) *Culture and the Bilingual Classroom: Studies in Classroom Ethnography*, pp. 212–30. Rowley, MA: Newbury House.

Mackay, D., Thompson, B. and Schaub, P. (1978) *Breakthrough to Literacy: The Theory and Practice of Teaching Initial Reading and Writing*. London: Longman and Schools Council.

Marsh, J. (2000) 'But I want to fly too!' Girls and superhero play in the infant classroom, *Gender and Education*, 12(2): 209–20.

Marsh, J. and Millard, E. (2000) *Literacy and Popular Culture: Using Children's Culture in the Classroom*. London: Sage/PCP.

Marsh, J. and Thompson, P. (2001) Parental involvement in literacy development: using media texts, *Journal of Reading Research*, 24(3): 266–78.

Maybin, J. (1999) Response to Gemma Moss: literacy and the social organisation of knowledge in and outside school, *Virtual Seminar 2: International Association of Applied Linguistics*, http://education.leeds.ac.uk/AILA/virtsem2.ma

Medwell, J., Wray, D., Poulson, I. and Fox, R. (1998) *The Effective Teachers of Literacy Project*. Exeter: University of Exeter.

Meek, M. (1982) *Learning to Read*. London: The Bodley Head.

Meek, M. (1988) *How Texts Teach What Readers Learn*. Stroud: Thimble Press.

Millard, E. and Marsh, J. (2001) Sending Minnie the Min home: comics and reading choices, *Cambridge Journal of Education*, 31(1): 25–38.

Moll, L.C. (2000) Inspired by Vygotksy: ethnographic experiments in education, in C.D. Lee and P. Smagorinsky (eds) *Vygotskian Perspectives on Literacy Research*, pp. 256–68. Cambridge: CUP.

Moon, C. (1990) Miscue made simple, *Child Education*, 43: 42.

Morgan, W. with Gilbert, P., Lankshear, C., Werba, S. and Williams, L. (1996) *Critical Literacy: Readings and Resources*. Norwood: Australian Association for the Teaching of English.

Morris, D., Ervin, C. and Conrad, K. (1996) A case study of middle school reading disability in teaching struggling readers, *The Reading Teacher*, 49(5): 368–77.

Morrow, L.M. (1992) The impact of a literature-based program on literacy achievement, use of literature and attitudes of children from minority backgrounds, *Reading Research Quarterly*, 27: 251–75.

Moss, G. (2000) Raising attainment: boys, reading and the national literacy hour, *Reading*, 34(3): 101–6.

Moss, G. and Attar, D. (1999) Boys and literacy: gendering the reading curriculum, in J. Prosser (ed.) *School Culture*. London: PCP/Sage.

Moustafa, M. (1993) Recoding in whole language reading instruction, *Language Arts*, 70: 483–7.

Moustafa, M. (1997) *Beyond Traditional Phonics: Research Discoveries and Reading Instruction*. Portsmouth, NH: Heinemann.

Newman, J. (1985) *Whole Language*. Portsmouth, NH: Heinemann.

NRP (National Reading Panel) (2000) *Teaching Children to Read: An Evidence-based assessment of the Scientific Research Literature on Reading and its Implications for Reading Instruction*. http://www.readingonline.org/critical/shanahan/panel.htm (accessed 14 November 2001).

Oakhill, J. and Beard, R. (eds) (1999) *Reading Development and the Teaching of Reading*. Oxford: Blackwell.

Ofsted (1996) *The Teaching of Reading in 45 Inner London Primary Schools: A Report of Her Majesty's Inspectors in Collaboration with the LEAs of Islington, Southwark and Tower Hamlets*. London: The Stationery Office.

Ogle, D. (1986) K-W-L: a teaching model that develops active reading of expository text, *The Reading Teacher*, 39: 564–70.

Palinscar, A. and Brown, A. (1984) Reciprocal teaching of comprehension-fostering and comprehension-monitoring activities, *Cognition and Instruction*, 1: 117–75.

Pearson, P.D. (1993) Teaching and learning reading: a research perspective, *Language Arts*, 70: 502–11.

Pearson, P.D. and Stephens, D. (1994) Learning about literacy? A 30-year journey, in R.B. Ruddell, M. Rapp Ruddell and H. Singer (eds) *Theoretical Models and Processes of Reading*, pp. 22–42. Newark, DE: International Reading Association.

Perfetti, C.K. (1995) Cognitive research can inform reading education, *Journal Research in Reading*, 18(2): 106–15.

Perfetti, C.K. and McCutchen, D. (1987) Schooled language competence: linguistic abilities in reading and writing, in S. Rosenberg (ed.) *Advances in Applied Psycholinguistics*, Vol. 2, pp. 105–41. Cambridge: CUP.

Phillips, M. (1990) Educashun still isn't working, *The Guardian*, 28 September.

Poulson, L., Wray, D. and Medwell, J. (1997) Subject knowledge and practice in primary literacy teaching. Paper presented at the annual conference of the British Educational Research Association, York, September.

Powell, R., Chambers-Cantrell, S. and Adams, S. (2001) Saving Black Mountain: the promise of critical literacy in a multicultural democracy, *The Reading Teacher*, 54(8): 772–81.

Pressley, M. (1998) *Reading Instruction that Works: The Case for Balanced Teaching*. New York, NY: Guilford.

Pressley, M. (2000) What should comprehension instruction be the instruction of? In M.L. Kamil, P.B. Mosenthal, P.D. Pearson and R. Barr (eds) *Handbook of Research*, Vol. 3, pp. 545–61. Hillsdale, NJ: Erlbaum.

Rasinski, T.V. (2000) Speed does matter in reading, *The Reading Teacher*, 51(2): 146–52.

Rasinski, T.V., Padak, N., Linek, W.L. and Sturtevant, E. (1994) Effects of fluency development on urban second-grade readers, *Journal of Educational Research*, 87: 158–65.

Rassool, N. (1999) *Literacy for Sustainable Development in the Age of Information*. Clevedon: Multilingual Matters.

Rosenblatt, L. (1991) Literature: S.O.S!, *Language Arts*, 68(6): 444–8.

Rumelhart, D. (1976) Toward an interactive model of reading, in S. Dornic (ed.) *Attention and Performance*. New York, NY: Academic Press.

Rumelhart, D. (1980) Schemata: the building blocks of cognition, in R.J. Spiro, B.C. Bruce and W.F. Brewer (eds) *Theoretical Issues in Reading Comprehension*, pp. 35–8. Hillsdale, NJ: Erlbaum.

Scribner, S. and Cole, M. (1981) *The Psychology of Literacy*. Cambridge: Cambridge University Press.

Scieszka, J. (1999) *The True Story of the Three Little Pigs*. New York: Viking.

Share, D., Jorm, A., Macleam, R. and Matthews, R. (1984) Sources of individual differences in reading acquisition, *Journal of Educational Psychology*, 76: 1309–24.

Smith, F. (1971) *Understanding Reading: A Psycholinguistic Analysis of Reading and Learning to Read*. New York, NY: Holt, Rinehart and Winston.

Smith, F. (ed.) (1973) *Psycholinguistics and Reading*. New York, NY: Holt, Rinehart and Winston.

Smith, F. (1978) *Reading*. Cambridge: CUP.

Smith, F. (1992) Learning to read: the never ending debate, *Phi Delta Kappan*, 73(6): 432–5.

Snow, C.E., Burns, S.M. and Griffin, P. (eds) (1998) *Preventing Reading Difficulties in Young Children*. Washington, DC: National Academy Press.

Solsken, J.W. (1993) *Literacy, Gender and Work in Families and School*. Norwood, NJ: Ablex.

Spiegel, D.L. (1992) Blending whole language and systematic direct instruction, *The Reading Teacher*, 46(1): 38–44.

Stahl, S.A. (1992) Saying the 'p' word: nine guidelines for exemplary phonics instruction, *The Reading Teacher*, 45(8): 618–25.

Stahl, S.A. (1997) Instructional models in reading: an introduction, in S.A. Stahl, *Instructional Models in Reading*, pp. 1–29. Hillsdale, NJ: Erlbaum.

Stahl, S.A. (1999) Why innovations come and go (and mostly go): the case of whole language, *Educational Researcher*, 28(8): 13–22.

Stahl, S.A. and Miller, P.D. (1989) Whole language and language experiences approaches for beginning reading: quantitative synthesis, *Review of Educational Research*, 16: 32–71.

Stahl, S.A., McKenna, M.C. and Pagnucco, J. (1994) The effects of whole-language instruction: an update and a reappraisal, *Educational Psychologist*, 29: 175–86.

Stanovich, K.E. (1986) Matthew effects in reading: some consequences of individual differences in the acquisition of literacy, *Reading Research Quarterly*, 21: 360–406.

Stanovich, K.E. (1991) Word recognition: changing perspectives, in R. Barr, M. Kamil, P. Mosenthal and D. Pearson (eds) *Handbook of Reading Research*, Vol. 2, pp. 418–52. New York, NY: Longman.

Stanovich, K.E. (1992) The psychology of reading: evolutionary and revolutionary developments, *Annual Review of Applied Linguistics*, 12: 3–30.

Stanovich, K.E. (1995) How research might inform the debate about early reading acquisition, *Journal of Research in Reading*, 18(2): 87–105.

Sulzby, E. and Teak, W. (1991) Emergent literacy, in R. Barr, M.L. Kamil, P. Mosenthal and P.D. Pearson (eds) *Handbook of Reading Research, Volume 2*. New Jersey: Erlbaum.

Tharp, R.G. (1982) The effective instruction of comprehension: results and description of the Kamehameha Early Education Program, *Reading Research Quarterly*, 17(4): 503–27.

Tierney, R.J. and Pearson, P.D. (1994) Learning to learn from text: a framework for improving classroom practice, in R.B. Ruddell and H. Singer (eds) *Theoretical Models and Processes of Reading*, pp. 496–513. Newark, DE: International Reading Association.

Tompkins, G.E. (1997) *Literacy for the Twenty-first Century: A Balanced Approach*. New Jersey: Merrill.

Topping, K. (1987) Paired reading: a powerful technique for parent use, *The Reading Teacher*, 40: 608–14.

Torgeson, J.K. and Mathes, P.G. (2000) *A Basic Guide to Understanding, Assessing, and Teaching Phonological Awareness*. Austin, TX: Pro-Ed.

Trachtenburg, P. (1990) Using children's literature to enhance phonics instruction, *The Reading Teacher*, May: 648–54.

Turner, M. (1990) *Sponsored Reading Failure*. Surrey: IPSET Education Unit.

Vygotsky, L.S. (1978) *Mind in Society: The Development of Higher Psychological Processes*. Cambridge, MA: Harvard University Press.

Wade, B. (1990) *Reading for Real*. Buckingham: Open University Press.

Waterland, L. (1988) *Read With Me: An Apprenticeship Approach to Reading*. Stroud: Thimble Press.

Watson, D.J. (1989) Defining and describing whole language, *Elementary School Journal*, 90(2): 129–41.

Wendon, L. (1992) *First Steps in Letterland.* Cambridge: Letterland Ltd.

Wixon, K. (1979) Miscue analysis: a critical review, *Journal of Reading Behavior,* 11(2): 163–75.

Wray, D. (1995) *English 7–11.* London: Routledge.

Wray, D. (1998) Teaching literacy: the foundations of good practice, *Education 3–13*, 27(1): 53–9.

Wray, D. and Lewis, M. (1995) *Developing Children's Non-fiction Writing.* Leamington Spa: Scholastic.

Wray, D. and Lewis, M. (1997) *Extending Literacy: Reading and Writing Non-fiction in the Primary School.* London: Routledge.

Wray, D., Medwell, J. and Poulson, L. (2001) *Teaching Literacy Effectively.* London: Routledge.

Yopp, H.K. (1995) Read-aloud books for developing phonemic awareness: an annotated bibliography, *The Reading Teacher*, 49(1): 20–9.

Yopp, R.H. and Yopp, H.K. (2001) *Literature-based Reading Activities*, 3rd edn. Boston: Allyn & Bacon.

Zipes, J. (1995) *Creative Storytelling: Building Community, Changing Lives.* London: Routledge.

INDEX